CliffsNotes®

Praxis II®: Middle School Mathematics Test (0069) Test Prep

by

Sandra Luna McCune, Ph.D.
E. Donice McCune, Ph.D.

WILEY

Wiley Publishing, Inc.

About the Authors

Sandra Luna McCune, Ph.D., is Regents professor and mathematics specialist in the Department of Elementary Education at Stephen F. Austin State University. E. Donice McCune, Ph.D., is Regents professor in the Department of Mathematics and Statistics at Stephen F. Austin State University. Regents professor is the highest honor the university is empowered to bestow upon a faculty member. Additionally, both Drs. E. Donice and Sandra Luna McCune have been named Distinguished Professor by the Stephen F. Austin State University Alumni Association. The Drs. McCune reside in Nacogdoches, Texas.

Authors' Acknowledgments

The authors wish to thank Grace Freedson for bringing us this project and the editors at Wiley Publishing, Inc., for their help in making this book the best that it can be. We also wish to thank our family, especially our children, our daughters-in-law, and our grandchildren—Richard, Rose, and Jude—for their loving support.

Publisher's Acknowledgments

Editorial

Project Editor: Kelly D. Henthorne

Acquisitions Editor: Greg Tubach

Production

Proofreaders: Toni Settle, Amanda Steiner

Wiley Publishing, Inc. Composition Services

CliffsNotes® Praxis II®: Middle School Mathematics Test (0069) Test Prep

Published by:
Wiley Publishing, Inc.
111 River Street
Hoboken, NJ 07030-5774
www.wiley.com

Copyright © 2009 Wiley, Hoboken, NJ

Published by Wiley, Hoboken, NJ
Published simultaneously in Canada

ISBN: 978-0-470-27822-2

WILEY

Table of Contents

PART II: PRACTICE TESTS

Introduction

General Description

The Praxis Middle School Mathematics test (0069) is designed to assess the mathematical knowledge and skills that an entry-level teacher of middle school mathematics needs to possess. As listed in the *Middle School Mathematics (0069) Test at a Glance* (www.ets.org/Media/Tests/PRAXIS/taag/0069/glance.htm), the test addresses five content categories:

    I. Arithmetic and Basic Algebra

    II. Geometry and Measurement

    III. Functions and Their Graphs

    IV. Probability, Data Analysis and Statistics, and Discrete Mathematics

    V. Problem Solving Exercises

The test consists of two parts: Part A (67 percent of total score) and Part B (33 percent of total score). Part A consists of 40 multiple-choice questions. Each multiple-choice question contains four response options. You record your answer choice in the separate answer booklet by filling in the space corresponding to **A, B, C,** or **D.** No penalty is imposed for wrong answers (you merely score a zero for that test question). Part B consists of three short constructed-response questions. You are given 2 hours to complete the test. The individual parts of the test are not timed, so you may allot your time between Parts A and B as you choose.

Allocation of the Test Content

According to the *Middle School Mathematics (0069) Test at a Glance,* the content categories for the test and approximate number of questions and percentage of the test for each content category are as follows:

Allocation of the Test Content		
Content Category	*Approximate Number of Questions*	*Approximate Percent of Test*
Arithmetic and Basic Algebra	12	20%
Geometry and Measurement	10	17%
Functions and Their Graphs	8	13%
Data, Probability, and Statistical Concepts; Discrete Mathematics	10	17%
Problem Solving Exercises	3	33%

In addition to mathematical knowledge and skills, the Praxis Middle School Mathematics test assesses five process categories: Mathematical Problem Solving, Mathematical Reasoning and Proof, Mathematical Connections, Mathematical Representation, and Use of Technology. These process categories refer to the ways through which mathematical knowledge is acquired and used. The first four process categories are adopted from the National Council of Teachers of Mathematics (NCTM) *Principles and Standards for School Mathematics* (2000–2004) process standards and are as described here:

Problem Solving (http://standards.nctm.org/document/chapter3/prob.htm)

- Build new mathematical knowledge through problem solving.
- Solve problems that arise in mathematics and in other contexts.
- Apply and adapt a variety of appropriate strategies to solve problems.
- Monitor and reflect on the process of mathematical problem solving.

Reasoning and Proof (http://standards.nctm.org/document/chapter3/reas.htm)

- Recognize reasoning and proof as fundamental aspects of mathematics.
- Make and investigate mathematical conjectures.
- Develop and evaluate mathematical arguments and proofs.
- Select and use various types of reasoning and methods of proof.

Connections (http://standards.nctm.org/document/chapter3/conn.htm)

- Recognize and use connections among mathematical ideas.
- Understand how mathematical ideas interconnect and build on one another.
- Recognize and apply mathematics in contexts outside of mathematics.

Representation (http://standards.nctm.org/document/chapter3/rep.htm)

- Create and use representations to organize, record, and communicate mathematical ideas.
- Select, apply, and translate among mathematical representations to solve problems.
- Use representations to model and interpret physical, social, and mathematical phenomena.

The description of the fifth process category as given in the *Middle School Mathematics (0069) Test at a Glance* is as follows:

Use of Technology

- Use technology appropriately as a tool for problem solving.
- Use technology as an aid to understanding mathematical ideas.

The process categories are integrated into the content questions. This circumstance means that you will not be asked explicit questions about the process categories, but rather you will be expected to use one or more of the processes in answering questions on the test.

Scoring of the Test

Educational Testing Service (ETS) does not release the exact details of the way the Praxis Middle School Mathematics test is scored. According to the *Middle School Mathematics (0069) Test at a Glance,* the multiple-choice part of the test is weighted 67 percent of the total score, and the short constructed-response part of the test is weighted 33 percent of the total score. Each short constructed response receives a score of 0 to 3 based on the following criteria:

- Correctly answered all parts of the question
- Gave a complete and full explanation for answers
- Demonstrated a strong understanding of the mathematical content relevant to the question
- Demonstrated a complete understanding of the most important aspects of any stimulus material provided

Your raw point score is obtained using a weighted formula, and then it is converted to a scaled score that adjusts for the difficulty level of the particular edition of the test that you took. Your score report for the test will show a scaled score ranging from 100 to 200. Read *Understanding Your Praxis Scores* (www.ets.org) for more information about the scoring of the test.

Calculators

You are allowed to bring a graphing calculator or a four-function scientific calculator to use while taking the Praxis Middle School Mathematics test. The testing company suggests that a graphing calculator could provide an advantage over a scientific calculator on certain questions, so you should plan to bring a graphing calculator to the test. *Note:* You must bring your own calculator because none will be provided at the test center.

You are *not* allowed to bring calculators with QWERTY keyboards (for example, TI-92 PLUS, Voyage 200); cell-phone calculators; minicomputers including powerbooks and portable/handheld computers; electronic writing pads or other pen-input/stylus-driven devices; or models that print, make noise, or require an electrical outlet.

Currently (in 2008) test administrators do not clear the memory of test takers' calculators before the test starts. You can find more information on the testing company's calculator use policy for Praxis tests at ww.ets.org/praxis/prxcalc.html.

The Role of the Praxis Middle School Mathematics Test in Teacher Certification/Licensure

The Praxis Middle School Mathematics test is one of the Praxis II Series subject assessment tests designed by ETS. The Praxis II tests are part of a national teacher assessment program and are used as part of the certification or licensing requirements in about 80 percent of the states. This means that you can transfer your score on the Praxis Middle School Mathematics test from state to state for those states that use it as a subject area assessment test.

If your state has selected the Praxis Middle School Mathematics test to assess middle school teacher candidates' mathematical knowledge and skills, then this *CliffsNotes* book will be invaluable in helping you achieve the passing score for your state. Test scores needed to obtain certification vary from state to state because each state sets its own passing score. ETS maintains a listing by state of links to test requirements for those states that require the Praxis II subject assessment tests for certification at www.ets.org/praxis/prxstate.html. ETS also publishes the most recent information it has regarding passing score requirements in a pamphlet titled *Understanding Your Praxis Scores* (www.ets.org/Media/Tests/PRAXIS/pdf/09706PRAXIS.pdf) and in a summary document *The Praxis Series Passing Scores* (www.ets.org). The following is a list of states that require the Praxis Middle School Mathematics test along with the current score (in 2008) as given in *The Praxis Series Passing Scores* that is needed to obtain certification in each state:

Alabama—149	Maryland—152	Pennsylvania—151
Alaska—145	Minnesota—152	Rhode Island—158
Connecticut—158	Mississippi—140	South Carolina—149
Delaware—148	Missouri—158	South Dakota—140
Hawaii—143	Nevada—139	Tennessee—143
Idaho—145	New Hampshire—151	Vermont—161
Indiana—156	New Jersey—152	Virginia—163
Kansas—158	North Carolina—141	Washington—152
Kentucky—148	North Dakota—148	West Virginia—148
Louisiana—148	Ohio—143	Wyoming—152
Maine—148	Oregon—156	

Questions Commonly Asked About the Praxis Middle School Mathematics Test

Q. What is the Praxis Middle School Mathematics test?

A. The Praxis Middle School Mathematics test is a Praxis II Series subject assessment test. Currently, it is used by 32 states as part of their teacher certification/licensure requirements.

Q. Who administers the Praxis Middle School Mathematics test?

A. The Praxis Middle School Mathematics test is administered by Educational Testing Service (ETS).

Q. When and where is the Praxis Middle School Mathematics test given?

A. Currently, Praxis II Series tests, including the Praxis Middle School Mathematics test, are administered seven times a year (usually in September, November, January, March, April, June, and July or August) at locations throughout the United States. You can find information on test dates, site locations, fees, registration procedures, and policies in the current *The Praxis Series Information and Registration Bulletin (Registration Bulletin)*, which you can download at www.ets.org/Media/Tests/PRAXIS/pdf/01361.pdf.

Q. How do I register to take to the test?

A. You can register online using a credit/debit card at the Praxis Website (www.ets.org/praxis) from 7 A.M. to 10 P.M. (EST), Monday through Friday; or Saturday, 7 A.M. through Sunday, 8 P.M. (EST).

You can register by mail by downloading the registration form available on the Praxis Website and then mailing the completed form to ETS-The Praxis Series, Box 382065, Pittsburgh, PA 15251–8065.

Q. Are special testing arrangements available?

A. If you have a disabling condition (visual, physical, hearing, or so on), special testing arrangements and test materials can be made available for you. Complete the registration form and follow the instructions at www.ets.org/praxis/prxdsabl.html.

If you are unable to take the test on Saturdays because of your religious convictions or because of duties as a member of the U.S. armed forces, you can request a Monday testing day by following the instructions in the *Registration Bulletin*. A copy of your military duties or a letter from your clergy on the clergy's letterhead, verifying the religious basis for your request, must be included with your registration application.

If your primary language is not English, you can request extended testing time by following the instructions in the *Registration Bulletin*.

You should write your name and contact information on all correspondence to ensure proper handling of your documentation. Don't forget to make copies of everything before you mail it.

Q. May I change my registration if I need to?

A. Yes, you may change tests, test sites, or transfer registration to a later test date by completing the appropriate forms, which you can download from the Praxis Website (www.ets.org/praxis). For test and test center changes, the form must be received by the late registration deadline. For test date changes, the form must be received within two weeks after your original test date. The current fee (in 2008) for this service is $45.

Q. What is the fee for the test?

A. The current fee (in 2008) for regular registration is $90. The fee for late registration is an additional $45 charge.

Q. What should I bring to the test site?

A. After you mail in your registration form, you should receive an admission ticket by one week before your scheduled test date. If you have not received your admission ticket by this time or if you have lost your admission ticket, contact Praxis Customer Service at 1-800-772-9476 or through email on its Website. If you register online, you must print your admission ticket. Your admission ticket will include your name, the tests you are registered to take, the test date, the test site address, and the reporting time. Check the information on your admission ticket to make sure that it is correct. You will not be allowed to make changes at the test site.

The day of the test, you should bring your admission ticket, a valid form of photo and signature identification (for example, driver's license or military identification), your graphing calculator, several sharpened, Number 2, soft lead pencils, a good eraser, a blue or black ink pen, and a watch to help pace yourself during the exam. Mechanical pencils cannot be used. No personal items such as handbags, cell phones, or study materials or other aids will be permitted in the testing room.

Q. Is the Praxis Middle School Mathematics test divided into timed sections?

A. No, you have two hours to complete both parts of the test: the 40 multiple-choice test items and the three short constructed-response questions. The testing company recommends that you plan to spend about 80 minutes on the 40 multiple-choice questions and about 40 minutes on the constructed response questions. Nonetheless, you may allot your time between the two parts as you choose as long as you stay within the two-hour timeframe.

Q. What is the passing score?

A. The passing score varies from state to state. Check the list of states and their passing score requirements given earlier in this chapter. You also should check with your preparation institution regarding the passing score in your state.

Q. When will I get my score report?

A. Your score report will be mailed approximately four weeks after the test administration date.

Q. How should I prepare?

A. If you have reached the point at which you need to test for certification/licensure, using this test prep book is your best preparation. This study guide gives you insights, reviews, and strategies for the question types. Some universities offer preparation programs to assist you in attaining a passing score. Check with them for further information.

Q. How do I get more information about the Praxis Middle School Mathematics test?

A. Check the Praxis Website (www.ets.org/praxis). If new information on the Praxis Middle School Mathematics test becomes available, it will be posted on this site.

How to Use This *CliffsNotes* Book

The review for the Praxis II Middle School Mathematics test in this CliffsNotes book is designed around the five content categories that are assessed on the test: Arithmetic and Basic Algebra, Geometry and Measurement, Functions and Their Graphs, Probability, Data Analysis and Statistics, Discrete Mathematics, and Problem Solving Exercises.

Three full-length practice tests follow the review chapters. Complete answer explanations are provided after each of the practice tests.

When you read through the list of content categories that are assessed on the Praxis Middle School Mathematics test, you may feel overwhelmed by the task of preparing for the test. Here are some suggestions for developing an effective study program using this book.

1. Set up a regular schedule of study sessions. Try to set aside approximately two hours for each session. If you complete one session per day (including weekends), it should take you about 4 to 6 weeks to work your way through the review and practice material provided in this book. Of course, if your test date is coming up soon, you might need to lengthen your study time per day.

2. Reserve a place for studying where you will have few distractions, so that you can concentrate. Make sure that you have adequate lighting and a room temperature that is comfortable—not too warm or too cold. Be sure that you have an ample supply of water to keep your brain hydrated, and you might also want to have some light snacks available. To improve mental alertness, choose snacks that are high in protein and low in carbohydrates (for example, nuts). Gather all the necessary study aids (paper, pencils, note cards, and so on) beforehand. Let your voicemail answer your phone during your study time.

3. Take Practice Test 1 before you begin reading the review material to help you discover your strengths and weaknesses. Read the answer explanations for all the questions, not just the ones you missed, because you might have gotten some of your correct answers by guessing. Make a list of the content categories with which you had the

most problems. Plan your study program so that you can spend more time on content categories that your Practice Test 1 results indicate are weak areas for you. For instance, if you did very well in arithmetic and basic algebra, but poorly in geometry and measurement, then you should plan to spend more time studying the review material on geometry and measurement.

4. Carefully study the review of the test areas in Part II of this book to refresh your memory about the key ideas for each of the content categories, being sure to concentrate as you go through the material. Work through the examples and exercises and make sure you understand them thoroughly.

5. Make flashcards to aid you in memorizing key definitions and formulas and keep them with you at all times. When you have spare moments of time, take out the flash cards and go over the information you've recorded on them. This is a particularly important strategy for the Praxis II Middle School Mathematics test because *no notation, definitions, and formulas sheet is provided for your reference during the test*.

6. Take several brief 2- to 3-minute breaks during your study sessions to give your mind time to absorb the review material you just read. According to brain research, you remember the first part and last part of something you've read more easily than you remember the middle part. Taking several breaks will allow you to create more beginnings and endings to maximize the amount of material you remember. It's best not to leave your study area during a break. Try stretching, closing your eyes for a few minutes, or getting a quick drink or snack.

7. Periodically review material you have already studied to reinforce what you have learned and to help you identify topics you might need to restudy.

8. When you complete your first review, take Practice Test 2. Use a timer and take the test under the same conditions you expect for the actual test, being sure to adhere to the 2-hour time limit for the test. When you finish taking the test, as you did for Practice Test 1, carefully study the answer explanations for *all* the questions. Then, go back and review again any topics in which you performed unsatisfactorily.

9. When you complete your second review, take Practice Test 3 under the same conditions you expect for the actual test, adhering to the 2-hour time limit. When you finish taking the test, carefully study the answer explanations for *all* the questions and do additional study, if needed.

10. Organize a study group, if possible. A good way of learning and reinforcing the material is to discuss it with others. If feasible, set up a regular time to study with one or more classmates or friends. Take turns explaining how to work problems to each other. This strategy will help you to clarify your own understanding of the problems and, at the same time, help you discover new insights into how to approach various problems.

After completing your study program, you should find yourself prepared and confident to achieve a passing score on the Praxis Middle School Mathematics test.

How to Prepare for the Day of the Test

There are several things you can do to prepare yourself for the day of the test.

1. Know how to get to the test center and how to get into the room where you will be testing at the test center.

2. Make sure you have dependable transportation that will get you to the test center and that you know where you should park (if you plan to go by car).

3. Keep all the materials you will need to bring to the test center—especially, your admission ticket and identification—in a secure place, so that you easily can find them on the day of the test.

4. The night before the test, try to get a good night's rest. Avoid taking nonprescription drugs or consuming alcohol as the use of these products might impair your mental faculties on test day.

5. On the day of the test, get to the testing center early—at least 30 minutes before your test is scheduled to begin.

6. Dress in comfortable clothing and wear comfortable shoes. Even if it is warm outside, wear layers of clothing that can be removed or put on, depending on the temperature in the test center.

7. Eat a light meal. Select foods that you have found usually give you the most energy and stamina.

8. Drink plenty of water to make sure that your brain remains hydrated during the test for optimal thinking.

9. Put fresh batteries in your calculator just before you leave to go to the testing center.

10. Make a copy of this list and post it in a strategic location. Check over it before you leave for the testing center.

Test Taking Strategies for the Praxis Middle School Mathematics Test

Here are some general test-taking strategies to help maximize your score on the test:

1. When you receive the test, briefly close your eyes, breathe in and out slowly, and mentally visualize yourself working through the test successfully.

2. During the test, read and follow all the directions. If you do not understand something in the directions, ask the test administrator for clarification.

3. Work through the test at a steady pace. Part I of the test consists of 40 multiple-choice items. As you begin the test, skim through the booklet to find multiple-choice question 20, mark this question as an approximate one-third-of-the-way point. When you get to question 20, check your watch to see how much time has passed. If more than 40 minutes have gone by, you will need to pick up the pace. Otherwise, continue to work as rapidly as you can without being careless, *but do not rush.*

4. Try to work the problems in order. Skipping around can waste time and might cause mistakes on your answer sheet. However, if a question is taking too much of your time, place a large check mark next to it in the test booklet (*not* on the answer booklet), mark your best guess in the answer booklet, and move on.

5. Read each question entirely. Skimming to save time can cause you to misread a question or miss important information.

6. Write in the test booklet. Mark on diagrams, draw figures, underline or circle key words or phrases, and do scratch work in the test booklet. Remember, however, to mark your answer choice in the separate answer booklet. Answers marked only in the test booklet are not scored.

7. Don't read too much into a question. For instance, don't presume a geometric figure is drawn accurately or to scale.

8. Use your calculator, but use it wisely. Keep in mind that graphing calculators are powerful tools, but they can make errors. See the discussion about graphing calculators that follows this section.

9. Be sure you are answering the question asked. Circle or underline what you are being asked to find, to help you stay focused on it.

10. Read all the answer choices before you select an answer. You might find an answer that immediately strikes you as correct, but this determination might have occurred because you jumped to a false conclusion or made an incorrect assumption.

11. Eliminate as many wrong choices as you can. Estimate the answer to help you decide which answers are unreasonable.

12. Change an answer only if you have a good reason to do so. Be sure to completely erase the old answer choice before marking the new one.

13. If you are trying to recall information during the test, close your eyes and try to visualize yourself in your study place. This might trigger your memory.

14. Remain calm during the test. If you start to feel anxious, briefly close your eyes, breathe in and out slowly, and mentally visualize yourself in a peaceful place, to help you relax.

15. Record your answers to the multiple-choice items in the answer booklet carefully. This part of the test is scored electronically, so it is critical that you mark your answer booklet accurately. As you go through the test questions, circle the letters of your answer choice in the test booklet. Then mark those answers in the answer booklet in bunches of 5 to 10 (unless time is running out, at which point you should start marking answers one by one).

16. Even though the testing company recommends that you spend only 40 minutes working the constructed-response questions, try to save at least 45 minutes for this part of the test—because it counts 33 percent of your test score.

17. Be sure you answer all parts of each constructed-response question and that you give complete and full explanations for your answers.

18. Before turning in your answer booklet, check that you have marked an answer for every multiple-choice test question. You are not penalized for a wrong answer (you merely score a zero for that test question), so even if you have no clue about how to work the problem, make a guess.

19. Before turning in your answer booklet, erase any stray marks in the answer booklet and brush off any loose eraser dust.

20. As you work through the practice tests provided in this book, consciously use the strategies suggested in this section as preparation for the actual Praxis Middle School Mathematics test. Try to reach the point where the strategies are automatic for you.

Graphing Calculators and the Praxis Middle School Mathematics Test

Because you likely will be bringing a graphing calculator to use when you take the Praxis Middle School Mathematics test, you should have your calculator on hand and use it, when needed, to work problems in the review material and practice tests in this book. Select a calculator that you will feel comfortable using. Don't purchase a high-powered calculator that will require an investment of your time to learn while you are preparing for the test. In this book, we use the TI-83 calculator to show special features of graphing calculators.

A word of caution: Graphing calculators are very powerful tools, but you should be aware that they can make errors!

One situation in which errors might occur is when the calculator is finding the roots or zeros of a high-degree polynomial (for example, a polynomial of degree eight). The algorithm that the calculator uses to find the roots of the polynomial forces the calculator to round numbers to a certain number of decimal places before the final result is obtained, thus yielding inaccurate answers.

Another situation in which errors commonly occur is when the calculator is drawing the graph of a function. Your choice of viewing window dimensions can give results that are visually very misleading. For instance, you can be led to believe that a function has only two zeros when, in fact, it has three zeros. Changing the dimensions for the viewing window can clear up the problem in most cases; however, not every time.

The point of this discussion is to make you aware that such mistakes can happen. Therefore, you should use your mathematical expertise to evaluate all your calculator's answers for reliability and accuracy.

You will benefit greatly from this *CliffsNotes* book. By using the recommendations in this chapter as you complete your study program, you will be prepared to walk into the testing room with confidence. Good luck on the test and on your new career as a middle school mathematics teacher!

PART I

TOPIC AREA REVIEWS

Arithmetic and Basic Number Concepts

This chapter provides a review of the key ideas and formulas of arithmetic and basic number concepts that are most important for you to know for the Praxis Middle School Mathematics test. Multiple-choice sample exercises, comparable to what might be presented on the Praxis Middle School Mathematics test, are given at the end of the chapter. The answer explanations for the sample exercises are provided immediately after the exercises.

Arithmetic Operations

Addition, subtraction, multiplication, and **division** are the four basic arithmetic operations. Each of the operations has special symbolism and terminology associated with it. The following table shows the terminology and symbolism you are expected to know.

Terminology and Symbolism for the Four Basic Arithmetic Operations			
Operation	**Symbols(s) Used**	**Name of Parts**	**Example**
Addition	+ (plus sign)	addend + addend = sum	$5 + 9 = 14$
Subtraction	− (minus sign)	sum − addend = difference	$14 - 5 = 9$
Multiplication	× (times sign)	factor × factor = product	$10 \times 6 = 60$
Multiplication	· (raised dot)	factor · factor = product	$10 \cdot 6 = 60$
Multiplication	( )( ) parentheses	(factor)(factor) = product	$(10)(6) = 60$
Division	÷ (division sign)	dividend ÷ divisor = quotient	$60 \div 10 = 6$
Division	⟌ (long division symbol)	$\text{divisor}\overline{)\text{dividend}}^{\text{quotient}}$	$10\overline{)60}^{\,6}$
Division	/ (slash or fraction bar)	dividend/divisor = quotient	$60/10 = 6$
Division	stacked fraction bar	$\dfrac{\text{dividend}}{\text{divisor}} = \text{quotient}$	$\dfrac{60}{10} = 6$

As you can see from the examples in the preceding table, addition and subtraction "undo" each other. Mathematicians express this relationship by saying that addition and subtraction are **inverses** of each other. Similarly, multiplication and division are **inverses** of each other; they "undo" each other, *as long as division by 0 is not involved.*

You must be *very* careful when division involves zero. Zero can be a dividend; that is, you can divide a nonzero number into zero. However, 0 *cannot* be a divisor, which means that you *cannot* divide by 0. The quotient of any number divided by zero has no meaning; that is, *division by zero is undefined—you can't do it!* Even zero divided by zero is undefined. Following is a summary of division involving zero.

Division Involving Zero		
Rule	**Meaning**	**Example**
You *cannot* divide by zero. Zero cannot be the divisor!	$\dfrac{\text{any number}}{0}$ = undefined	$\dfrac{21}{0}$ = undefined
You *cannot* divide by zero. Zero cannot be the divisor!	$\dfrac{0}{0}$ = undefined	$\dfrac{0}{0}$ = undefined
You can divide zero by a nonzero number. Zero can be the dividend as long as the divisor is not zero.	$\dfrac{0}{\text{any nonzero number}}$ = 0	$\dfrac{0}{47}$ = 0

Counting Numbers

The **counting numbers** or **natural numbers** are 1, 2, 3, and so on. Counting numbers that are greater than 1 are either *prime* or *composite*. A **prime number** is a whole number greater than 1 that has exactly two distinct factors: itself and 1. Thus, the primes are 2, 3, 5, 7, 11, 13, and so on.

The counting numbers greater than 1 that are *not* prime are called the **composite numbers.** They are 4, 6, 8, 9, 10, 12, and so on.

The counting number 1 is neither prime nor composite.

Besides classifying a counting number as prime or composite, a counting number can be classified as either *even* or *odd*. Counting numbers that divide evenly by 2 are called **even.** The **even counting numbers** are 2, 4, 6, 8, and so on.

Counting numbers that do *not* divide evenly by 2 are called **odd.** The **odd counting numbers** are 1, 3, 5, 7, 9, and so on.

The **principle of mathematical induction** states that any set of counting numbers that contains the number 1 and $k + 1$, whenever it contains the counting number k, contains all the counting numbers.

The **Fundamental Theorem of Arithmetic** states that every counting number ≥ 2 is either a prime or can be factored into a product of primes in one and only one way, except for the order in which the factors appear. To find the prime factors of a number, you can use a **factor tree.** Here is an example of using a factor tree to find the prime factors of the number 36.

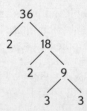

The numbers at the tips of the "branches" are prime factors—you cannot factor them any further. So the prime factors of 36 are 2 and 3. You can write 36 as the product of its prime factors like this: $36 = 2 \cdot 2 \cdot 3 \cdot 3$.

Divisibility rules can help with factoring numbers. A counting number is **divisible by** another counting number if, after dividing by that number, the remainder is zero. You write $a|b$ to mean a divides b evenly or, equivalently, b "is divisible by" a. For example $3|36$, which means 36 is divisible by 3. Therefore, 3 is a factor of 36. The following table shows some common divisibility rules that you will find helpful.

Some Common Divisibility Rules		
Divisibility by	**Rule**	**Example**
2	A number is divisible by 2 if and only if the last digit of the number is even.	2|2,347,854 since 4 (the last digit) is even.
3	A number is divisible by 3 if and only if the sum of its digits is divisible by 3.	3|151,515 since 3 divides 1+5+1+5+1+5 = 18 (the sum of the digits).
4	A number is divisible by 4 if and only if the last 2 digits form a number that is divisible by 4.	4|47,816 since 4 divides 16 (the number formed by the last two digits).
5	A number is divisible by 5 if and only if the last digit of the number is 0 or 5.	5|42,115 since the last digit is 5.
6	A number is divisible by 6 if and only if it is divisible by both 2 and 3.	6|18,122,124 since 2|18,122,124 (the last digit is even) and 3|18,122,124 (21, the sum of the digits, is divisible by 3).
7	To test for divisibility by 7, double the last digit and subtract the product from the number formed by the remaining digits. If the results is a number divisible by 7, the original number is also divisible by 7.	7|875 since 87−10 = 77, which is divisible by 7.
8	A number is divisible by 8 if and only if the last 3 digits form a number that is divisible by 8.	8|55,864 since 8 divides 864 (the number formed by the last three digits).
9	A number is divisible by 9 if and only if the sum of its digits is divisible by 9.	9|151,515 since 9 divides 1+5+1+5+1+5 = 18 (the sum of the digits).
10	A number is divisible by 10 if and only if the last digit of the number is 0.	10|66,660 since the last digit is 0.
11	To test for divisibility by 11, alternately add and subtract the digits. If the results is a number divisible by 11, the original number is also divisible by 11.	11|2,574 since 11 divides 2−5+7−4 = 0 (the sum of the digits).

The **greatest common factor** of two or more counting numbers is the greatest product that will divide evenly into each of the counting numbers. It can be obtained by writing the prime factorization of each counting number and building a product consisting of each factor the *highest* number of times it appears as a *common* factor of the counting numbers in the set. The greatest common factor of two counting numbers m and n is denoted **gcf(m,n)**. For example, since $24 = 2 \cdot 2 \cdot 2 \cdot 3$ and $36 = 2 \cdot 2 \cdot 3 \cdot 3$, the gcf(24, 36) $= 2 \cdot 2 \cdot 3 = 12$.

The **greatest common divisor** of two counting numbers m and n, denoted **gcd(m,n),** is the greatest common factor of m and n. Thus, the gcd(24, 36) $= 12$.

Tip: The greatest common divisor of two numbers is the greatest number that will divide evenly into both numbers.

The **least common multiple** of a set of counting numbers is the least product that is a multiple of each of the counting numbers. It can be obtained by factoring each counting number and building a product consisting of each factor the *most* number of times it appears as a factor in any *one* of the counting numbers in the set. The least common multiple of two counting numbers m and n is denoted **lcm (m,n)**. For example, since $24 = 2 \cdot 2 \cdot 2 \cdot 3$ and $36 = 2 \cdot 2 \cdot 3 \cdot 3$, the lcm(24, 36) $= 2 \cdot 2 \cdot 2 \cdot 3 \cdot 3 = 72$.

> **Tip:** The least common multiple of a set of numbers is the least number that is divisible by each of the numbers in the set.

Rational Numbers

The **rational numbers** are the numbers that you are familiar with from school and from your everyday experiences with numbers. The rational numbers include the whole numbers, integers, and positive and negative fractions, decimals, and percents.

The **whole numbers** are the numbers 0, 1, 2, 3, . . .

The **integers** are the numbers . . ., –3, –2, –1, 0, 1, 2, 3, . . .

Integers are either **positive** (1, 2, 3, . . .), **negative** (. . ., –3, –2, –1), or **zero**. Negative numbers have a small horizontal line (–) on the left of the number.

> **Tip:** You do not have to write the + sign on positive numbers (although it's not wrong to do so). If no sign is written with a nonzero number, then you know that it is a positive number. The number zero is neither positive nor negative.

Integers that are divisible by 2 are called **even** integers. The **even integers** are . . .,–8, –6, –4, –2, 0, 2, 4, 6, 8, ...

> **Tip:** Notice that zero is an even integer because 0 divided by 2 is 0 (no remainder).

Integers that are *not* divisible by 2 are called **odd** integers. The **odd integers** are. . ., –9, –7, –5, –3, –1, 1, 3, 5, 7, 9, ...

The **rational numbers** are all the numbers that can be written as a ratio of two integers, where zero is *not* the denominator of the ratio. Here are examples: $\frac{3}{4}$, $-\frac{2}{5}$, $\frac{325}{1000}$, $\frac{15}{7}$, and $-\frac{75}{100}$.

All the counting numbers, whole numbers, and integers are rational numbers because you can write each as a ratio whose denominator is 1 as shown here.

$$. . ., \ -3 = \frac{-3}{1}, \ -2 = \frac{-2}{1}, \ -1 = \frac{-1}{1}, \ 0 = \frac{0}{1}, \ 1 = \frac{1}{1}, \ 2 = \frac{2}{1}, \ 3 = \frac{3}{1}, . . .$$

Rational numbers can be expressed as **fractions, decimals,** or **percents.**

Fractions

Equivalent fractions are fractions that have the same value. For example, $\frac{3}{4}$ and $\frac{75}{100}$ are equivalent fractions.

If the numerator and denominator of a fraction have one or more common factors (other than 1), you can **reduce** the fraction to an equivalent fraction in **lowest terms** by dividing the numerator and denominator by the greatest common factor, as in $\frac{75 \div 25}{100 \div 25} = \frac{3}{4}$. In this case, gcf(75,100) = 25.

To write a fraction as an equivalent fraction with a larger denominator, you multiply the numerator and denominator by the same whole number (greater than 1). For example, $\frac{3 \cdot 25}{4 \cdot 25} = \frac{75}{100}$.

A **proper fraction** is a fraction in which the numerator is less than the denominator. For example, $\frac{1}{2}$, $\frac{9}{10}$, and $\frac{24}{36}$ are **proper fractions.** An **improper fraction** is one in which the numerator is greater than or equal to the denominator. For example, $\frac{3}{2}$, $\frac{29}{10}$, and $\frac{36}{36}$ are **improper fractions.** Any improper fraction has a value greater than or equal to one.

A **mixed number** is the sum of a whole number and a fraction, written together like these examples: $1\frac{1}{2}$ and $2\frac{9}{10}$. When you read a mixed number, you say the word *and* between the whole number and the fraction. For instance, $2\frac{9}{10}$ is read as "two and nine-tenths."

You change an improper fraction to a mixed number or a whole number by dividing the numerator by the denominator and writing the remainder, if any, like this: $\frac{\text{remainder}}{\text{denominator}}$. For example, $\frac{29}{10} = 2 \text{ R } 9 = 2\frac{9}{10}$.

Even though you are allowed to use a calculator on the Praxis Middle School Mathematics test, you still need to know and understand how to perform computations with fractions. Understanding the process will make it less likely that you will make an error when performing a calculation and will also help you evaluate the reasonableness of the result of your computation.

The following table summarizes the rules for addition and subtraction of fractions.

Rules for Addition and Subtraction of Fractions

Operation	Rule	Example
Addition/Subtraction— Like Denominators	Add/subtract the numerators of the fractions to obtain the numerator of the answer, which is placed over the common denominator. Reduce to lowest terms, if needed.	$\frac{5}{8} + \frac{1}{8} = \frac{5+1}{8} = \frac{6}{8} = \frac{6 \div 2}{8 \div 2} = \frac{3}{4}$ $\frac{5}{8} - \frac{1}{8} = \frac{5-1}{8} = \frac{4}{8} = \frac{4 \div 4}{8 \div 4} = \frac{1}{2}$
Addition/Subtraction— Unlike Denominators	Find a common denominator. The common denominator is the least common multiple (lcm) of the denominators. Write each fraction as an equivalent fraction having the common denominator as a denominator. Add/subtract the numerators of the fractions to obtain the numerator of the answer, which is placed over the common denominator. Reduce to lowest terms, if needed.	$\frac{1}{4} + \frac{2}{3} = \frac{3}{12} + \frac{8}{12} = \frac{3+8}{12} = \frac{11}{12}$ $\frac{3}{4} - \frac{2}{3} = \frac{9}{12} - \frac{8}{12} = \frac{9-8}{12} = \frac{1}{12}$

The following table summarizes the rules for multiplication and division with fractions.

Rules for Multiplication and Division of Fractions

Operation	Rule	Example
Multiplication— Proper Fractions or Improper Fractions	Multiply the numerators to obtain the numerator of the product and multiply the denominators to obtain the denominator of the product. Reduce to lowest terms, if needed.	$\frac{1}{3} \times \frac{3}{4} = \frac{1 \times 3}{3 \times 4} = \frac{3}{12} = \frac{3 \div 3}{12 \div 3} = \frac{1}{4}$

(continued)

Rules for Multiplication and Division of Fractions *(continued)*		
Operation	*Rule*	*Example*
Multiplication— Proper Fraction and Whole Number	Write the whole number as an equivalent fraction with denominator 1 and then multiply as with proper fractions.	$\frac{3}{4} \times 12 = \frac{3}{4} \times \frac{12}{1} = \frac{3 \times 12}{4 \times 1} = \frac{36}{4} = \frac{36 \div 4}{4 \div 4} = \frac{9}{1} = 9$
Multiplication— One or More Mixed Numbers	Change the mixed numbers to improper fractions and then multiply as with proper fractions.	$2\frac{3}{4} \times 1\frac{1}{3} = \frac{11}{4} \times \frac{4}{3} = \frac{11 \times 4}{4 \times 3} = \frac{44}{12} = \frac{44}{12} = \frac{44 \div 4}{12 \div 4} = \frac{11}{3}$ or $3\frac{2}{3}$
Division—Proper Fractions or Improper Fractions	Multiply the first fraction by the *reciprocal* of the second fraction.	$\frac{4}{3} \div \frac{1}{2} = \frac{4}{3} \times \frac{2}{1} = \frac{4 \times 2}{3 \times 1} = \frac{8}{3}$ or $2\frac{2}{3}$
Division—Whole Number Divisor	Write the whole number as an equivalent fraction with denominator 1 and then multiply the first fraction by the *reciprocal* of the whole number fraction.	$\frac{4}{5} \div 3 = \frac{4}{5} \div \frac{3}{1} = \frac{4}{5} \times \frac{1}{3} = \frac{4 \times 1}{5 \times 3} = \frac{4}{15}$
Multiplication— One or More Mixed Numbers	Change the mixed numbers to improper fractions and then multiply the first fraction by the *reciprocal* of the second fraction.	$2\frac{1}{3} \div 1\frac{1}{2} = \frac{7}{3} \div \frac{3}{2} = \frac{7}{3} \times \frac{2}{3} = \frac{7 \times 2}{3 \times 3} = \frac{14}{9}$ or $1\frac{5}{9}$

Tip: Here is a mnemonic to help you remember division of fractions: "Keep it, change it, flip it" meaning "*Keep* the first fraction, *change* the division symbol to a multiplication symbol, and then *change* the second fraction to its reciprocal."

You can make multiplying fractions easier by reducing to lowest terms before any multiplication is performed. You simply divide out factors common to a numerator and denominator (as in reducing) before multiplying.

Here is an example.

$$2\frac{3}{4} \times 1\frac{1}{3} = \frac{11}{\overset{1}{\cancel{4}}} \times \frac{\overset{1}{\cancel{4}}}{3} = \frac{11}{3} = \text{ or } 3\frac{2}{3}$$

Decimals

Decimals are rational numbers that are written using a base-10 place-value system. In a decimal number, the number of digits to the right of the decimal point up to and including the final digit is the number of decimal places in the number. For instance, a whole number such as 376 has zero decimal places; the number 37.6 has one decimal place; the number 3.76 has two decimal places; and the number 3.760 has three decimal places.

You can obtain the decimal representation of a fractional number by dividing the numerator by the denominator. Here is an example.

$$\frac{3}{5} = 0.6 \text{ because } 5\overline{)3.0}^{\,0.6}.$$

In this case, the decimal **terminates** (eventually has a zero remainder). For some rational numbers, the decimal keeps going, but eventually in a block of one or more digits that repeats over and over again. These decimals are **repeating.**

Here is an example of a repeating decimal.

$$\frac{2}{3} = 3\overline{)2.000\ldots}^{0.666\ldots}$$

No matter how long you continue to add zeroes and divide, the 6s in the quotient continue without end. Put a bar over the repeating digit (or digits when more than one digit repeats) to indicate the repetition. Thus, $\frac{2}{3} = 0.\overline{6}$. When decimals repeat, they are usually rounded to a specified degree of accuracy (for example, 0.6666. . . is 0.67 when rounded to 2 decimal places). All terminating and repeating decimals are rational numbers.

You should do your decimal computations with your calculator when you take the Praxis Middle School Mathematics test. Just for review, the following two tables summarize the rules for decimal computations.

Rules for Computations with Decimals		
Operation	**Rule**	**Example**
Addition/subtraction	Line up the decimal points vertically. Add/subtract as you would with whole numbers. Place the decimal point in the answer directly under the decimal points in the problem.	$65.3 + 0.34 = 65.30$ $65.3 - 0.34 = 65.30$ $+ 0.34$ $- 0.34$ 65.64 64.96
	Tip: Fill in empty decimal places with zeroes.	
Multiplication	Multiply the numbers as whole numbers. Place the decimal point in the proper place in the product. The number of decimal places in the product is the sum of the number of decimal places in the numbers being multiplied. If there are not enough places, insert one or more zeros at the *left* end of the number.	$55.7 \times 0.25 = 13.925$
Division	Rewrite the problem as an equivalent problem with a whole number divisor. Do this by multiplying the divisor and dividend by the power of 10 that makes the divisor a whole number, annexing additional zeroes after the dividend, if needed. Divide as with whole numbers. Place the decimal point in the quotient directly above the decimal point in the dividend.	$2.04 \div 0.002 = 0.002\overline{)2.040} = 0002\overline{)2040.}^{1020.} = 1020$

Percents

You can also write rational numbers as percents. *Percent* means "per hundred." The percent sign is a short way to write $\frac{1}{100}$ or 0.01. When you see a percent sign, you can substitute $\frac{1}{100}$ or 0.01 for the percent sign.

A **percent** is a way of writing a fraction as an equivalent fraction in which the denominator is 100. Thus, $25\% = 25 \cdot \frac{1}{100} = \frac{25}{100} = 0.25$. You can think of percents as special ways to write ordinary decimals or fractions. For instance, 100% is just a special way to write the number 1—because $100\% = 100 \cdot \frac{1}{100} = \frac{100}{100} = 1$. If you have 100% of something, you have all of it. A percent that is less than 100% is less than 1. When you have less than 100% of something, you have less than one whole thing. A percent that is greater than 100% is greater than 1. When you have more than 100% of something, you have more than one whole thing.

You can write a percent as an equivalent fraction by writing the number immediately to the left of the percent sign as the numerator of a fraction in which the denominator is 100. The resulting fraction may then be reduced to lowest terms. Here are examples.

$$50\% = \frac{50}{100} = \frac{50 \div 50}{100 \div 50} = \frac{1}{2} \; ; \; 75\% = \frac{75}{100} = \frac{75 \div 25}{100 \div 25} = \frac{3}{4} \; ; \; 1\% = \frac{1}{100} \; ; \; 125\% = \frac{125}{100} = \frac{125 \div 25}{100 \div 25} = \frac{5}{4} = 1\frac{1}{4}$$

When percents contain decimal fractions, multiply the numerator and denominator by 10, 100, or 1000, and so on, to remove the decimal in the numerator, and then reduce the resulting fraction, if possible. Here are examples.

$$12.5\% = \frac{12.5}{100} = \frac{12.5 \times 10}{100 \times 10} = \frac{125}{1000} = \frac{125 \div 125}{1000 \div 125} = \frac{1}{8} \; ; \; 0.2\% = \frac{.2}{100} = \frac{.2 \times 10}{100 \times 10} = \frac{2}{1000} = \frac{2 \div 2}{1000 \div 2} = \frac{1}{500}$$

If a percent contains a simple common fraction, replace the percent sign with $\frac{1}{100}$, multiply, and then reduce, if possible. Here are examples.

$$\frac{1}{2}\% = \frac{1}{2} \times \frac{1}{100} = \frac{1}{200} \; ; \; \frac{3}{4}\% = \frac{3}{4} \times \frac{1}{100} = \frac{3}{400} \; ; \; \frac{5}{8}\% = \frac{5}{8} \times \frac{1}{100} = \frac{5}{800} = \frac{5 \div 5}{800 \div 5} = \frac{1}{160}$$

When percents contain mixed fractions, change the mixed fraction to an improper fraction, replace the percent sign with $\frac{1}{100}$, multiply, and then reduce, if possible. Here are examples.

$$12\frac{1}{2}\% = \frac{25}{2} \times \frac{1}{100} = \frac{25}{200} = \frac{25 \div 25}{200 \div 25} = \frac{1}{8} \; ; \; 33\frac{1}{3}\% = \frac{100}{3} \times \frac{1}{100} = \frac{100}{300} = \frac{100 \div 100}{300 \div 100} = \frac{1}{3}$$

You can write a percent as an equivalent decimal by changing it to an equivalent fraction in which the denominator is 100 and then dividing by 100. For example, $75\% = \frac{75}{100} = 100 \overline{)75.00}^{0.75}$. A shortcut for this process is to move the decimal point two places to the left (which is the same as dividing by 100) and drop the percent sign. Here are examples.

$$25\% = 0.25; \; 32\% = 0.32; \; 45.5\% = 0.455; \; 8\% = 0.08; \; 200\% = 2.00 = 2$$

Conversely, to write a decimal in percent form, move the decimal point two places to the right (which is the same as multiplying by 100) and attach the percent sign (%) at the end of the resulting number. Why does this make sense? Recall that the percent sign is a short way to write $\frac{1}{100}$, which means 1 divided by 100. Since the percent sign has division by 100 built into it, when you put the percent sign at the end of the number, you undo the multiplication by 100 that you did earlier. Thus, the value of the original number does not change. Here are examples.

$$0.45 = 45\%; \; 0.01 = 1\%; \; 0.125 = 12.5\%; \; 2 = 2.00 = 200\%; \; 0.0025 = 0.25\%$$

To write a fraction in percent form, first write the fraction as an equivalent decimal by performing the indicated division and then change the resulting decimal to a percent. When the quotient is a repeating decimal, carry the division to two decimal places and then write the remainder as a fraction like this: $\frac{\text{remainder}}{\text{divisor}}$. Here are examples.

$$\frac{1}{4} = 4 \overline{)1.00}^{0.25} = 25\%; \; \frac{3}{5} = 5 \overline{)3.00}^{0.60} = 60\%; \; \frac{1}{3} = 3 \overline{)1.00}^{0.33 \text{ R } 1} = 0.33\frac{1}{3} = 33\frac{1}{3}\%$$

Before you take the Praxis Middle School Mathematics test, it would be to your advantage to memorize the following list of common percents with their fraction and decimal equivalents. Make a set of flashcards to carry with you and drill on these when you have spare time.

$100\% = 1.00 = 1$, $75\% = 0.75 = \frac{3}{4}$, $50\% = 0.5 = \frac{1}{2}$, $25\% = 0.25 = \frac{1}{4}$, $33\frac{1}{3}\% = 0.33\frac{1}{3}$, $66\frac{2}{3}\% = 0.66\frac{2}{3} = \frac{2}{3}$,

$20\% = 0.20 = 0.2 = \frac{1}{5}$, $40\% = 0.40 = 0.4 = \frac{2}{5}$, $60\% = 0.60 = 0.6 = \frac{3}{5}$, $80\% = 0.80 = 0.8 = \frac{4}{5}$,

$10\% = 0.10 = 0.1 = \frac{1}{10}$, $30\% = 0.30 = 0.3 = \frac{3}{10}$, $5\% = 0.05 = \frac{1}{20}$.

Irrational Numbers

Irrational numbers are numbers that *cannot* be written as the ratio of two integers. They have nonterminating, nonrepeating decimal representations. There are infinitely many decimals that are neither terminating nor repeating decimals. For example, $0.343344333444\ldots$ is such a decimal. Even though, you can predict that, if the pattern in the digits to the right of the decimal point was to continue, four 3s followed by four 4s would come next in the decimal representation, the number is not a repeating decimal because a *block of digits* do not repeat. Therefore, $0.343344333444\ldots$ is an irrational number. Other examples of irrational numbers are $\sqrt{6}$ (the square root of 6) and $\sqrt[3]{-75}$ (the cube root of -75), e (Euler's number), and $-\pi$ (negative pi). With these numbers, there is no discernible repeating pattern in the decimal representation. You can use the ellipsis ($\ldots$) to indicate digits are missing as shown here.

$$\sqrt{6} = 2.449490\ldots, \quad \sqrt[3]{-75} = -4.217163\ldots, \quad e = 2.718281\ldots, \quad -\pi = -3.141593\ldots$$

Tip: Some roots of rational numbers are rational, and others are not. For example, $\sqrt{6}$ is irrational; but $\sqrt{4}$ is 2, a rational number. $\sqrt[3]{-75}$ is irrational; but $\sqrt[3]{-8}$ is −2, a rational number. Furthermore, be cautious with *even* roots of rational numbers. When working with real numbers, be aware that taking the square root, fourth root, eighth root, and so forth of a *negative* number will *not* yield a real number.

For computational purposes, you can only approximate irrational numbers. For example, if you want to use $\sqrt{6}$, $\sqrt[3]{-75}$, e, or $-\pi$ in computations, you can obtain an approximate value for each using a preselected number of decimal places. For example, their decimal representations to 3 places are as follows:

$$\sqrt{6} \cong 2.449, \quad \sqrt[3]{-75} \cong -4.217, \quad e \cong 2.718, \quad -\pi \cong -3.142$$

Note: The symbol $\cong$ is read "is approximately equal to."

However, it is important to remember that if the *exact* value of an irrational root is desired, the radical symbol must be retained. For instance, if the area of a square is 6 cm², then the exact length of each side of the square is $\sqrt{6}$ cm. See "Radicals and Roots" in this chapter for an additional discussion of roots.

Tip: For the Praxis Middle School Mathematics test, you can use the π key on your calculator for problems involving π.

Real Numbers

The real numbers, denoted *R,* are the numbers that describe the world in which we live. They are made up of all the rational numbers plus all the irrational numbers. The counting numbers, whole numbers, integers, rational numbers, and irrational numbers are all subsets of the real numbers. The relationship of the subsets of the real numbers is illustrated in the following figure. Each set in the figure contains those sets below it to which it is connected.

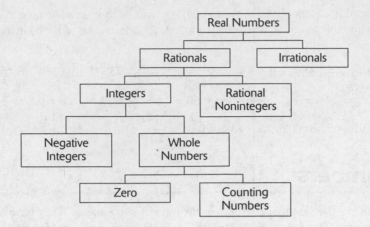

The real numbers can be represented on a number line. Every point on the number line corresponds to a real number. Positive numbers are located to the right of zero, and negative numbers are to the left of zero. Here are examples.

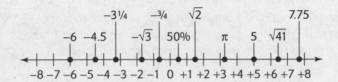

Absolute Value

The **absolute value** of a real number is its distance from zero on the number line. Distance always has a *nonnegative* (*positive* or *zero*) value. The absolute value is indicated by two vertical bars (| |), one on either side of the number. For example, $|5| = |-5| = 5$.

Formally, **absolute value** is defined as follows:

For any real number x, the absolute value of x is given by $|x| = \begin{cases} x, \text{ if } x \geq 0 \\ -x, \text{ if } x < 0 \end{cases}$.

Thus, for every real number x, its absolute value, denoted $|x|$, is either x or $-x$, whichever is a *nonnegative* number (that is, whichever one is farther to the right on the number line).

The following figure illustrates the absolute value definition graphically.

$$x < 0: |x| = -x \qquad x > 0: |x| = x$$

$$-7 \ -6 \ -5 \ -4 \ -3 \ -2 \ -1 \ \ 0 \ \ 1 \ \ 2 \ \ 3 \ \ 4 \ \ 5 \ \ 6 \ \ 7$$

$$x = 0:$$
$$|x| = 0$$

> **Tip:** Remember, $-x$ can be a positive number. Don't be confused by the $-$ symbol to the left of x. The $-$ symbol to the immediate left of x tells you to change the sign of x. When x itself is *nonnegative* (positive or zero), $|x|$ is the *nonnegative* number x; but when x is *negative*, $|x|$ is the *positive* number $-x$.

Absolute value has the following properties for all real numbers x and y.

$$|0| = 0 \qquad |x| = |-x| \qquad |xy| = |x||y| \qquad \left|\frac{x}{y}\right| = \frac{|x|}{|y|}, \text{ provided } y \neq 0 \qquad |x + y| \leq |x| + |y|$$

If c is any positive number, $|x| = c$ if and only if $x = c$ or $x = -c$.

If c is any positive number, $|x| < c$ if and only if $-c < x < c$ (called **conjunction**).

If c is any positive number, $|x| > c$ if and only if $x < -c$ or $x > c$ (called **disjunction**).

Radicals and Roots

A number a such that $a^2 = x$ is called a **square root** of x. Finding the square root of a number is the reverse of squaring a number. Every positive number has two square roots that are equal in absolute value and opposite in sign. For example, since $(5)^2 = 25$ and $(-5)^2 = 25$, 5 and -5 are square roots of 25. The positive square root is called the **principal square root** of the number.

A number a such that $a^3 = x$ is called a **cube root** of x. Finding the cube root of a number is the reverse of cubing a number. Every real number has exactly one real cube root. For example, since $(-5)^3 = -125$, -5 is a cube root of -125.

In general, if $a^n = x$ where n is a counting number, a is called an ***n*th root** of x, written $a = \sqrt[n]{x}$. The expression $\sqrt[n]{x}$ is called a **radical**, x is called the **radicand**; n is called the **index** and indicates which root is desired. If no index is written, it is understood to be 2, and the radical expression indicates the *principal* square root of the radicand. Thus, $\sqrt{x^2} = |x|$. For example, $\sqrt{25} = 5$, not ± 5, and $\sqrt{(-5)^2} = 5$, not -5. As a rule, a *positive* real number x has exactly one real positive *n*th root whether n is even or odd; and *every* real number x has exactly one real *n*th root when n is odd. Negative numbers do not have real *n*th roots when n is even. Thus,

$$\sqrt{36} = 6 \,;\; \sqrt[3]{125} = 5 \,;\; \sqrt[3]{-64} = -4 \,;\; \sqrt{-64} \text{ is not a real number; } \sqrt[4]{-16} \text{ is not a real number.}$$

Finally, the *n*th root of zero is zero, whether n is even or odd : $\sqrt[n]{0} = 0$ (always).

Following are the rules for radicals when x and y are real numbers, m and n are positive integers, and the radical expression denotes a real number:

$$\sqrt[n]{x^n} = x \text{ if } n \text{ is odd} \qquad \sqrt[n]{x^n} = |x| \text{ if } n \text{ is even} \qquad \sqrt[n]{x^m} = \left(\sqrt[n]{x}\right)^m \qquad \left(\sqrt[n]{x}\right)\left(\sqrt[n]{y}\right) = \sqrt[n]{xy}$$

$$\frac{\sqrt[n]{x}}{\sqrt[n]{y}} = \sqrt[n]{\frac{x}{y}}, \, (y \neq 0) \qquad \sqrt[m]{\sqrt[n]{x}} = \sqrt[mn]{x} \qquad \sqrt[pn]{x^{pm}} = \sqrt[n]{x^m} \qquad a\left(\sqrt[n]{x}\right) + b\left(\sqrt[n]{x}\right) = (a + b)\left(\sqrt[n]{x}\right)$$

These rules form the basis for simplifying radical expressions. (See Appendix A for a discussion on simplifying radicals.)

Comparing and Ordering Real Numbers

When you are comparing two real numbers, think of their relative locations on the number line. The number that is farther to the right is the greater number. For example, $-7 < -2$ because as you can see on the number line, -2 lies to the right of -7.

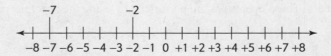

When you compare decimals, compare the digits in each place value from left to right. If the decimals do not have the same number of decimal places, annex or delete zeros after the last digit to the right of the decimal point to make the number of decimal places the same. Remember, annexing or deleting zeros after the last digit to the right of the decimal point does not change the value of a decimal.

For example, 2.5 = 2.50 = 2.500 = 2.5000 and so on. Thus, 2.28 < 2.5 because 2.28 < 2.50.

When comparing fractions that have the same denominator, compare the numerators. For example, $\frac{7}{8} > \frac{5}{8}$ because 7 > 5.

If the denominators of the fractions are not the same, write the fractions as equivalent fractions using a common denominator. For example, $\frac{3}{4} < \frac{7}{8}$ because $\frac{6}{8} < \frac{7}{8}$.

To compare a mixture of decimals and fractions, use your calculator to change the fractions to decimals. Round them off if they repeat. When you are instructed to **order** a list of numbers, you put them in order from **least to greatest** or from **greatest to least**, depending on how the question is stated.

Here is an example:

Order the numbers $\frac{7}{8}$, 0.35, 4.8, $\frac{2}{3}$ from least to greatest.

Before proceeding, write $\frac{7}{8}$ as a decimal by performing the division on your calculator like this: 7 ÷ 8 = 0.875.

Similarly, write $\frac{2}{3}$ as 0.667 (rounding to 3 places). Write 0.35 as 0.350 and 4.8 as 4.800. Next, compare the transformed numbers and put them in order as follows: 0.350, 0.667, 0.875, 4.800. Lastly, substitute the original numbers for their stand-ins to obtain the final answer: 0.35, $\frac{2}{3}$, $\frac{7}{8}$, 4.8.

Here are some tips for handling situations that might occur in problems that involve comparing and ordering real numbers.

- If negative numbers are involved, they will be less than all the positive numbers and 0.
- If percents are involved, change the percents to decimals.
- If the problem contains exponential expressions, evaluate them before making comparisons.
- If you have square roots that are rational numbers, find the square roots before making comparisons.
- If you have irrational square roots, use your calculator to estimate the square roots before comparing them to other numbers.

Here is an example:

Order the following series of numbers from least to greatest.

$\sqrt{37}$, 2^3, 4.39, –4, $\frac{9}{2}$

You do not have to proceed in the order the numbers are listed. Clearly, –4 is less than all the other numbers. Evaluate 2^3 to obtain 8. Write $\frac{9}{2}$ as 4.50, which is greater than 4.39. In order from least to greatest, these four numbers are –4, 4.39, 4.50, 8. Estimate $\sqrt{37}$ to be approximately 6.08, which puts it between 4.50 and 8 in the list. Thus, your final answer is –4, 4.39, $\frac{9}{2}$, $\sqrt{37}$, 2^3.

Operations with Signed Numbers

The real numbers are often called **signed numbers** because they may be positive (+), negative (–), or zero (no sign). On the Praxis Middle School Mathematics test, you will need to know how to perform addition, subtraction, multiplication, and division with signed numbers. These operations are performed by using the absolute values, which are always positive or zero, of the numbers.

Addition of Signed Numbers

When you add two signed numbers, you must note whether the two numbers have the same sign (both positive or both negative) or have different signs (one positive and one negative). How you do the addition depends on which of these situations is the case. This type of addition is called **algebraic addition.** The following summarizes the rules for algebraic addition of two signed numbers.

Rules for Algebraic Addition of Two Signed Numbers		
If the signs are:	*The rule is:*	*Examples*
the same—both positive or both negative	Add the absolute values of the two numbers and attach the common sign to the sum.	4 + 6 = 10; −4 + −6 = −10
different—one positive and one negative	Subtract the lesser absolute value from the greater absolute value and indicate that the result has the same sign as the number with the greater absolute value; if both numbers have the same absolute value, the sum is 0.	−4 + 6 = 2; 4 + −6 = −2; −4 + 4 = 0

As you can see, algebraic addition is different from arithmetic addition; particularly, because you don't always "add" to get the sum. In fact, if the signs are different, you subtract to find the sum. How does this make sense? Keep in mind that the numbers you worked with in arithmetic were amounts only—they had no signs. Real numbers have an amount *and* a sign. The sign adds a direction to the number. Every real number has an amount and a direction. The number +5 is 5 units in the positive direction. The number −5 is 5 units in the negative direction. When you add signed numbers, you have to take into account both the amount and the direction of the number.

If you have three or more signed numbers to add together, you may find it convenient to first add all the positive numbers; second, add all the negative numbers; and then add the resulting two answers. Here is an example:

$$14 + -35 + 6 + -25 = 20 + -60 = -40$$

Other times, you might look for opposites that sum to zero. Here is an example:

$$1200 + -450 + 5 + -1200 + 450 = 1200 + -1200 + -450 + 450 + 5 = 0 + 0 + 5 = 5$$

Subtraction of Signed Numbers

You do not have to memorize a set of new rules for subtraction of signed numbers! The reason is that you subtract signed numbers by changing the subtraction problem in a special way to an algebraic addition problem, so that the rules for addition of signed numbers will apply. Here's how you do it.

Algebraic Subtraction of Signed Numbers		
Operation	*Rule*	*Example*
Subtraction	To subtract two signed numbers: Change the minus (−) symbol to a plus (+) symbol. Change the sign of the second number. Perform algebraic addition according to the rules for addition of signed numbers.	−10 − 4 = −10 + Change 4 to −4. −10 + −4 = −14

Think of the minus symbol as "+ opposite of." Incorrectly interpreting subtraction is a common mistake. Here are examples of correctly rewriting subtraction problems.

$$10 - 16 = 10 + \text{opposite of } 16 = 10 + -16$$
$$26 - 15 = 26 + \text{opposite of } 15 = 26 + -15$$
$$-5 - 20 = -5 + \text{opposite of } 20 = -5 + -20$$
$$2 - -6 = 2 + \text{opposite of } -6 = 2 + 6$$
$$-8 - -4 = -8 + \text{opposite of } -4 = -8 + 4$$

Tip: Here is a mnemonic to help you remember how to rewrite a subtraction problem: "Keep it, change it, change it," meaning "*Keep* the first number, *change* the minus symbol to a plus symbol, and then *change* the second number to its opposite."

Here are examples of algebraic subtraction. Recite "Keep it, change it, change it" as you rewrite the problems.

$$10 - 16 = 10 + -16 = -6$$
$$26 - 15 = 26 + -15 = 11$$
$$-5 - 20 = -5 + -20 = -25$$
$$2 - -6 = 2 + 6 = 8$$
$$-8 - -4 = -8 + 4 = -4$$

Multiplication and Division of Signed Numbers

Algebraic multiplication and division of signed numbers share the same pattern. The following summarizes the rules for multiplication or division of two signed numbers.

Rules for Algebraic Multiplication or Division of Two Signed Numbers		
If the signs are:	*The rule is:*	*Examples*
the same—both positive or both negative	Multiply or divide the absolute values of the two numbers, and indicate the answer is positive (no sign is necessary).	$2 \cdot 5 = 10$; $-2 \cdot -5 = 10$; $12 \div 4 = 3$; $-12 \div -4 = 3$
different—one positive and one negative	Multiply or divide the absolute values of the two numbers, and use a negative sign as the sign for the answer.	$-2 \cdot 5 = -10$; $2 \cdot -5 = -10$; $-12 \div 4 = -3$; $12 \div -4 = -3$

Tip: Unlike algebraic addition, for algebraic multiplication/division when the signs are the same, it doesn't matter what the common sign is, the product/quotient is positive no matter what. Similarly, unlike algebraic addition, for algebraic multiplication/division when the signs are different, it doesn't matter which number has the greater absolute value—the product/quotient is negative no matter what.

The two rules for multiplication tell you how to multiply two numbers, but often you will want to find the product of more than two numbers. To do this, multiply in pairs. You can keep track of the appropriate sign as you proceed, or you can use the following:

When *zero* is one of the factors, the product is *always* zero; otherwise; products involving an *even* number of *negative* factors are *positive*, whereas, those involving an *odd* number of *negative* factors are *negative*.

Here are examples:

$(-10)(2)(0)(-5) = 0$

$(-10)(2)(3)(-5) = 300.$

$(-10)(2)(3)(-5)(-1) = -300.$

The rules for algebraic addition, subtraction, multiplication, and division apply to all real numbers. Here are examples:

$$-\frac{5}{8} + -\frac{1}{8} = -\frac{6}{8} = -\frac{3}{4}$$

$$\frac{2}{3} - \frac{3}{4} = \frac{8}{12} - \frac{9}{12} = -\frac{1}{12}$$

$$24.5 + 134.28 = 158.78$$

$$-18.5 + 7.25 = -11.25$$

$$\frac{3}{4} \times -12 = \frac{3}{\underset{1}{4}} \times \frac{-\overset{3}{12}}{1} = -\frac{9}{1} = -9$$

$$-2\frac{3}{4} \times -1\frac{1}{3} = -\frac{11}{\underset{1}{4}} \times -\frac{\overset{1}{4}}{3} = \frac{11}{3} \text{ or } 3\frac{2}{3}$$

$$(-0.75)(400) = -300$$

$$(-125.43)(-0.005) = 0.62715$$

Exponentiation of Signed Numbers

In mathematical expressions, **exponentiation** is indicated by a small raised number, called the **exponent,** written to the upper right of a quantity, which is called the **base** for the exponential expression. The most common exponents that you will need to know for the Praxis Middle School Mathematics test are summarized in the following table.

Exponents		
Type of Exponent	*Definition*	*Example*
Positive Integer	If x is any real number and n is a positive integer, then $x^n = \underbrace{x \cdot x \cdot x \cdots \cdots x}_{n \text{ factors of } x}$, where x^n is read "x to the nth power" or as "x to the n."	$2^5 = 2 \cdot 2 \cdot 2 \cdot 2 \cdot 2 = 32$
Zero	For any real number x (except zero), $x^0 = 1$.	$(-12.78)^0 = 1$
Fractional Number	If x is any real number (except zero) and m and n are natural numbers, then $x^{\frac{1}{n}} = \sqrt[n]{x}$; and $x^{\frac{m}{n}} = \left(\sqrt[n]{x}\right)^m$ or $\sqrt[n]{x^m}$; provided, in all cases, that $x \geq 0$ when n is even .	$16^{\frac{1}{2}} = \sqrt{16} = 4$ and $64^{\frac{3}{4}} = \left(\sqrt[4]{64}\right)^3 = (2)^3 = 8$
Negative Number	If x is any real number (except zero) and $-n$ is a negative number, then $x^{-n} = \frac{1}{x^n}$ and $\frac{1}{x^{-n}} = x^n$	$2^{-3} = \frac{1}{2^3} = \frac{1}{8}$ and $\frac{1}{2^{-3}} = 2^3 = 8$

> **Tip:** The exponent, 2, on a number is usually read "squared" rather than as "to the second power;" likewise, the exponent, 3, is usually read "cubed" rather than as "to the third power."

The following **rules for exponents** hold:

For real numbers x and y and integers m, n, and p:

$$x^1 = x \qquad x^0 = 1, x \neq 0 \qquad 0^0 \text{ is undefined} \qquad x^{-n} = \frac{1}{x^n} \qquad \left(\frac{x}{y}\right)^{-1} = \frac{y}{x} \qquad \left(\frac{x}{y}\right)^{-n} = \left(\frac{y}{x}\right)^n$$

$$\left(x^n\right)^p = x^{np} \qquad \left(\frac{x}{y}\right)^p = \frac{x^p}{y^p} \qquad (xy)^p = x^p y^p \quad x^m x^n = x^{m+n} \text{ (product rule)} \qquad \frac{x^m}{x^n} = x^{m-n} \text{ (quotient rule)},$$

provided, in all cases, that division by zero does not occur.

Here are some points to remember about exponents.

The product and quotient rules for exponential expressions apply only when the exponential expressions have exactly the same base:

$$x^2 x^3 = x^{2+3} = x^5 \text{ and } \frac{x^5}{x^3} = x^{5-3} = x^2 \text{; but } x^2 y^3 \text{ and } \frac{x^5}{y^3} \text{ cannot be simplified further.}$$

Exponentiation is not "commutative": $2^5 \neq 5^2$.

Exponentiation does not distribute over addition (or subtraction): $(3 + 2)^3 = 5^3 = 125$; $(3 + 2)^3 \neq 3^3 + 2^3 = 27 + 8 = 35$.

An exponent applies only to the base it is attached to: $3 \cdot 5^2 = 3 \cdot 25 = 75$; $3 \cdot 5^2 \neq 3^2 \cdot 5^2 = 9 \cdot 25 = 225$; $-3^2 = -(3 \cdot 3) = -9$, $-3^2 \neq (-3)^2 = -3 \cdot -3 = 9$.

Use parentheses around the factors for which the exponent applies: $(3 \cdot 5)^2 = 3^2 \cdot 5^2 = 9 \cdot 25 = 225$.

A negative number raised to an even power yields a positive product: $(-2)^4 = -2 \cdot -2 \cdot -2 \cdot -2 = 16$.

A negative number raised to an odd power yields a negative product: $(-2)^5 = -2 \cdot -2 \cdot -2 \cdot -2 \cdot -2 = -32$.

Any nonzero quantity raised to the zero power is 1: $\left(\text{nonzero quantity}\right)^0 = 1$, ALWAYS!

Only exponential expressions that are factors can be moved from the numerator to the denominator (or from the denominator to the numerator) of a fraction simply by changing the sign of the exponent:

$$\frac{1}{2^{-1} 3^{-1}} = \frac{2 \cdot 3}{1} = \frac{6}{1} = 6 \text{, but } \frac{1}{2^{-1} + 3^{-1}} = \frac{1}{\frac{1}{2} + \frac{1}{3}} = \frac{1}{\frac{5}{6}} = \frac{6}{5} = 1\frac{1}{5} \text{; } \frac{1}{2^{-1} + 3^{-1}} \neq \frac{2 + 3}{1} = \frac{5}{1} = 5.$$

In general, when you have zero or negative exponents in a mathematical expression, you should rewrite it as an equivalent expression that no longer contains zero or negative exponents:

$$\frac{x^3 y^{-4} z^{-1}}{u^0 x^{-2} y^3 z^{-3}} = \frac{x^3 x^2 z^3}{1 y^4 y^3 z} = \frac{x^5 z^2}{y^7}.$$

The Order of Operations

When more than one operation is involved in a numerical expression, you must follow the **order of operations** to **simplify** the expression:

1. Do computations inside **parentheses.** If there is more than one operation inside the parentheses, follow the order of operations given here as you do the computations inside the parentheses.

2. Evaluate any terms with **exponents.**

3. **Multiply** and **divide** in the order in which these operations occur from left to right.

4. **Add** and **subtract** in the order in which these operations occur from left to right.

Here are examples of using the order of operations to simplify numerical expressions:

Simplify: $90 - 5 \cdot 3^2 + 42 \div (5 + 2)$

$$90 - 5 \cdot 3^2 + 42 \div (5 + 2) = 90 - 5 \cdot 3^2 + 42 \div (7) \quad \text{First, do computations inside parentheses.}$$

$$= 90 - 5 \cdot 9 + 42 \div (7) \quad \text{Next, evaluate exponents.}$$

$$= 90 - 45 + 6 \quad \text{Then, multiply and divide from left to right.}$$

$$= 51 \quad \text{Finally, add and subtract from left to right.}$$

When simplified, the numerical expression $90 - 5 \cdot 3^2 + 42 \div (5 + 2) = 51$.

Simplify: $-50 + 40 \div 2^3 - 5(4 + 6)$

$$-50 + 40 \div 2^3 - 5(4 + 6) = -50 + 40 \div 2^3 - 5(10) \quad \text{First, do computations inside parentheses.}$$

$$= -50 + 40 \div 8 - 5(10) \quad \text{Next, evaluate exponents.}$$

$$= -50 + 5 - 50 \quad \text{Then, multiply and divide from left to right.}$$

$$= -95 \quad \text{Finally, add and subtract from left to right.}$$

When simplified, the numerical expression $-50 + 40 \div 2^3 - 5(4 + 6) = -95$.

Simplify: $8 - 4 \div (7 - 5) - (7 + 3) \div 2$

$$8 - 4 \div (7 - 5) - (7 + 3) \div 2 = 8 - 4 \div 2 - 10 \div 2 \quad \text{First, do computations inside parentheses.}$$

$$= 8 - 4 \div 2 - 10 \div 2 \quad \text{Next, evaluate exponents—none, so skip this step.}$$

$$= 8 - 2 - 5 \quad \text{Then, divide from left to right.}$$

$$= 1 \quad \text{Finally, subtract from left to right.}$$

When simplified, the numerical expression : $8 - 4 \div (7 - 5) - (7 + 3) \div 2 = 1$.

Properties of Number Systems

The set of real numbers has the following **field properties** under addition and multiplication:

Field Properties	
Field Property	**Explanation**
Closure property: $a + b$ and ab are real numbers.	The sum or product of any two real numbers is a real number.
Commutative property: $a + b = b + a$ and $ab = ba$.	You can switch the order of any two numbers when you add or multiply without changing the answer.
Associative property: $(a + b) + c = a + (b + c)$ and $(ab)c = a(bc)$.	The way the addends or factors are grouped does not affect the final sum or product.
Additive identity property: There exists a real number, denoted 0, such that $a + 0 = a$ and $0 + a = a$.	This property ensures that zero is a real number and that its sum with any real number is the number.
Multiplicative identity property: There exists a real number, denoted 1, such that $a \cdot 1 = a$ and $1 \cdot a = a$.	This property ensures that one is a real number and that its product with any real number is the number.
Additive inverse property: For every real number a, there exists a real number, denoted $-a$, such that $a + (-a) = 0$ and $(-a) + a = 0$.	This property ensures that for every real number, there is another real number, opposite to it in sign, which when added to the number gives 0.
Multiplicative inverse property: For every nonzero real number a, there exists a real number, denoted a^{-1}, such that $a \cdot a^{-1} = 1$ and $a^{-1} \cdot a = 1$.	This property ensures that for every real number, *except zero*, there is another real number, which when multiplied by the number gives 1.
Distributive property: $a(b + c) = ab + ac$ and $(b + c)a = ba + ca$.	When you have a factor times a sum, you can either add first and then multiply, or multiply first and then add. Either way, the answer works out to be the same.

Subtraction and division are defined as follows.

Subtraction: $a - b = a + (-b)$.

Division: $a \div b = \dfrac{a}{b} = a \cdot b^{-1} = a \cdot \dfrac{1}{b}$.

> **Tip:** Have you ever wondered why subtraction and division are given *new* definitions in algebra? Why not do it the old way—like you learned in arithmetic? The simple reason is that arithmetic subtraction is neither commutative nor associative over the real numbers and neither is arithmetic division. (Make up examples to convince yourself about this.) That's why changing to algebraic addition or multiplication, whichever one is applicable, is better—because these two operations have *all* the useful properties we've discussed in this section.

For the Praxis Middle School Mathematics test, you might be asked to identify field properties used in a calculation.

Here is an example:

Which property of the real numbers is used in the following calculation: $8(215) = 1720$?

Since $8(215) = 8(200 + 10 + 5) = 8 \cdot 200 + 8 \cdot 10 + 8 \cdot 5 = 1600 + 80 + 40 = 1720$, you can see that the distributive property is used in the calculation.

In general, a system consisting of a set S and two binary operations defined on S is called a **field** if the field properties are satisfied for *all* elements in S under the two operations. On the Praxis Middle School Mathematics test, you might be asked whether a defined operation has a given field property. Symbols commonly used for defined operations are $\oplus$, $\otimes$, $*$, $\circ$, and #.

Here is an example.

Consider the operation $\oplus$ defined by $a \oplus b = 2a + 3b$, where the operations on the right side of the equal sign denote the standard arithmetic operations. Is the operation $\oplus$ commutative over the set of real numbers?

To determine whether $\oplus$ is commutative over the set of real numbers, you should ask the question, "Does $a \oplus b$ equal $b \oplus a$ for all real numbers a and b?" In other words, you need to determine whether $2a + 3b = 2b + 3a$ for all real numbers a and b. Clearly, the answer is no. For instance, when $a = 2$ and $b = 5$, $2 \cdot 2 + 3 \cdot 5 = 19 \neq 2 \cdot 5 + 3 \cdot 2 = 16$. Therefore, the operation $\oplus$ is not commutative over the set of real numbers.

> **Tip:** Even though commutativity (associativity and so on) might hold for some numbers from a given set, if it does not hold for *all* numbers from the set, the operation under consideration is not commutative (associative and so on) over the given set of numbers.

Scientific Notation

Scientific notation is a way to write real numbers in a shortened form. When the numbers are very large or very small, scientific notation helps keep track of the decimal places and makes performing computations with these numbers easier.

A number written in scientific notation is written as a product of two factors. The first factor is a number that is greater than or equal to 1, but less than 10. The second factor is a power of 10. The idea is to make a product that will equal the given number. Any decimal number can be written in scientific notation. Here are examples of numbers written in scientific notation.

Written in scientific notation, 34,000 is $3.4 \cdot 10^4$.

Written in scientific notation, 6.5 is $6.5 \cdot 10^0$.

Written in scientific notation, 0.00047 is $4.7 \cdot 10^{-4}$.

Follow these steps to write a number in scientific notation:

Step 1. Move the decimal point to the immediate right of the first *nonzero* digit of the number.

Step 2. Indicate multiplication by the proper power of 10. The exponent for the power of 10 is the number of places you moved the decimal point in Step 1.

- If you moved the decimal point to the *left,* make the exponent positive.
- If you moved the decimal point to the *right,* make the exponent negative.

As long as you make sure your first factor is greater than or equal to 1 and less than 10, you can always check to see whether you did it right by multiplying out your answer to see whether you get your original number back. Look at these examples.

$$254,000 = 2.54 \cdot 10^5 \text{ (in scientific notation)} = 2.54 \cdot 10{,}000 = 254{,}000$$

$$0.00015 = 1.5 \cdot 10^{-4} \text{ (in scientific notation)} = 1.5 \cdot \frac{1}{10^4} = 1.5 \cdot \frac{1}{10000} = 0.00015$$

Complex Numbers

The set of **complex numbers** consists of all those numbers that can be written in the form $x + yi$, where x and y are real numbers and $i^2 = -1$. The real number coefficients x and y, are called the **real part** and **imaginary part,** respectively, of a complex number. When x is zero, the numbers in the resulting set are called **pure imaginary** numbers. When y is zero, the resulting set of numbers consists of the **real numbers.** Thus, the real numbers are a subset of the complex numbers.

The complex numbers can be represented on the complex plane, where the horizontal axis is called the **real axis** and the vertical axis is called the **imaginary axis.** The complex numbers $z_1 = 2 + i$, $z_2 = 3 - 2i$, $z_3 = -4 + 2i$, and $z_4 = -2 - 3i$ are shown on the complex plane in the following figure.

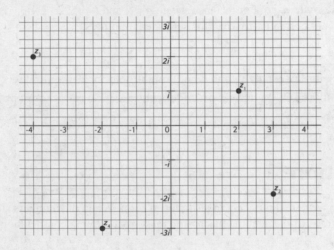

Some basic concepts for complex numbers are the following:

$i^2 = -1$ Examples: $6i^2 = 6(-1) = -6$; $64 - 9i^2 = 64 + -9(-1) =$
                                                                  $64 + 9 = 73$.

$\sqrt{-b} = \sqrt{b} \cdot i \ (b \geq 0)$ Examples: $\sqrt{-25} = 5i$; $\sqrt{-3} = \sqrt{3}i$.

$-x + -yi$ and $x + yi$ are mutual additive inverses.   Example: $8 + 3i$ and $-8 + -3i$ are mutual additive inverses.

$x + yi$ and $x - yi$ are mutual complex conjugates.   Example: $8 + 3i$ and $8 - 3i$ are mutual complex conjugates.

The following table summarizes the definitions for performing operations with any two complex numbers, represented by $(x + yi)$ and $(u + vi)$ in the table.

Definitions for Operations with Complex Numbers		
Operation	*Definition*	*Example*
Addition	$(x + yi) + (u + vi) = (x + u) + (y + v)i$	$(-5 + 2i) + (8 + 3i) = (-5 + 8) + (2i + 3i) = 3 + 5i$
	Tip: Add the real parts. Add the imaginary parts.	
Subtraction	$(x + yi) - (u + vi) = (x + yi) + (-u + -vi) =$ $(x + -u) + (y + -v)i$	$(-5 + 2i) - (8 + 3i) = (-5 + 2i) + (-8 + -3i) =$ $(-5 + -8) + (2i + -3i) = -13 + -1i = -13 - 1i$
	Tip: Add the additive inverse of the second number.	

Operation	Definition	Example
Multiplication	$(x + yi)(u + vi) = (xu - yv) + (xv + yu)i$ Tip: Use F.O.I.L. (first terms, outer terms, inner terms, and last terms) to perform the multiplication. $(x + yi)(x - yi) = x^2 + y^2$	$(-5 + 2i)(8 + 3i) = (-5)(8) + (-5)(3i) + (2i)(8) +$ $(2i)(3i) = -40 + -15i + 16i + 6i^2 =$ $-40 + -15i + 16i + -6 = -46 + 1i$ $(8 + 3i) \cdot (8 - 3i) = (8)(8) + (8)(-3i) + (3i)(8) +$ $(3i)(3i) = 64 + -24i + 24i - 9i^2 = 64 + -9(-1) =$ $64 + 9 = 73$
	Tip: The product of a complex number and its conjugate is a real number.	
Division	$\dfrac{x + yi}{u + vi} = \dfrac{(x + yi)(u - vi)}{(u + vi)(u - vi)} =$ $\dfrac{(xu + yv) + (yu - xv)i}{u^2 + v^2} = \dfrac{(xu + yv)}{u^2 + v^2} + \dfrac{(yu - xv)}{u^2 + v^2}i$	$\dfrac{-5 + 2i}{8 + 3i} = \dfrac{(-5 + 2i)(8 - 3i)}{(8 + 3i)(8 - 3i)} =$ $\dfrac{-46 + 1i}{73} = -\dfrac{46}{73} + \dfrac{1}{73}i$
	Tip: Multiply the numerator and denominator by the conjugate of the denominator.	

Tip: Keep in mind that since the coefficients *x* and *y* in a complex number *x* + *yi* are real numbers, the computations involving the real number coefficients must follow the rules for computations with real numbers that are given in the section "Operations with Signed Numbers," earlier in this chapter.

The field properties apply also to the set of complex numbers for the operations of addition and multiplication.

Sample Exercises

1. Find the greatest common factor of 18 and 30.

   A. 2
   B. 3
   C. 6
   D. 90

2. Simplify $7 + 3(4^2) - 8$.

   A. 23
   B. 32
   C. 47
   D. 152

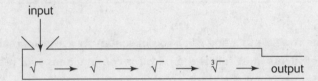

3. If x^6, where x is a positive number, is used as the input for the sequence of root operations shown in the function machine diagram, which of the following is equivalent to the output?

   A. $x^{\frac{11}{6}}$
   B. $x^{\frac{1}{4}}$
   C. $x^7 \cdot x^{\frac{1}{6}}$
   D. x^{11}

   $$23 + 39 + 77 + 11 = 23 + 77 + 39 + 11 = 100 + 50 = 150$$

4. Which of the following properties of the real numbers are illustrated by the preceding computation sequence?

   I. commutativity
   II. associativity
   III. distributive property

   A. I and II only
   B. I and III only
   C. II and III only
   D. I, II, and III

5. What is the product of the complex numbers $2 + 3i$ and $2 - 3i$?

   A. −5
   B. 13
   C. $13 - 12i$
   D. $13 + 12i$

Answer Explanations for Sample Exercises

1. C. The greatest common factor of 18 and 30 is the greatest product that will divide evenly into each of them. It can be obtained by writing the prime factorization of both 18 and 30 and building a product consisting of each factor the *highest* number of times it appears as a *common* factor in 18 and 30. Since $18 = 2 \cdot 3 \cdot 3$ and $30 = 2 \cdot 3 \cdot 5$, the gcf(18, 30) = $2 \cdot 3 = 6$, Choice C.

2. C. To simplify the expression $7 + 3(4^2) - 8$, follow the order of operations using the mnemonic "<u>P</u>lease <u>E</u>xcuse <u>M</u>y <u>D</u>ear <u>A</u>unt <u>S</u>ally."

$$7 + 3(4^2) - 8 = 7 + 3(16) - 8$$ First, do the exponentiation inside the parentheses.

$$= 7 + 48 - 8$$ Next, multiply.

$$= 47$$ Finally, add and subtract from left to right.

3. B. Since the answer choices are given as exponential expressions, the best way to work this problem is to perform on x^6 the sequence of root operations shown in the diagram, using the exponential form for the radicals:

$$\left(\left(\left(\left(x^6\right)^{\frac{1}{2}}\right)^{\frac{1}{2}}\right)^{\frac{1}{2}}\right)^{\frac{1}{3}} = x^{\frac{6}{24}} = x^{\frac{1}{4}} \text{ output, Choice B.}$$

4. A. This question is an example of a multiple response set question. One approach to answering this type of question is to do the following steps. First, read the question carefully to make sure you understand what the question is asking; next, identify choices that you know are incorrect from the Roman numeral options, and then draw a line through every answer choice that contains a Roman numeral you have eliminated; next examine the remaining answer choices to determine which Roman numeral options you are sure are correct. Eliminate answer choices, if any, that do not contain correct options.

Looking at the three properties given in the Roman numeral options, you can immediately eliminate III because there are no parentheses in the computation sequence, meaning that the distributive property did not come into play. Draw a line through choices B, C, and D because each of these answer choices contains option III. This leaves answer Choice A as the correct response. This choice includes commutativity (I) and associativity (II), both of which are used in the computation sequence.

5. B. $(2 + 3i)(2 - 3i) = 4 - 9i^2 = 4 - 9(-1) = 4 + 9 = 13$, Choice B.

Basic Algebra

This chapter provides a review of the key ideas and formulas of basic algebra that are most important for you to know for the Praxis Middle School Mathematics test. Multiple-choice sample exercises, comparable to what might be presented on the Praxis Middle School Mathematics test, are given at the end of the chapter. The answer explanations for the sample exercises are provided immediately following.

Basic Algebraic Terminology

A **variable** holds a place open for a number and is represented by a symbol (usually a letter). A variable does not represent a single fixed quantity; rather it is used to represent in turn a collection of numbers in a given discussion. A **constant** is a quantity whose value remains fixed throughout a discussion. For example, all the real and complex numbers are constants. Each has a fixed, definite value. Thus, when a letter is used to name a constant, the letter has one fixed value. For instance, the Greek letter π stands for the number that equals the ratio of the circumference of a circle to its diameter, which is approximately 3.14159.

A **numerical expression** is any constant or combination of two or more constants joined by operational symbols. For example, 100, 3.5, $\frac{3 \cdot 25}{4 \cdot 5}$, 0.75(2000) + 2500, and $\pi(6)^2$ are numerical expressions.

An **algebraic expression,** or **symbolic expression,** is a symbol or combination of symbols that represents a number. Algebraic expressions consist of one or more variables joined by one or more operations with or without constants (explicitly) included. For example, $7x$, uv, $-t$, $6x + 3$, $5x^4 + 3x^3 - 12x^2 + 15$, $6(a + 5) - 3$, $7abc$, $y(2x + 3)$, $\frac{8xy}{4(y + 2z)}$, and $\frac{3}{a+3} + \frac{10}{t-25}$ are algebraic expressions.

A **term** is a constant, variable, or product of constants or variables. For instance, x, $8ab$, $-9z$, $10xyz$, $x(-6x)$, and 11 are terms. The algebraic expression $6x^4 + 3x^3 - 12x^2 + 15$, has four terms. The terms $6x^4$, $3x^3$, $12x^2$, and 15 are separated by either + or – symbols. Quantities enclosed within grouping symbols are considered single terms, even though they may contain + or – symbols. Thus, the algebraic expression $6(a + 5) - 3$ has two terms.

In a term that is a product of two or more factors, the **coefficient** of a factor is the product of the other factors in that term. For instance, in the term $4y(2x + 3)$, $4y$ is the coefficient of $(2x + 3)$, and $4(2x + 3)$ is the coefficient of y. The product of the numerical factors of a term is called the **numerical coefficient** of the term. If no numerical coefficient is explicitly written, then the numerical coefficient is understood to be 1.

A **monomial** is an algebraic expression of one term, such as $6x^4y$, consisting of the product of a numerical coefficient and one or more variables each raised to a nonnegative power. The **degree of a monomial** is the sum of the exponents of its variables. For instance, the degree of the monomial $6x^4y$ is 5. The degree of a nonzero constant c is zero because $c = x^0$ for any constant c. The degree of the monomial 0 is undefined. **Like terms** are monomial terms that differ only in their numerical coefficients. For instance, $6x^4y$ and $-4x^4y$ are like terms; however, $6x^4y$ and $-4xy^4$ are **unlike terms.** All constants are like terms.

A **polynomial** is an algebraic expression of one or more terms. Thus, a **monomial** is a polynomial of one term. A **binomial** is a polynomial of two terms, such as $x + 3$. A **trinomial** is a polynomial of three terms, such as $9x^4 - 24x^2 + 16$.

Performing Operations with Polynomials

The following table summarizes the rules for addition and subtraction of polynomials.

Rules for Addition and Subtraction of Polynomials		
Operation	*Rule*	*Example*
Addition	Combine *like* monomial terms by adding or subtracting their numerical coefficients, use the result as the coefficient of the common variable factor or factors, and simply indicate the sum or difference of *unlike* terms.	$(5x^2 + 10x - 6) + (3x^2 - 2x + 4) =$ $5x^2 + 10x - 6 + 3x^2 - 2x + 4 =$ $8x^2 + 8x - 2$
Subtraction	*Mentally* change the subtraction symbol to addition, *change the sign of every term* in the second polynomial, and proceed as in addition.	$(5x^2 + 10x - 6) - (3x^2 - 2x + 4) =$ $5x^2 + 10x - 6 - 3x^2 + 2x - 4 =$ $2x^2 + 12x - 10$

Tip: When simple parentheses (or brackets or braces) are immediately preceded by a + symbol, they can be removed without changing the signs of the terms within, but if the parentheses are immediately preceded by a – symbol, the sign of *every* term within the grouping must be changed when the parentheses are removed. In the second case, you *mentally* change the – symbol that precedes the parentheses to a + symbol and do not explicitly write the change because $+ \cdot + = +$ and $+ \cdot - = -$.

The following table summarizes the rules for multiplication of polynomials.

Rules for Multiplication of Polynomials		
Operation	*Rule*	*Example*
Multiplication—Monomial by Monomial	Multiply both the numerical coefficients and the variable factors.	$(-5x^2y)(10xy) = -50x^3y^2$
Multiplication—Polynomial by Monomial	Use the distributive property to multiply *each* term of the polynomial by the monomial.	$2x^2(3x^2 - 5x + 1) = 6x^4 - 10x^3 + 2x^2$
Multiplication—Polynomial by Polynomial	Use the distributive property to multiply each term in the second polynomial by each term of the first polynomial, and then combine like terms.	$(x + 2)(x^2 - 2x + 4) = x^3 - 2x^2 + 4x +$ $2x^2 - 4x + 8 = x^3 + 8$
Multiplication—Binomial by Binomial	Use the distributive property to multiply each term in the second binomial by each term of the first binomial and then combine like terms.	$(2x - 3)(x + 4) = 2x^2 + 8x - 3x - 12 =$ $2x^2 + 5x - 12$
	Tip: Use F.O.I.L. (first terms, outer terms, inner terms, and last terms) to perform the multiplication.	

Tip: Remember that when you multiply variable factors, you *add* (not multiply) the exponents of like bases.

Tip: When multiplying polynomials, if possible, arrange the terms of the polynomials in descending or ascending powers of a common variable.

Some special products that are important to know for the Praxis Middle School Mathematics test are given in the following table.

Special Products		
Special Name	**Special Product**	**Example**
Perfect Trinomial Square	$(x + y)^2 = (x + y)(x + y) = x^2 + 2xy + y^2$	$(x + 3)^2 = x^2 + 6x + 9$
Perfect Trinomial Square	$(x - y)^2 = (x - y)(x - y) = x^2 - 2xy + y^2$	$(2x - 5)^2 = 4x^2 - 20x + 25$
The Difference between Two Squares	$(x + y)(x - y) = x^2 - y^2$	$(x + 3)(x - 3) = x^2 - 9$
The Sum of Two Cubes	$(x + y)(x^2 - xy + y^2) = x^3 + y^3$	$(x + 2)(x^2 - 2x + 4) = x^3 + 8$
The Difference between Two Cubes	$(x - y)(x^2 + xy + y^2) = x^3 - y^3$	$(x - 2)(x^2 + 2x + 4) = x^3 - 8$
Perfect Cube	$(x + y)^3 = x^3 + 3x^2y + 3xy^2 + y^3$	$(x + 2)^3 = x^3 + 6x^2 + 12x + 8$
Perfect Cube	$(x - y)^3 = x^3 - 3x^2y + 3xy^2 - y^3$	$(x - 2)^3 = x^3 - 6x^2 + 12x - 8$

Tip: It is a common mistake to omit the middle terms when squaring or cubing binomials. The square of a binomial has three terms (a trinomial), and the cube of a binomial has four terms. Just remember that the number of terms is *one more* than the exponent used.

Simplifying Polynomials

A polynomial is **simplified** when all indicated operations have been performed, and it contains no uncombined like terms. The **degree of a polynomial** is the same as the greatest of the degrees of its monomial terms after the polynomial has been simplified.

To simplify a polynomial expression, follow these three steps:

Step 1. When grouping symbols are present, perform all operations within grouping symbols, starting with the innermost grouping symbol and working outward.

Step 2. Perform all indicated multiplication, starting with exponentiation, being sure to enclose the product in parentheses if it is to be multiplied by an additional factor.

Step 3. Remove all remaining parentheses and combine like terms using addition or subtraction as indicated.

Tip: Simplifying polynomials follows PE(MD)(AS), which makes sense since the variables in the polynomials represent numbers.

Here are examples.

$$2 + 4(x + 3y - 10) = 2 + 4x + 12y - 40 = 4x + 12y - 38$$

Don't make the mistake of writing $2 + 4(x + 3y - 10)$ as $6(x + 3y - 10)$. Remember PE(MD)(AS)—multiplication must be performed before addition (or subtraction) unless grouping symbols indicate otherwise.

$$2(x + 3)(x - 3) - (x + 3)^2 = 2(x^2 - 9) - (x^2 + 6x + 9) = 2x^2 - 18 - x^2 - 6x - 9 = x^2 - 6x - 27$$

Enclosing the products in parentheses will help prevent careless errors.

Dividing Polynomials

The following table summarizes division of polynomials by monomials.

Rules for Division by a Monomial		
Operation	*Rule*	*Examples*
Division—Monomial by Monomial	Divide the numerical coefficients. Divide the variable factors that have a common base. Leave other variable factors alone. Use the quotient of the numerical coefficients as the coefficient for the answer.	$\dfrac{-50x^3y^2z}{-5x^2y} = 10xyz$
Division—Polynomial by Monomial	Divide each term of the polynomial by the monomial.	$\dfrac{25x^5y^3 + 35x^3y^2 - 10x^2y}{-5x^2y} =$ $-5x^3y^2 - 7xy + 2$

You do **long division of polynomials** in a manner analogous to long division in arithmetic. The result is usually written as a mixed expression: quotient + $\dfrac{\text{remainder}}{\text{divisor}}$. Long division of polynomials is often a tedious process, and you are unlikely to have to do it on the Praxis Middle School Mathematics test. **Synthetic division** is a shortcut method commonly used to divide a polynomial by a binomial of the form $x - r$. See Appendix B for an example of long division and a discussion of synthetic division.

Factoring Polynomials

Factoring a polynomial means to write the polynomial as a product of two or more polynomial factors, if possible. A polynomial that cannot be written as a product of two or more polynomial factors is said to be **prime**. To factor a polynomial that is not prime, you must find two or more polynomials whose product is the original polynomial. For example, $(2x - 3)(x + 4)$ is a **factorization** of $2x^2 + 5x - 12$ because $(2x - 3)(x + 4) = 2x^2 + 5x - 12$. The polynomials $(2x - 3)$ and $(x + 4)$ cannot be factored further, so they are **prime polynomial factors** of $2x^2 + 5x - 12$. **Factoring a polynomial completely** means writing it as a product of prime polynomial factors. When factoring polynomials, proceed systematically as follows:

1. Check for a greatest common monomial factor.
2. If a factor is a binomial, check for
   difference of two squares: $x^2 - y^2 = (x + y)(x - y)$.
   sum of two cubes: $x^3 + y^3 = (x + y)(x^2 - xy + y^2)$.
   difference of two cubes: $x^3 - y^3 = (x - y)(x^2 + xy + y^2)$.
3. If a factor is a trinomial, check for
   general factorable quadratic: $x^2 + (a + b)x + ab = (x + a)(x + b)$
   $\qquad\qquad\qquad\qquad\qquad\qquad acx^2 + (ad + bc)x + bd = (ax + b)(cx + d)$
   perfect trinomial square: $a^2x^2 + 2abxy + b^2y^2 = (ax + by)^2$
   $\qquad\qquad\qquad\qquad\qquad\quad a^2x^2 - 2abxy + b^2y^2 = (ax - by)^2$
4. If a factor has four terms, try grouping some of the terms together and factoring the groups separately first, and then factoring the entire expression.
5. Write the original polynomial as the product of all the factors obtained. Check to make sure that all polynomial factors except monomial factors are prime.
6. Check by multiplying the factors to obtain the original polynomial.

Here are examples.

$$x^2 - 3x - 4 = (x - 4)(x + 1)$$

$$16a^2b^2 - 4a^2 = 4a^2(4b^2 - 1) = 4a^2(2b + 1)(2b - 1).$$

$$18x^2 + 24xy + 8y^2 = 2(9x^2 + 12xy + 4y^2) = 2(3x + 2y)^2.$$

$$80x^3y - 270y^4 = 10y(8x^3 - 27y^3) = 10y(2x - 3y)(4x^2 + 6xy + 9y^2).$$

$$3x^4y + 3x^3y - 27x^2y - 27xy = 3xy(x^3 + x^2 - 9x - 9) = 3xy[(x^3 + x^2) - (9x + 9)] = 3xy[x^2(x + 1) - 9(x + 1)] =$$

$$3xy[(x + 1)(x^2 - 9)] = 3xy[(x + 1)(x + 3)(x - 3)] = 3xy(x + 1)(x + 3)(x - 3).$$

Rational Expressions

A **rational expression** is an algebraic fraction in which both the numerator and denominator are polynomials. Values for which the denominator is zero are **excluded.** For instance, $\frac{2x}{5}$ (no excluded value), $\frac{5}{2x}$ ($x \neq 0$), $\frac{10x}{x-1}$ ($x \neq 1$),

$\frac{x^2 - 4}{x^2 - 3x - 4} = \frac{(x+2)(x-2)}{(x-4)(x+1)}$ (($x \neq 4$, $x \neq -1$), $x^4y^{-3} = \frac{x^4}{y^3}$ ($y \neq 0$), and all polynomials (no excluded values) are

rational expressions. Hereafter, whenever a rational expression is written, it will be understood that any values for which the expression is undefined are excluded.

To perform computations with algebraic fractions, often you will need to factor the polynomials that are used in the algebraic fractions. For instance, factoring is frequently necessary when reducing algebraic fractions to lowest terms and when finding a common denominator for algebraic fractions. The following table summarizes the process.

Reducing Algebraic Fractions to Lowest Terms		
Type of Algebraic Fraction	**Rule**	**Example**
$\frac{\text{monomial}}{\text{monomial}}$	Divide numerator and denominator by the greatest common factor of the two monomials.	$\frac{9x^5y^2z}{12x^2y^3} = \frac{3x^2y^2 3x^3z}{3x^2y^2 4y} = \frac{3x^3z}{4y}$
$\frac{\text{monomial}}{\text{polynomial}}$ or $\frac{\text{polynomial}}{\text{mononomial}}$	Factor out the greatest monomial factor, if any, from the polynomial, and then divide numerator and denominator by the greatest common factor.	$\frac{-9x^2y}{12x^3y - 36x^2y - 48xy} =$ $\frac{-9x^2y}{12xy(x^2 - 3x - 4)} = \frac{-3x}{4(x^2 - 3x - 4)}$; $\frac{12x^3y - 36x^2y - 48xy}{9x^2y} =$ $\frac{12xy(x^2 - 3x - 4)}{9x^2y} = \frac{4(x^2 - 3x - 4)}{3x}$
$\frac{\text{polynomial}}{\text{polynomial}}$	Factor the polynomials completely, and then divide numerator and denominator by the greatest common factor.	$\frac{9x^2y - 9y}{12x^3y - 36x^2y - 48xy} = \frac{9y(x^2 - 1)}{12xy(x^2 - 3x - 4)}$ $\frac{9y(x+1)(x-1)}{12xy(x+1)(x-4)} = \frac{3(x-1)}{4x(x-4)}$

When reducing algebraic fractions, make sure that you divide by factors only. For instance, $\dfrac{x+2}{4}$ cannot be reduced further. Even though 2 is a factor of the denominator, it is not a factor of the numerator—it is a term of the numerator. Remember, divide by factors, *not* terms.

The following table summarizes computations with algebraic fractions.

Rules for Computations with Algebraic Fractions		
Operation	*Rule*	*Example*
Addition/Subtraction— Like Denominators	Add/subtract the numerators to find the numerator of the answer, which is placed over the common denominator. Simplify and reduce to lowest terms, if needed.	$\dfrac{x+2}{x-3}+\dfrac{2x-11}{x-3} = \dfrac{3x-9}{x-3}=\dfrac{3(x-3)}{x-3}=\dfrac{3}{1}=3$ $\dfrac{5x^2}{3(x-1)}-\dfrac{4x^2+1}{3(x+1)} = \dfrac{5x^2-4x^2-1}{3(x+1)} =$ $\dfrac{x^2-1}{3(x+1)}=\dfrac{(x+1)(x-1)}{3(x+1)}=\dfrac{x-1}{3}$ Show sign changing step. When subtracting, you must change the sign of *every* term of the numerator of the second fraction.
Addition/Subtraction— Unlike Denominators	Factor each denominator completely. Find the common denominator, which is the product of each prime factor the *highest* number of times it is a factor in any one denominator. Write each algebraic fraction as an equivalent fraction having the common denominator as a denominator. Add/subtract the numerators to find the numerator of the answer, which is placed over the common denominator. Simplify and reduce to lowest terms, if needed.	$\dfrac{1}{x^2-3x-4}+\dfrac{2}{x^2-1} =$ $\dfrac{1}{(x+1)(x-4)}+\dfrac{2}{(x+1)(x-1)} =$ $\dfrac{1(x-1)}{(x+1)(x-4)(x-1)} + \dfrac{2(x-4)}{(x+1)(x-1)(x-4)} =$ $\dfrac{x-1}{(x+1)(x-4)(x-1)} + \dfrac{2x-8}{(x+1)(x-1)(x-4)} =$ $\dfrac{3x-9}{(x+1)(x-1)(x-4)} = \dfrac{3(x-3)}{(x+1)(x-1)(x-4)}$
Multiplication	Factor all numerators and denominators completely and then divide numerators and denominators by their common factors (as in reducing). The product of the remaining numerator factors is the numerator of the answer and the product of the remaining denominator factors is the denominator of the answer.	$\dfrac{a^2+4a+4}{a^2+a-2}\cdot\dfrac{a^2-2a+1}{a^2-4} =$ $\dfrac{(a+2)(a+2)}{(a+2)(a-1)}\cdot\dfrac{(a-1)(a-1)}{(a+2)(a-2)} = \dfrac{a-1}{a-2}$
Division	Multiply the first algebraic fraction by the reciprocal of the second algebraic fraction.	$\dfrac{a^2+4a+4}{a^2+a-2}\div\dfrac{a^2-4}{a^2-2a+1} =$ $\dfrac{a^2+4a+4}{a^2+a-2}\cdot\dfrac{a^2-2a+1}{a^2-4} =$ $\dfrac{(a+2)(a+2)}{(a+2)(a-1)}\cdot\dfrac{(a-1)(a-1)}{(a+2)(a-2)} = \dfrac{a-1}{a-2}$

A **complex fraction** is a fraction that has fractions in its numerator, denominator, or both. One way to simplify a complex fraction is to interpret the fraction bar of the complex fraction as meaning division. For instance,

$$\frac{\dfrac{1}{x}+\dfrac{1}{y}}{\dfrac{1}{x}-\dfrac{1}{y}} = \frac{\dfrac{y}{xy}+\dfrac{x}{xy}}{\dfrac{y}{xy}-\dfrac{x}{xy}} = \frac{\dfrac{y+x}{xy}}{\dfrac{y-x}{xy}} = \frac{y+x}{xy}\div\frac{y-x}{xy} = \frac{y+x}{xy}\cdot\frac{xy}{y-x} = \frac{y+x}{y-x}.$$

Another way to simplify a complex fraction is to multiply its numerator and denominator by the least common denominator of all the fractions used in its numerator and denominator. For instance,

$$\frac{\dfrac{1}{x}+\dfrac{1}{y}}{\dfrac{1}{x}-\dfrac{1}{y}} = \frac{xy\left(\dfrac{1}{x}+\dfrac{1}{y}\right)}{xy\left(\dfrac{1}{x}-\dfrac{1}{y}\right)} = \frac{xy\cdot\dfrac{1}{x}+xy\cdot\dfrac{1}{y}}{xy\cdot\dfrac{1}{x}-xy\cdot\dfrac{1}{y}} = \frac{y+x}{y-x}.$$

Solving One-Variable Linear Equations

An **equation** is a mathematical sentence stating equality between two expressions. Equations containing only numerical expressions can be assigned a **truth value** of either true or false. For instance, $1 + 2 = 3$ is an equation whose truth value is true, but $1 + 2 = 5$ is an equation whose truth value is false. (See "Basic Concepts of Logic" in the chapter "Discrete Mathematics" for an additional discussion of truth value.) An equation containing one or more variables is an **open sentence.** For instance, $x + 2 = 3$ and $x + 2y = 8$ are open sentences. The truth value of an open sentence can be determined only after numerical quantities are substituted for the variables in the sentence.

A **solution,** or **root,** of a one-variable equation is a number that when substituted for the variable makes the equation true. To determine whether a number is a solution of a one-variable equation, replace the variable with the number and perform all operations indicated on each side of the equation. If the resulting statement is true, the number is a solution of the equation. This process is called **checking** a solution. The **solution set** of an equation is the set consisting of all the solutions of the equation. To **solve an equation** means to find its solution set. An **identity** is an equation whose solution set is the set of all possible values of the variable. If the solution set is empty, the equation has no solution. **Equivalent equations** are equations that have the same solution set.

A **one-variable linear equation** is an equation that can be written in the form $ax + b = 0$, where $a \neq 0$ and b is a constant in the discussion. For instance, $2x + 6 = 0$, $12x + 1 = 5(x - 4)$, $\dfrac{2y}{3} - 45 = y$, and $0.05x = 200 + 0.06(1500 - x)$ are one-variable linear equations.

A one-variable equation is **solved** when the variable is by itself on one and only one side of the equation and has a coefficient of 1. Two main strategies used in solving equations are the following:

1. Addition or subtraction of the same quantity on both sides of the equation.
2. Multiplication or division by the same *nonzero* quantity on both sides of the equation.

When you use one of these strategies, the resulting equation is equivalent to the original equation. The process of solving a one-variable linear equation uses a series of steps to produce an equivalent equation of the form: $x =$ solution (or solution $= x$). To solve a one-variable linear equation, use the following steps:

1. Remove grouping symbols, if any, by applying the distributive property and then simplify.
2. *Eliminate fractions, if any, by multiplying both sides of the equation by the least common denominator of all the fractions in the equation; and then simplify.
3. Undo indicated addition or subtraction to isolate the variable on one side—that is, get all terms containing the variable on one side and all other terms on the other side—and then simplify.
4. If necessary, factor the side containing the variable so that one of the factors is the variable.

5. Divide both sides by the coefficient of the variable.

6. Check the solution in the original equation.

*This step is optional; but when fractions are involved, it usually simplifies the process to include it.

Here are examples. [*Note:* The symbol $\Rightarrow$ is used hereafter to indicate a sequence of logical steps.]

Solve $12x + 1 = 5(x - 4)$.

$12x + 1 = 5(x - 4) \Rightarrow 12x + 1 = 5x - 20 \Rightarrow 12x + 1 - 5x = 5x - 20 - 5x \Rightarrow 7x + 1 = -20 \Rightarrow$

$7x + 1 - 1 = -20 - 1 \Rightarrow 7x = -21 \Rightarrow \dfrac{7x}{7} = \dfrac{-21}{7} \Rightarrow x = -3$

Check: $12(-3) + 1 \overset{?}{=} 5(-3 - 4) \Rightarrow -35 \overset{\checkmark}{=} -35$

Solve $\dfrac{2y}{3} - 45 = y$.

$\dfrac{2y}{3} - 45 = y \Rightarrow 3 \cdot \dfrac{2y}{3} - 3 \cdot 45 = 3 \cdot y \Rightarrow 2y - 135 = 3y \Rightarrow 2y - 135 - 2y = 3y - 2y \Rightarrow -135 = y$

Check: $\dfrac{2(-135)}{3} - 45 \overset{?}{=} -135 \Rightarrow -135 \overset{\checkmark}{=} -135$

As you become proficient in solving equations, you can do some steps mentally. Just always make sure that you are doing the same operation to both sides of the equation, whether or not you show all your work!

Solving One-Variable Inequalities

An **inequality** is a mathematical sentence stating that two expressions are not equal. You use the symbols > (greater than), < (less than), $\geq$ (greater than or equal to), and $\leq$ (less than or equal to) to write one-variable linear inequalities. The solution sets of one-variable linear inequalities are subsets of the real numbers. (See "Set Terminology" in the chapter "Discrete Mathematics" for a discussion of the term *subset*.)

You solve an inequality just as you would an equation *except* for one difference: If you multiply or divide both sides of the inequality by a *negative* number, *reverse* the direction of the inequality.

Here are examples.

Solve $12x + 1 < 5(x - 4)$.

$12x + 1 < 5(x - 4) \Rightarrow 12x + 1 < 5x - 20 \Rightarrow 12x + 1 - 5x < 5x - 20 - 5x \Rightarrow 7x + 1 < -20 \Rightarrow$

$7x + 1 - 1 < -20 - 1 \Rightarrow 7x < -21 \Rightarrow \dfrac{7x}{7} < \dfrac{-21}{7} \Rightarrow x < -3$

Thus, using **set-builder notation**, the solution set is $\{x \mid x < -3\}$, which is read "The set of all real numbers x such that x is less than -3." (See "Basic Set Operations and Venn Diagrams" in the chapter "Discrete Mathematics" for an additional discussion of set-builder notation.) You can graph this set on a number line. You shade the numbers to the left of -3; and to indicate that the number 3 does *not* belong in the solution set, you put in a small *open* circle at the point -3.

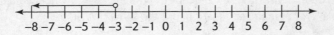

Solve $3x + 5 \geq 5x - 7$.

$3x + 5 \geq 5x - 7 \Rightarrow 3x + 5 - 5x \geq 5x - 7 - 5x \Rightarrow -2x + 5 \geq -7 \Rightarrow -2x + 5 - 5 \geq -7 - 5 \Rightarrow$

$-2x \geq -12 \Rightarrow \dfrac{-2x}{-2} \leq \dfrac{-12}{-2} \Rightarrow x \leq 6$ (Reverse the inequality since you divided both sides by a negative number.)

Thus, the solution set is $\{x \mid x \le 6\}$. To graph the solution set, you shade the numbers to the left of 6 and to indicate that the number 6 also belongs in the solution set, you put a small *shaded* circle at the point 6.

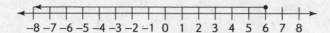

Solving Literal Equations and Formulas

A **literal equation** is an equation in which all constants are represented by letters. A **formula** is an equation that expresses the relationship between two or more variables. You can use the procedure for solving one-variable linear equations to solve a literal equation or a formula for a specific variable in terms of the other variable(s). Also, you can use the procedure to solve a formula for a specific variable when the value(s) of the other variable(s) are known. What you must keep in mind when using the procedure for these purposes is that, when the word *variable* is used, it is referring only to the variable *for which you are solving*. In general, isolate your variable of interest and treat all other variable(s) as constants.

Here are examples.

Solve $C = \frac{5}{9}(F - 32)$ for F.

$C = \frac{5}{9}(F - 32) \Rightarrow C = \frac{5}{9}F - \frac{160}{9} \Rightarrow 9 \cdot C = 9 \cdot \frac{5}{9}F - 9 \cdot \frac{160}{9} \Rightarrow 9C = 5F - 160 \Rightarrow 9C + 160 = 5F - 160 + 160 \Rightarrow$

$9C + 160 = 5F \Rightarrow \frac{9C + 160}{5} = F \Rightarrow \frac{9}{5}C + 32 = F$ or $F = \frac{9}{5}C + 32$

Solve $ax + b = c$ for x.

$ax + b = c \Rightarrow ax + b - b = c - b \Rightarrow ax = c - b \Rightarrow \frac{ax}{a} = \frac{c-b}{a} \Rightarrow x = \frac{c-b}{a}$.

The procedure for solving one-variable linear equations can be used to solve a two-variable linear equation for one variable in terms of the other variable. For example, the procedure can be used to transform the two-variable linear equation $ax + by = c$ into the form: $y = mx + b$, where m and b are constants in the discussion.

Here is an example.

Express $3x - 2y = 8$ in the form $y = mx + b$.

$3x - 2y = 8 \Rightarrow 3x - 2y - 3x = 8 - 3x \Rightarrow -2y = 8 - 3x \Rightarrow y = \frac{8 - 3x}{-2} \Rightarrow y = -4 + \frac{3}{2}x \Rightarrow y = \frac{3}{2}x - 4$

Solving One-Variable Absolute Value Equations and Inequalities

You can solve one-variable absolute value equations using the procedure for solving one-variable linear equations and the following:

$|ax + b| = 0$ if and only if $ax + b = 0$; or

if c is any positive number: $|ax + b| = c$ if and only if either $ax + b = c$ or $ax + b = -c$.

Tip: Notice that for equations like $|ax + b| = c$, you must solve *two* linear equations. Don't forget the second equation!

43

Here are examples.

Solve $|2x + 6| = 0$.

$|2x + 6| = 0$ if and only if $2x + 6 = 0 \Rightarrow 2x + 6 - 6 = 0 - 6 \Rightarrow 2x = -6 \Rightarrow \dfrac{2x}{2} = \dfrac{-6}{2} \Rightarrow x = -3$

Solve $|2x + 6| = 10$.

$|2x + 6| = 10$ if and only if either $2x + 6 = 10$ or $2x + 6 = -10$. Now solve each of these two linear equations.

$2x + 6 = 10 \Rightarrow 2x + 6 - 6 = 10 - 6 \Rightarrow 2x = 4 \Rightarrow \dfrac{2x}{2} = \dfrac{4}{2} \Rightarrow x = 2$ is a solution.

$2x + 6 = -10 \Rightarrow 2x + 6 - 6 = -10 - 6 \Rightarrow 2x = -16 \Rightarrow \dfrac{2x}{2} = \dfrac{-16}{2} \Rightarrow x = -8$ is a solution.

Therefore, the solution set for $|2x + 6| = 10$ is $\{x \mid x = -8 \text{ or } x = 2\}$.

You can solve one-variable absolute value inequalities using the procedure for solving one-variable linear inequalities and the following:

If c is any positive number:

$|ax + b| < c$ if and only if $-c < ax + b < c$; and

$|ax + b| > c$ if and only if either $ax + b < -c$ or $ax + b > c$.

The expression $-c < ax + b < c$ is called a **double inequality** because it is a concise way to express the two inequalities: $-c < ax + b$ and $ax + b < c$.

Note: You can replace $<$ with $\leq$ and $>$ with $\geq$ everywhere in the given inequalities, and the statements will still hold.

> **Tip: Notice that for absolute value inequalities, you must solve *two* linear inequalities. Don't forget the second inequality!**

Here are examples.

Solve $|2x + 6| < 10$.

$|2x + 6| < 10$ if and only if $-10 < 2x + 6 < 10$.

You can solve this double inequality by applying the techniques for solving inequalities to the two inequalities simultaneously. Focus on isolating the variable in the middle variable expression. Whatever you do to the middle expression, you must also do to each of the two expressions on either side as shown here.

$-10 < 2x + 6 < 10 \Rightarrow -10 - 6 < 2x + 6 - 6 < 10 - 6 \Rightarrow -16 < 2x < 4 \Rightarrow \dfrac{-16}{2} < \dfrac{2x}{2} < \dfrac{4}{2} \Rightarrow -8 < x < 2$ is the solution.

Thus, the solution set for $|2x + 6| < 10$ is $\{x \mid -8 < x < 2\}$.

Solve $|2x + 6| > 10$.

$|2x + 6| > 10$ if and only if either $2x + 6 < -10$ or $2x + 6 > 10$. Now solve each of these two linear inequalities.

$2x + 6 > 10 \Rightarrow 2x + 6 - 6 > 10 - 6 \Rightarrow 2x > 4 \Rightarrow \dfrac{2x}{2} < \dfrac{4}{2} \Rightarrow x > 2$ is a solution.

$2x + 6 < -10 \Rightarrow 2x + 6 - 6 < -10 - 6 \Rightarrow 2x < -16 \Rightarrow \dfrac{2x}{2} < \dfrac{-16}{2} \Rightarrow x < -8$ is a solution.

Thus, the solution set for $|2x + 6| > 10$ is $\{x \mid x < -8 \text{ or } x > 2\}$.

Solving Quadratic Equations

A **one-variable quadratic equation** is an equation that can be written in the **standard form** $ax^2 + bx + c = 0$, where $a \neq 0$ and a, b, and c are real-valued constants in the discussion. Specifically, a is the numerical coefficient of x^2, b is the numerical coefficient of x, and c is the constant coefficient, or simply the constant term. The solutions of a quadratic equation are called its **roots.** A quadratic equation may have exactly *one* real root, exactly *two* real unequal roots, or *no* real roots.

[*Note:* Quadratic equations in which a, b, or c is not an element of the real numbers are not covered on the Praxis Middle School Mathematics test.]

Three algebraic methods for solving quadratic equations are (1) by **factoring,** (2) by **completing the square,** and (3) by using the **quadratic formula.**

The procedure for solving a quadratic equation by factoring is based on the **property of zero products** for numbers:

> **If the product of two quantities is zero, at least one of the quantities is zero.**

To solve a quadratic equation by factoring use the following procedure.

1. Express the equation in standard form: $ax^2 + bx + c = 0$.
2. Factor the left side of the equation completely.
3. Set each factor containing the variable equal to zero.
4. Solve each of the resulting two linear equations.
5. Check each root in the original equation.

Here is an example.

Solve $x(x + 8) = 20$ by factoring.

$x^2 + 8x - 20 = 0$	Express the equation in standard form.
$(x + 10)(x - 2) = 0$	Factor the left side.
$x + 10 = 0$ or $x - 2 = 0$	Set each factor equal to zero.
$x = -10$ or $x = 2$	Solve the resulting two equations.
$(-10)^2 + 8(-10) - 20 \overset{?}{=} 0 \qquad (2)^2 + 8(2) - 20 \overset{?}{=} 0$	Check each root.
$100 - 80 - 20 \overset{?}{=} 0 \qquad 4 + 16 - 20 \overset{?}{=} 0$	
$0 = 0 \qquad\qquad 0 = 0$	

Thus, $x(x + 8) = 20$ has two roots, -10 and 2.

Note: Now that you understand the checking process, hereafter, checking will be omitted.

> **Tip:** Some beginners start solving $x(x + 8) = 20$ by setting each factor on the left equal to 20. This is incorrect. The property of zero products can only be applied when the product is *zero*, not 20 or any other nonzero number!

When solving by completing the square, it is of use to know that quadratic equations that can be written in the form: $x^2 = C$, where C is a constant, can be solved by observing that x must be one of the square roots of C. Thus, $x^2 = C$ has solution $x = \pm\sqrt{C}$. If C is *zero,* there is *one* real root that has the value zero; if *positive,* there are *two* unequal real roots; and if *negative,* there are *no* real roots.

Here is an example.

Solve $4x^2 - 9 = 0$.
$$4x^2 - 9 = 0 \Rightarrow 4x^2 = 9 \Rightarrow x^2 = \frac{9}{4} \Rightarrow x = \pm\frac{3}{2}$$

Thus, $4x^2 - 9 = 0$ has two roots, $-\frac{3}{2}$ and $\frac{3}{2}$.

This process can be extended to quadratic equations when they are rewritten in the form $(x + k)^2 = C$, where C is a constant. For such equations, it is evident that $x + k$ must be one of the square roots of C; and, thus, $x + k = \pm\sqrt{C}$.

To solve a quadratic equation by completing the square, use the following procedure:

1. Express the equation in the form: $ax^2 + bx =$ numerical expression.

2. If the coefficient a is not 1, divide each term by a to obtain an equation of the form $x^2 + \dfrac{b}{a}x =$ numerical expression.

3. Add the square of half the coefficient of x to both sides of the equation and then simplify to obtain an equation of the form $x^2 + \dfrac{b}{a}x + \left(\dfrac{b}{2a}\right)^2 = C$, where C is a constant.

4. Factor the perfect trinomial square on the left side of the equation as the square of a binomial, so that you have an equation of the form $\left(x + \dfrac{b}{2a}\right)^2 = C$.

5. Recognizing that $x + \dfrac{b}{2a}$ must be one of the square roots of C, write $x + \dfrac{b}{2a} = \pm\sqrt{C}$, being sure to prefix a $\pm$ symbol to the square root of the right side of the equation.

6. Solve each of the resulting two linear equations.

7. Check each root in the original equation.

Here is an example.

Solve $x(x + 8) = 20$ by completing the square.

$x^2 + 8x = 20$	Express the equation in the form: $ax^2 + bx =$ numerical expression.
$x^2 + 8x + 4^2 = 20 + 4^2$	Add 4^2, the square of half of 8 to both sides.
$x^2 + 8x + 16 = 36$	Simplify.
$(x + 4)^2 = 36$	Factor the left side as the square of a binomial.
$x + 4 = \pm 6$	Write $x + 4$ equal to $\pm$ the square root of the right side of the equation. Don't forget the $\pm$ symbol!
$x + 4 = -6 \quad$ or $\quad x + 4 = 6$	Solve the resulting two linear equations.
$x = -10 \quad$ or $\qquad x = 2$	

Thus, $x(x + 8) = 20$ has two roots, -10 and 2, the same as obtained when $x(x + 8) = 20$ was solved by factoring.

To solve a quadratic equation by using the quadratic formula, use the following procedure:

1. Express the equation in standard form: $ax^2 + bx + c = 0$.

2. Determine the values of a, b, and c.

3. Substitute into the quadratic formula: $x = \dfrac{-b \pm \sqrt{b^2 - 4ac}}{2a}$.

4. Evaluate and simplify each of the two resulting expressions on the right side of the equation.

5. Check each root in the original equation.

Here is an example.

Solve $x(x + 8) = 20$ by using the quadratic formula.

$x^2 + 8x - 20 = 0$	Express in standard form.
$a = 1, b = 8, c = -20$ (include the $-$ sign)	Determine the values of a, b, and c.

$$x = \frac{-8 \pm \sqrt{8^2 - 4(1)(-20)}}{2(1)} = \frac{-8 \pm \sqrt{64 + 80}}{2} = \frac{-8 \pm \sqrt{144}}{2} = \frac{-8 \pm 12}{2}$$

Substitute into the quadratic formula.

Evaluate each of the two resulting expressions.

$$x = \frac{-8 + 12}{2} = \frac{4}{2} = 2 \text{ or}$$

$$x = \frac{-8 - 12}{2} = \frac{-20}{2} = -10$$

Thus, the two roots are –10 and 2, the same as obtained previously.

> **Tip:** When solving quadratic equations, *never* divide both sides of the equation by the variable or by an expression containing the variable.

The quantity $b^2 - 4ac$ is called the **discriminant** of the quadratic equation. The quadratic equation $ax^2 + bx + c = 0$ has exactly *one* real root if $b^2 - 4ac = 0$, *two* real unequal roots if $b^2 - 4ac > 0$, and *no* real roots if $b^2 - 4ac < 0$.

You also can solve linear and quadratic equations that have real zeros by using features of your graphing calculator. Check your owner's manual for instructions. For example, the **Trace** feature of a graphing calculator is one way to find the roots. When the trace cursor moves along the function, the y-value is calculated from the x-value. You can move the trace cursor to the point or points where the graph appears to cross the x-axis (that is, where $y = 0$). You might need to **Zoom in** to obtain better resolution and more accurate results. Most likely, you will have to approximate the zeros because you are limited by the pixel resolution of your viewing screen. (Pixels are the small cells that light up when you graph an equation.)

Systems of Equations and Inequalities

A set of equations, each with the same set of variables, is called a **system** when the set of equations are considered simultaneously. The system possesses a **solution** when the equations in the system are all satisfied by at least one set of values of the variables. A system that has a solution is said to be **consistent.** A system that has no solution is said to be **inconsistent.**

A **system of two linear equations in two variables** consists of a pair of linear equations in the same two variables. To **solve a system** of linear equations in two variables means to find all pairs of values for the two variables that make *both* equations true simultaneously. A pair of values—for example, an x-value paired with a corresponding y-value—is called an **ordered pair** and is written as (x, y). An ordered pair that makes an equation true is said to **satisfy** the equation. When an ordered pair makes both equations in a system true, the ordered pair **satisfies** the system. The **solution set** is the collection of all solutions. There are three possibilities: the system has exactly *one solution*, *no solution,* or *infinitely many solutions*.

Two algebraic methods for solving a system of linear equations that has a solution are **substitution** and **elimination.** To solve a system of linear equations by using **substitution,** use the following procedure:

1. Select the simpler equation and solve it for one of the variables in terms of the other.
2. Using the other given equation, replace the variable solved for in Step 1 with the expression obtained, simplify, and solve for the second variable.
3. Using the simpler equation, substitute the value obtained in Step 2 for the second variable, simplify, and solve for the first variable.
4. Check the solution in the original equations.

Here is an example.

Solve $\begin{cases} 3x - y = 1 \\ x + y = -5 \end{cases}$ by using substitution.

$x + y = -5 \Rightarrow x = -5 - y$	Solve the simpler equation for x in terms of y.
$3x - y = 1 \Rightarrow 3(-5 - y) - y = 1$	In the other given equation, replace x with $-5 - y$.
$3(-5 - y) - y = 1 \Rightarrow -15 - 3y - y = 1 \Rightarrow -4y = 16 \Rightarrow y = -4$	Solve for y.
$x + y = -5 \Rightarrow x + (-4) = -5$	Substitute -4 for y into $x + y = -5$.
$x + (-4) = -5 \Rightarrow x = -1$	Solve for x.

Thus, the ordered pair $(-1, -4)$ is the solution for the system $\begin{cases} 3x - y = 1 \\ x + y = -5 \end{cases}$.

To solve a system of linear equations by using **elimination,** use the following procedure:

1. Write both equations in standard form: $Ax + By = C$.
2. If necessary, multiply one or both of the equations by a nonzero constant or constants to make the coefficients of one of the variables sum to zero.
3. Add the resulting equations and then solve for the remaining variable.
4. Substitute the value obtained in Step 3 into one of the equations, simplify, and solve for the other variable.
5. Check the solution in the original equations.

Here is an example.

Solve $\begin{cases} 2x - 3y = 12 \\ 5x + 2y = 11 \end{cases}$ by using elimination:

$\begin{cases} 4x - 6y = 24 \\ 15x + 6y = 33 \end{cases}$ Multiply the first equation by 2 and the second equation by 3.

$\begin{array}{l} 4x - 6y = 24 \\ \underline{15x + 6y = 33} \\ 19x + 0 = 57 \end{array}$ Add the equations.

$19x = 57 \Rightarrow \dfrac{19x}{19} = \dfrac{57}{19} \Rightarrow x = 3$ Solve for x.

$2x - 3y = 12 \Rightarrow 2(3) - 3y = 12$ Substitute 3 for x into one of the equations.

$2(3) - 3y = 12 \Rightarrow 6 - 3y = 12 \Rightarrow -3y = 6 \Rightarrow y = -2$ Solve for y.

Thus, the ordered pair $(3, -2)$ is the solution for the system $\begin{cases} 2x - 3y = 12 \\ 5x + 2y = 11 \end{cases}$.

You can use the methods of this section to solve systems of equations in two variables when one of the equations is nonlinear.

Here is an example.

Solve $\begin{cases} 5x - y = 12 \\ 2x^2 + y = 0 \end{cases}$.

Observe that the coefficients of y sum to zero.

$\begin{array}{l} 5x - y = 12 \\ \underline{2x^2 + y = 0} \\ 2x^2 + 5x = 12 \end{array}$ Add the equations.

$2x^2 + 5x = 12$ Solve the resulting quadratic equation using a convenient method.

$2x^2 + 5x = 12 \Rightarrow 2x^2 + 5x - 12 = 0 \Rightarrow (2x - 3)(x + 4) = 0 \Rightarrow 2x - 3 = 0 \text{ or } x + 4 = 0 \Rightarrow 2x = 3 \text{ or } x = -4 \Rightarrow x = 1.5 \text{ or } x = -4$

Tip: Do not make the mistake of stopping at this point and writing (1.5, −4) as the solution. You have obtained two distinct values for x and now must obtain the corresponding y value for each.

Substitute $x = 1.5$ and $x = -4$ into $5x - y = 12$, to find the corresponding y value for each.

$$5(1.5) - y = 12 \quad \text{or} \quad 5(-4) - y = 12$$
$$-y = 4.5 \quad \text{or} \quad -y = 32$$
$$y = -4.5 \quad \text{or} \quad y = -32$$

Thus, two ordered pairs, $(1.5, -4.5)$ and $(-4, -32)$, satisfy the system $\begin{cases} 5x - y = 12 \\ 2x^2 + y = 0 \end{cases}$.

Sample Exercises

1. $(3xy^3)(-2x^2y^4) =$

    A. $-6x^2y^{12}$
    B. $-6x^3y^7$
    C. x^3y^7
    D. $6x^3y^7$

2. Simplify $\dfrac{18x^2 + 54}{3x^2 + 6}$.

    A. 15
    B. $6x + 9$
    C. $\dfrac{6x^2 + 9}{x^2 + 1}$
    D. $\dfrac{6x^2 + 18}{x^2 + 2}$

3. Which of the following is a factor of $2x^2 + x - 6$?

    A. $x - 2$
    B. $x + 2$
    C. $2x + 3$
    D. $2x - 6$

4. If $\dfrac{1}{2}x - 5 = 14$, what is the value of $3x - 1$?

    A. 19
    B. 38
    C. 113
    D. 114

5. What is the sum of the roots of $x^2 + x - 20 = 0$?

    A. -9
    B. -1
    C. 1
    D. 9

6. What is the y value of the ordered pair that is a solution to the system $\begin{cases} 2x - 3y = 12 \\ 4x + 5y = 2 \end{cases}$?

    A. -3
    B. -2
    C. 2
    D. 3

Answer Explanations for Sample Exercises

1. B. Follow the rules for multiplying two monomials.

$(3xy^3)(-2x^2y^4) = (3)(-2)\ (xy^3)(x^2y^4) = -6x^{1+2}y^{3+4} = -6x^3y^7$, Choice B.

> **Tip: Remember that when you multiply variable factors, you *add* (not multiply) the exponents of like bases.**

2. D. To simplify the expression $\dfrac{18x^2 + 54}{3x^2 + 6}$, follow the procedure for simplifying polynomials.

$\dfrac{18x^2 + 54}{3x^2 + 6} = \dfrac{18(x^2 + 3)}{3(x^2 + 2)} = \dfrac{6(x^2 + 3)}{(x^2 + 2)} = \dfrac{6x^2 + 18}{x^2 + 2}$, Choice D.

3. B. Factor $2x^2 + x - 6$ into the product of two binomials by using F.O.I.L. in reverse.

$2x^2 + x - 6 = (2x - 3)(x + 2)$, which means Choice B is the correct response.

> **Tip: After factoring, mentally multiply the two factors to check your work.**

4. C. First use the procedure for solving linear equations to solve $\frac{1}{2}x - 5 = 14$.

$\frac{1}{2}x - 5 = 14 \Rightarrow 2 \cdot \frac{1}{2}x - 2 \cdot 5 = 2 \cdot 14 \Rightarrow x - 10 = 28 \Rightarrow x = 38$.

Next, substitute 38 for x in $3x - 1$ and evaluate: $3(38) - 1 = 113$, Choice C.

5. B. First solve the quadratic equation $x^2 + x - 20 = 0$ using a convenient method.

$x + x - 20 = 0 \Rightarrow (x + 5)(x - 4) = 0 \Rightarrow (x + 5) = 0$ or $(x - 4) = 0 \Rightarrow x = -5$ or $x = 4$.

Next, sum the two roots: $-5 + 4 = -1$, Choice B.

6. B. First solve the system $\begin{cases} 2x - 3y = 12 \\ 4x + 5y = 2 \end{cases}$ using a convenient method. Be clever! Since you want to determine

the y value, solve by eliminating the x variable.

$\begin{cases} -4x + 6y = -24 \\ \ \ \ 4x + 5y = 2 \end{cases}$ Multiply the first equation by -2.

$\begin{aligned} -4x + 6y &= -24 \qquad \text{Add the equations, and then solve for } y. \\ \underline{4x + 5y} &= \underline{2} \\ 11y &= -22 \end{aligned}$

$11y = -22 \Rightarrow y = -2$, Choice B.

Geometry

This chapter provides a review of the key ideas and formulas of geometry that are most important for you to know for the Praxis Middle School Mathematics test. Multiple-choice sample exercises, comparable to what might be presented on the Praxis Middle School Mathematics test, are given at the end of the chapter. The answer explanations for the sample exercises are provided immediately following.

General Relationships Involving Geometric Figures

Congruent (symbolized by ≅) geometric figures have exactly the same size and same shape. They are superimposable, meaning that they will fit exactly on top of each other. Corresponding parts of congruent figures are congruent. Here are examples of congruent figures.

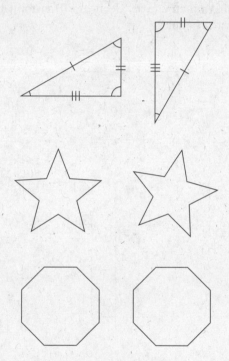

Note: Hash marks (as shown in the first pair of congruent figures) can be used to draw attention to corresponding congruent parts.

Similar (symbolized by ~) geometric figures have the same shape, but not necessarily the same size. According to the 2008 *National Mathematics Advisory Panel Report of the Task Group on Learning Processes* (www.ed.gov/about/bdscomm/list/mathpanel/index.html), a more "mathematically correct" definition of similarity is to say that two geometric "figures are similar if one of the figures is congruent to a dilated version of the other" (p. 95). (See "Geometric Transformations" in this chapter for a discussion of *dilation*.) Here are examples of similar figures.

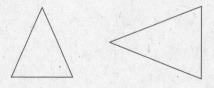

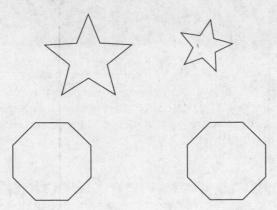

Symmetry describes the shape of a figure or object. A figure has **reflective** (or **bilateral**) **symmetry** if it can be folded exactly in half and the resulting two parts are congruent. The line along the fold is the **line of symmetry.** A figure has **rotational symmetry** if it can be rotated onto an exact copy of itself before it comes back to its original position. The center of rotation is called the **center of symmetry.** (See "Geometric Transformations" in this chapter for a discussion of *rotation* of geometric figures.) Here are examples.

Reflective Symmetry Only

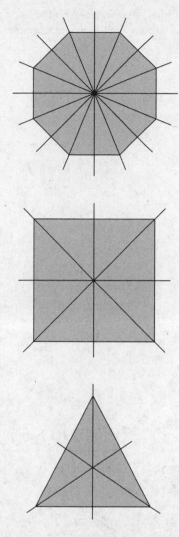

Both Reflective and Rotational Symmetry

Lines and Angles

In geometry, the terms **point**, **line,** and **plane** are undefined. You can think of a point as a location in space. You can think of a line as a set of points that extends infinitely in both directions. You can think of a plane as a set of points that form a flat infinite surface. *Note:* For discussions in this chapter, unless specifically stated otherwise, all figures and objects are considered to lie in the same plane.

A **ray** is a line extending from a point. When two rays meet at a common point, they form an **angle.** The point where the rays meet is called the **vertex** of the angle.

The number of degrees in an angle is called its **measure.** If there are k degrees in angle A, then you write $m\angle A = k$. You can classify angles by the number of degrees in their measurement. An **acute angle** measures between 0° and 90°; that is if angle A is acute, $0° < m\angle A < 90°$. A **right angle** measures exactly 90°; that is, if angle C is a right angle, $m\angle C = 90°$. An **obtuse angle** measures between 90° and 180°; that is if angle B is obtuse, $90° < m\angle B < 180°$. A **straight angle** measures exactly 180°. Two angles whose measures sum to 90° are **complementary angles.** Two angles whose measures sum to 180° are **supplementary angles.** Two angles with the same measure are **congruent. Adjacent angles** are angles that have a common vertex and a common side. Here are examples.

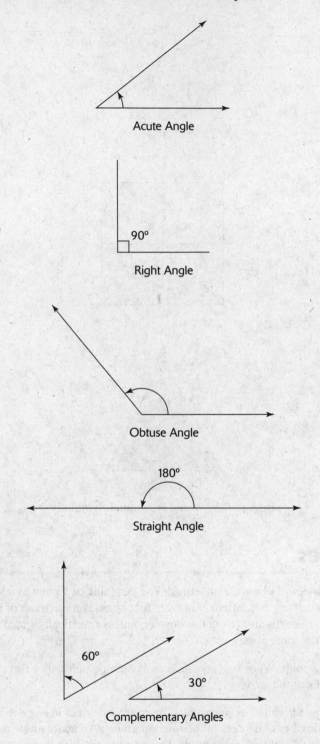

Acute Angle

90°

Right Angle

Obtuse Angle

180°

Straight Angle

60°   30°

Complementary Angles

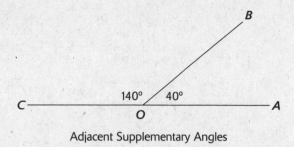

Adjacent Supplementary Angles

A **bisector of an angle** is a line that passes through the vertex of the angle and divides it into two congruent angles.

Lines in a plane can be parallel or intersecting. **Intersecting lines** cross at a point in the plane. Two nonadjacent angles formed by intersecting lines are called **vertical angles.** Vertical angles formed by two intersecting lines are congruent. In the figure shown, ∠A and ∠B are congruent vertical angles; and ∠C and ∠D are congruent vertical angles.

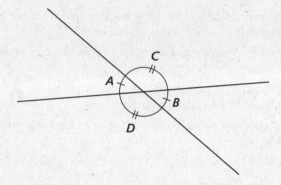

Parallel lines (in a plane) never meet. The distance between them is always the same. A shorthand way to indicate that a line *AB* is parallel to a line *CD* is to write *AB//CD*. A **transversal** is a straight line that intersects two or more given lines. When two parallel lines, such as *l* and *m* shown here, are cut by a transversal, eight angles are formed.

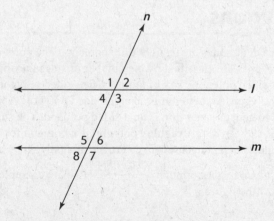

The **interior angles** are ∠3, ∠4, ∠5, and ∠6. The **exterior angles** are ∠1, ∠2, ∠7, and ∠8. The **corresponding angles** are the pair of angles ∠1 and ∠5, the pair of angles ∠2 and ∠6, the pair of angles ∠4 and ∠8, and the pair of angles ∠3 and ∠7. The **alternate exterior angles** are the pair of angles ∠1 and ∠7 and the pair of angles ∠2 and ∠8. The **alternate interior angles** are the pair of angles ∠4 and ∠6 and the pair of angles ∠3 and ∠5.

Perpendicular lines intersect at right angles. A shorthand way to indicate that a line *AB* is perpendicular to a line *CD* is to write *AB⊥CD*. The **perpendicular bisector** of a line segment is the set of all points in the plane of the line segment that are equidistant from the end points of the line segment. In the figure shown, line *m* is the perpendicular bisector of line segment $\overline{AB}$.

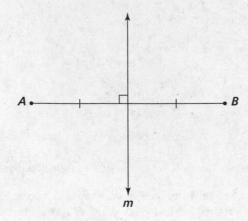

Following are theorems about lines that are useful to know.

- **Euclid's Parallel Postulate:** Given a line and a point in the same plane but not on the line, there is one and only one line through the given point that is parallel to the given line.

- If two parallel lines are cut by a transversal, then any pair of corresponding angles, alternate exterior angles, or alternate interior angles are congruent.

- If two lines are cut by a transversal and if any pair of corresponding angles, alternate exterior angles, or alternate interior angles are congruent, then the two lines are parallel.

- If two lines are cut by a transversal and a pair of interior angles on the same side of the transversal are supplementary, then the two lines are parallel.

- The shortest distance from a point to a line is the measure of the perpendicular line segment from the point to the line.

- Two distinct lines (in a plane) that are perpendicular to the same line are parallel.

- If a line in a plane is perpendicular to one of two parallel lines, it is perpendicular to the other parallel line.

Properties of Polygons

A **polygon** is a closed plane figure, whose **sides** are straight line segments. The point at which the two sides of a polygon intersect is called a **vertex.** Polygons are classified by the number of sides they have. A **triangle** is a three-sided polygon. A **quadrilateral** is a four-sided polygon. A **pentagon** is a five-sided polygon. A **hexagon** is a six-sided polygon. A **heptagon** is a seven-sided polygon. An **octagon** is an eight-sided polygon. A **nonagon** is a nine-sided polygon. A **decagon** is a ten-sided polygon. In general, an **n-gon** is an n-sided polygon. The sum of the measures of the interior angles of an n-sided polygon equals $(n-2)180°$. A **regular polygon** is a polygon for which all sides and angles are congruent. A line segment that connects two nonconsecutive vertices of a polygon is called a **diagonal.** The number of diagonals of an n-sided polygon is given by the formula: $\dfrac{n(n-3)}{2}$. Here are examples of regular polygons with the number of diagonals indicated below the figure.

Triangle

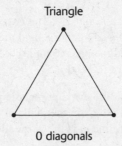

0 diagonals

Quadrilateral

2 diagonals

Pentagon

5 diagonals

Hexagon

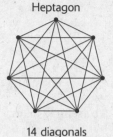
Heptagon

Octagon

9 diagonals

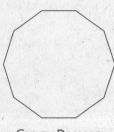
14 diagonals

20 diagonals

If all the diagonals of a polygon lie within the interior of the polygon, the polygon is **convex;** otherwise, the polygon is **concave.** Here are examples.

Convex Hexagon   Concave Hexagon   Convex Decagon   Concave Decagon

Properties of Quadrilaterals

Quadrilaterals are commonly classified as trapezoids or parallelograms.

A **trapezoid** has two definitions, both of which are widely accepted. One definition is that a trapezoid is a quadrilateral that has *exactly* one pair of opposite sides that are parallel. This definition would exclude parallelograms as a special case. The other definition is that a trapezoid is a quadrilateral that has *at least* one pair of parallel sides. This definition would allow any parallelogram to be considered a special kind of trapezoid. This situation is one of the few times that mathematicians do not agree on the definition of a term. For purposes of this CliffsTestPrep book, you will have to assume that answers to problems involving trapezoids on the Praxis Middle School Mathematics test will not hinge on the definition for trapezoid you choose to use during the test.

A **parallelogram** is a quadrilateral that has two pairs of opposite sides that are parallel. Some useful properties of parallelograms are the following: opposite sides are congruent; the sum of the four interior angles is 360°; opposite interior angles are congruent; consecutive interior angles are supplementary; the diagonals bisect each other; and each diagonal divides the parallelogram into two congruent triangles.

Some parallelograms have special names because of their special properties. A **rhombus** is a parallelogram that has four congruent sides. A **rectangle** is a parallelogram that has four right angles. A **square** is a parallelogram that has four right angles and four congruent sides. These three figures have all the general properties of parallelograms. In addition, their diagonals are equal. In the rhombus and square, the diagonals intersect at right angles.

Here are examples of quadrilaterals.

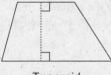
Trapezoid

Trapezoid

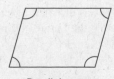
Parallelogram

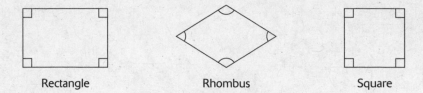

Rectangle   Rhombus   Square

Following are theorems about quadrilaterals that are useful to know.

- The sum of the angles of a quadrilateral is 360°.
- If the diagonals of a quadrilateral bisect each other, the quadrilateral is a parallelogram.
- If two sides of a quadrilateral are parallel and congruent, the quadrilateral is a parallelogram.
- If the diagonals of a quadrilateral are perpendicular bisectors of each other, the quadrilateral is a rhombus.
- If a parallelogram has one right angle, it has four right angles and is a rectangle.
- If a rhombus has one right angle, it has four right angles and is a square.

Properties of Triangles

Triangles can be classified in two different ways. You can classify triangles according to their sides as scalene, isosceles, or equilateral. A **scalene** triangle has no two sides congruent. An **isosceles** triangle has at least two congruent sides, and the angles opposite the congruent sides are called the **base angles.** An **equilateral** triangle has three congruent sides. Another way to classify triangles is according to the measures of their interior angles. The sum of the measures of the interior angles of a triangle is 180°. An **acute** triangle has three acute interior angles. A **right** triangle has exactly one right interior angle. An **obtuse** triangle has exactly one obtuse interior angle. Here are examples.

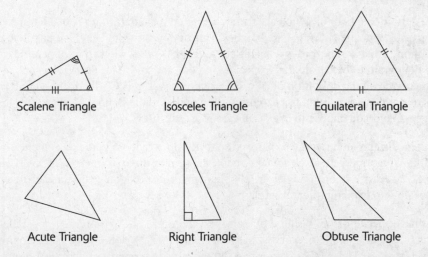

Scalene Triangle   Isosceles Triangle   Equilateral Triangle

Acute Triangle   Right Triangle   Obtuse Triangle

An **altitude** of a triangle is a line segment drawn from a vertex of the triangle perpendicular to the side, called the **base,** opposite that vertex. The **height** of a triangle is the length of the altitude. *Note:* The term *altitude* is sometimes used to mean the *height* of the triangle, rather than the line segment that determines the height. On the Praxis Middle School Mathematics test, you will be able to tell from the context of the problem what meaning is intended for the term altitude. Every triangle has three altitudes, one from each vertex. The lines containing the altitudes of a triangle are **concurrent,** meaning they intersect in a point. This point of concurrency of the altitudes of a triangle is called the **orthocenter** of the triangle.

A **median** of a triangle is a line segment connecting a vertex of the triangle to the midpoint of the side opposite that vertex. The lines containing the medians of a triangle are concurrent, and their point of concurrency, called the **centroid,** is two-thirds of the way along each median, from the vertex to the opposite side.

A **perpendicular bisector** of the side of a triangle is a line perpendicular to that side at its midpoint. The perpendicular bisectors of the sides of a triangle are concurrent, and their point of concurrency, called the **circumcenter,** is equidistant from the vertices of the triangle. Thus, if a circle is circumscribed about the triangle, the circumcenter is the center of the circumscribed circle.

The **angle bisectors** of the interior angles of a triangle are concurrent, and their point of concurrency, called the **incenter,** is equidistant from the three sides. Thus, if a circle is inscribed in a triangle, the incenter is the center of the inscribed circle.

Here are examples.

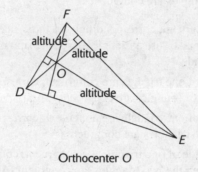

Orthocenter *O*

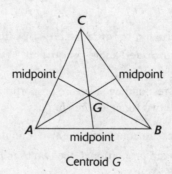

Centroid *G*

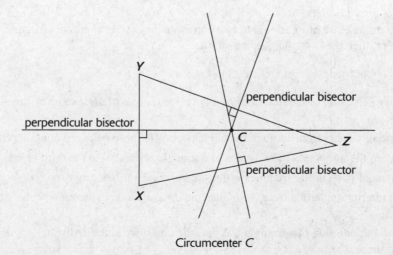

Circumcenter *C*

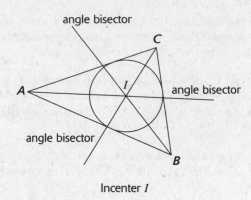

Incenter I

Congruent triangles are triangles for which corresponding sides and corresponding angles are congruent. The following theorems can be used to prove two triangles are congruent.

- If three sides of one triangle are congruent, correspondingly, to three sides of another triangle, then the two triangles are congruent (**SSS**). *Note:* To make sure a triangle exists, the sum of the lengths of any two sides must be greater than the length of the third side.
- If two sides and the included angle of one triangle are congruent, correspondingly, to two sides and the included angle of another triangle, then the two triangles are congruent (**SAS**).
- If two angles and the included side of one triangle are congruent, correspondingly, to two angles and the included side of another triangle, then the two triangles are congruent (**ASA**).
- If two angles and the nonincluded side of one triangle are congruent, correspondingly, to two angles and the nonincluded side of another triangle, then the two triangles are congruent (**AAS**).

Tip: Two methods that do NOT work for proving congruence are AAA (three corresponding angles congruent) and SSA (two corresponding sides and the *nonincluded* angle congruent).

Similar triangles are triangles for which corresponding sides are proportional and corresponding angles are congruent. The following theorems can be used to prove two triangles are similar.

- If corresponding angles of two triangles are congruent, the two triangles are similar.
- If corresponding sides of two triangles are proportional, the two triangles are similar.
- If two angles of one triangle are congruent to two corresponding angles of another triangle, then the two triangles are similar.
- If two sides of one triangle are proportional to two corresponding sides of another triangle, and the included angles are congruent, then the two triangles are similar.

Here are other theorems about triangles that are useful to know.

- **Triangle inequality:** The sum of the measures of any two sides of a triangle must be greater than the measure of the third side.
- If two sides of a triangle are congruent, then the angles opposite those sides are congruent, and conversely.
- The segment between the midpoints of two sides of a triangle is parallel to the third side and half as long.
- The ratio of the areas of two similar triangles is the square of the ratio of any two corresponding sides.
- The bisector of an interior angle of a triangle divides the opposite side in the ratio of the sides that form the angle bisected.
- A line that is parallel to one side of a triangle and cuts the other two sides in distinct points cuts off segments that are proportional to these two sides.

The Pythagorean Theorem

In a right triangle the side opposite the right angle is called the **hypotenuse** of the right triangle. The hypotenuse is *always* the longest side of the right triangle. The other two sides are called the **legs** of the right triangle. Commonly, the letter c is used to represent the hypotenuse of a right triangle and the letters a and b to represent the legs. A special relationship, named after the famous Greek mathematician Pythagoras, exists between the sides of a right triangle. This special relationship is the **Pythagorean Theorem,** which states that $c^2 = a^2 + b^2$. Here is an illustration.

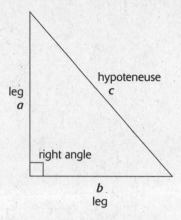

The Pythagorean relationship applies only to right triangles. If you know any two sides of a right triangle, you can find the third side by using the formula $c^2 = a^2 + b^2$. Here is an example.

Find the hypotenuse of a right triangle that has legs 9 cm and 12 cm.

Plugging into the formula, you have $c^2 = a^2 + b^2 = c^2 = (9 \text{ cm})^2 + (12 \text{ cm})^2 = 81 \text{ cm}^2 + 144 \text{ cm}^2 = 225 \text{ cm}^2 \Rightarrow c = 15$ cm.

If the measures of the three sides of a triangle satisfy the Pythagorean relationship, the triangle is a right triangle. Numbers, such as 3, 4, and 5, which satisfy the Pythagorean relationship, are called **Pythagorean triples.** After you identify a Pythagorean triple, any multiple of the three numbers is also a Pythagorean triple. For example, since 3, 4, and 5 is a Pythagorean triple, then so is 30, 40, and 50.

The altitude to the hypotenuse of a right triangle divides the triangle into two right triangles that are similar to each other and to the original right triangle. Furthermore, the length of the altitude is the geometric mean of the lengths of the two segments into which it separates the hypotenuse. In the figure shown, $\triangle ACB \sim \triangle AHC \sim \triangle CHB$; and $\dfrac{\overline{AH}}{h} = \dfrac{h}{HB}$.

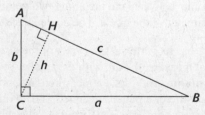

Here are additional theorems about right triangles that are useful to know.

- The sides of a 45°- 45°- 90° right triangle are in the ratio $1:1:\sqrt{2}$.
- The sides of a 30°- 60°- 90° right triangle are in the ratio $1:\sqrt{3}:2$, where the shortest side is opposite the 30-degree angle.
- Given two right triangles, if the hypotenuse and one leg of one triangle are congruent to the hypotenuse and the corresponding leg of the other triangle, then the two right triangles are congruent.

Properties of Circles

A **circle** is a closed plane figure for which all points are the same distance from a point within, called the **center.** A **radius** of a circle is a line segment joining the center of the circle to any point on the circle. A **chord** of a circle is a line segment with both endpoints on the circle. A **diameter** is a chord that passes through the center of the circle. The diameter of a circle is twice the radius. Conversely, the radius of a circle is half the diameter. Here is an illustration.

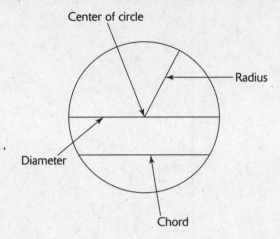

In a circle, a radius that is perpendicular to a chord bisects the chord. Consequently, the perpendicular bisector of a chord passes through the center of the circle. Here is an illustration.

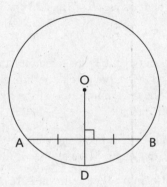

An **arc** is part of a circle; it is the set of points between and including two points on the circle. A **semicircle** is an arc whose endpoints are the endpoints of a diameter of the circle. The degree measure of a semicircle is 180°.

A **central angle** of a circle is an angle that has its vertex at the center of the circle. A central angle determines two arcs on the circle. If the two arcs are of unequal measure, the arc with the smaller measure is called the **minor arc** and the arc with the greater measure is called the **major arc.** Arcs are measured in degrees. The measure of a minor arc is equal to the measure of its central angle. The measure of a major arc equals 360° minus the measure of the minor arc's central angle. In the circle shown, the measure of minor arc $\overset{\frown}{AB}$ is 80°, and the measure of major arc $\overset{\frown}{AB}$ is 360°– 80° = 280°. Here is an illustration.

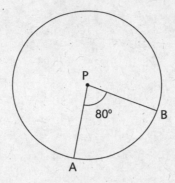

An **inscribed angle** is an angle whose vertex is on a circle and whose sides are chords of the circle. The arc of the circle that is in the interior of the inscribed angle and whose endpoints are on the sides of the angle is its **intercepted arc.** The measure of an inscribed angle is half the measure of its intercepted arc. An angle inscribed in a semicircle is a right angle. Look at these examples.

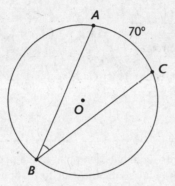 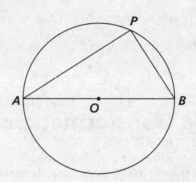

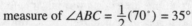

measure of $\angle ABC = \frac{1}{2}(70°) = 35°$ measure of $\angle APB = 90°$

If two chords intersect within a circle, each of the angles formed equals one-half the sum of its intercepted arcs. Furthermore, the product of the lengths of the segments formed for one chord equals the product of the lengths of the segments formed for the other chord. In the circle shown, $\angle SVT = \frac{1}{2}(70° + 50°) = \frac{1}{2}(120°) = 60°$; and $\overline{RV} \cdot \overline{VS} = \overline{UV} \cdot \overline{VT}$.

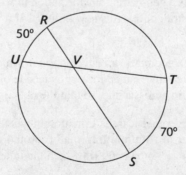

A **secant** to a circle is a line that contains a chord. A **tangent** to a circle is a line in the plane of the circle that intersects the circle in only one point. The point of contact is called the **point of tangency.** If a straight line is tangent to a circle, then the radius drawn to the point of tangency will be perpendicular to the tangent. Here is an illustration.

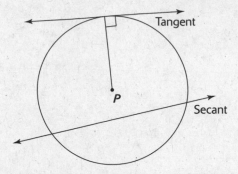

An angle formed outside a circle by the intersection of two secants, two tangents, or a tangent and a second equals one-half the difference of the intercepted arcs.

Concentric circles are circles that have the same center.

A **sector** of a circle is a region bounded by two radii and an arc of the circle.

A polygon is **inscribed** in a circle if each of its vertices lies on the circle.

A polygon is **circumscribed** about a circle if each of its sides is tangent to the circle.

Geometric Transformations

A **geometric transformation** is a mapping between two sets of points such that each point in the **preimage** has a unique **image** and that each point in the image has exactly one preimage. The four geometric transformations are **translations, reflections, rotations,** and **dilations.** Translations, reflections, and rotations are **rigid motions,** meaning that the transformation preserves distances and angles. Thus, the image and the preimage of translations, reflections, and rotations are congruent. The situation is different for dilations. In general, a dilation is not a rigid motion. A dilation preserves angles, but in only one special circumstance does a dilation preserve distances. Thus, the image and preimage of a dilation are similar, but not necessarily congruent. You can think of geometric transformations as ways to change geometric figures without changing their basic properties.

A **translation** of a plane geometric figure is a geometric transformation in which every point P is "moved" the same distance and in the same direction along a straight line to a new point P'. Informally, a translation is a **slide** in a horizontal or vertical direction.

A **reflection** of a plane geometric figure is a geometric transformation in which every point P is "moved" to a new point P' that is the same distance from a fixed line, but on the opposite side of the line. The fixed line is called the **line of reflection.** Informally, a reflection is a **flip** across a line, so that the new figure is a mirror image of the original.

A **rotation** of a plane geometric figure is a geometric transformation in which every point P is "rotated" through an angle around a fixed point, called the **center of rotation.** Informally, a rotation is a **turn** around a point. A figure has **rotational symmetry** if there is a rotation of less than 360° in which the image and its preimage coincide under the rotation.

A **dilation** of a plane geometric figure is a geometric transformation in which every point P is mapped to a new point P', where the point P' lies on a ray through a fixed point O and the point P, so that the $\overline{OP'} = |k|\,\overline{OP}$, where k is a nonzero real number, called the **scale factor.** Informally, a **dilation** is an expanding ($|k| > 1$) or contracting ($|k| < 1$) of a geometric shape using a scale factor, while its shape, location, and orientation remain the same. In the case that $|k| = 1$, the dilated image is congruent to the original geometric shape, and the dilation is a rigid motion.

[*Note:* Some sources insist that a dilation must change a figure's size. This requirement would exclude the scale factor k, where $|k| = 1$. However, to be consistent with the 2008 *National Mathematics Advisory Panel Report of the Task Group on Learning Processes* (**www.ed.gov/about/bdscomm/list/mathpanel/index.html**), which suggests the use of dilation in defining similarity, the case that results in congruency between the image and preimage must be included (since similar figures can be congruent).]

Here are examples.

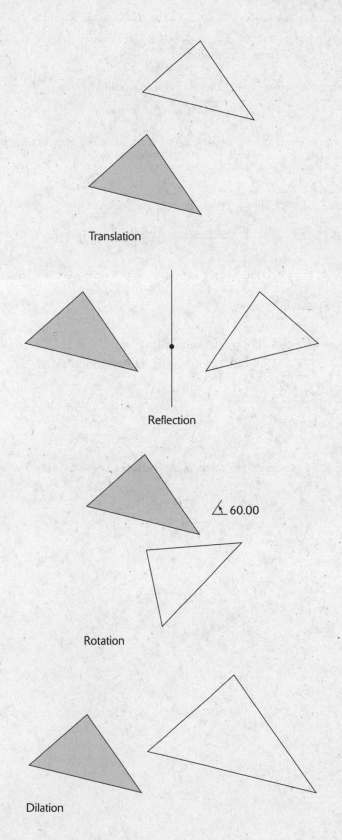

Translation

Reflection

△ 60.00

Rotation

Dilation

Formulas Used in Two- and Three-Dimensional Coordinate Systems

To find the distance between two points, (x_1, y_1) and (x_2, y_2) on a coordinate graph, use the formula: Distance between two points $= \sqrt{(x_2 - x_1)^2 + (y_2 - y_1)^2}$. Here is an example.

Find the distance between the points $(1, -2)$ and $(4, 2)$ on a coordinate graph.

Distance $= \sqrt{(4-1)^2 + (2-(-2))^2} = \sqrt{(3)^2 + (4)^2} = \sqrt{25} = 5$ units.

To find the midpoint between two points (x_1, y_1) and (x_2, y_2) on a coordinate graph, use the formula: Midpoint between two points $= \left(\dfrac{x_1 + x_2}{2}, \dfrac{y_1 + y_2}{2} \right)$. Here is an example.

Find the midpoint between $(1, -2)$ and $(4, 2)$ on a coordinate graph.

Midpoint $= \left(\dfrac{x_1 + x_2}{2}, \dfrac{y_1 + y_2}{2} \right) = \left(\dfrac{1+4}{2}, \dfrac{-2+2}{2} \right) = \left(\dfrac{5}{2}, \dfrac{0}{2} \right) = (2.5, 0)$.

To find the distance d from point (x_1, y_1) to the line whose equation is $Ax + By + C = 0$, use the formula: $d = \dfrac{|Ax_1 + By_1 + C|}{\sqrt{A^2 + B^2}}$. Here is an example.

Find the distance, d, from the point $(1, -2)$ to the line whose equation is $3x - 4y = 1$.

First, rewrite $3x - 4y = 1$ as $3x - 4y - 1 = 0$, and then plug into the formula:

$$d = \frac{|Ax_1 + By_1 + C|}{\sqrt{A^2 + B^2}} = \frac{|3(1) - 4(-2) - 1|}{\sqrt{3^2 + (-4)^2}} = \frac{|10|}{\sqrt{9 + 16}} = \frac{10}{5} = 2 \text{ units.}$$

Tip: When substituting values into formulas, enclose in parentheses any substituted value that is negative to avoid making a sign error.

Sample Exercises

1. The center of a circle that is inscribed in a triangle coincides with which of the following points associated with the triangle?

   A. centroid
   B. circumcenter
   C. incenter
   D. orthocenter

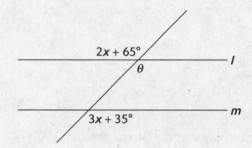

2. In the preceding figure, lines l and m are parallel. What is the measure of angle θ?

   A. 125°
   B. 97°
   C. 30°
   D. 16°

3. A length of cable is attached to the top of a 12-foot pole. The cable is anchored 9 feet from the base of the pole. What is the length of the cable?

   A. 13 feet
   B. 21 feet
   C. $3\sqrt{7}$ feet
   D. 15 feet

4. What is the sum of the measures of the interior angles of an octagon?

   A. 720°
   B. 900°
   C. 1080°
   D. 1440°

5. In the figure shown, $\triangle ABC \sim \triangle EFG$, line segment $\overline{AB}$ is 4 cm, line segment $\overline{EG}$ is 7 cm, and line segment $\overline{AC}$ is 2 cm. Find the length of line segment $\overline{EF}$.

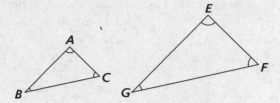

A. $\frac{2}{7}$ cm

B. $\frac{6}{7}$ cm

C. $3\frac{1}{2}$ cm

D. 14 cm

6. What is the measure of an inscribed angle whose intercepted arc is 100°?

A. 50°

B. 100°

C. 130°

D. 200°

Answer Explanations for Sample Exercises

1. **C.** Analyze the problem. The angle bisectors of a triangle are concurrent, and their point of concurrency, called the **incenter,** is equidistant from the three sides. Thus, if a circle is inscribed in a triangle, the incenter is the center of the inscribed circle, Choice C.

2. **A.** Analyze the problem. From the figure, you can see that the angle whose measure is $2x + 65°$ and θ are vertical angles, so they are congruent. Angle θ and the angle whose measure is $3x + 35°$ are corresponding angles of parallel lines, so they are congruent. Thus, the angles whose measures are $2x + 65°$ and $3x + 35°$ are congruent and have the same measure. Devise a plan. To find the measure of θ will take two steps. First, set the expressions $2x + 65°$ and $3x + 35°$ equal to each other, and then solve the resulting equation for x. Next, substitute the value obtained for x into one of the expressions, $2x + 65°$ or $3x + 35°$, to find the measure of angle θ.

   Step 1. Solve for x: $2x + 65° = 3x + 35° \Rightarrow 30° = x$.

   Step 2. Substitute the value obtained for x into $2x + 65°$.

   $2x + 65° = 2(30°) + 65° = 125°$, Choice A.

Tip: Be sure to answer the question! Choice C results if you fail to do Step 2 above.

3. **D.** First sketch a diagram to illustrate the problem.

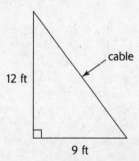

   Analyze the problem. The pole, the cable, and the ground form a right triangle. From the diagram, you can see that the length of the cable is the hypotenuse of a right triangle that has legs of 12 feet and 9 feet. You can use the Pythagorean theorem to find the hypotenuse. Devise a plan. To find the length of the cable, plug into the formula for the Pythagorean theorem and solve for the hypotenuse, denoted by c:

   $c = $ hypotenuse $= ?$, $a = 12$ ft, and $b = 9$ ft.

   $c^2 = a^2 + b^2 = (12 \text{ ft})^2 + (9 \text{ ft})^2 = 144 \text{ ft}^2 + 81 \text{ ft}^2 = 225 \text{ ft}^2 \Rightarrow c = 15$ ft, Choice D.

Tip: Sketching a figure for problems dealing with geometric figures is a smart test-taking strategy.

4. **C.** Analyze the problem. The sum of the measures of the interior angles of an n-sided polygon equals $(n - 2)180°$. An octagon has eight sides, so the sum of the measures of its interior angles is $(8 - 2)180° = 1080°$, Choice C.

5. C. Analyze the problem. The two triangles are similar. Therefore, corresponding sides are proportional. Devise a plan. Set up a proportion and solve for $\overline{EF}$. Carry out the plan.

$$\frac{\overline{EF}}{\overline{AC}} = \frac{\overline{EG}}{\overline{AB}} \Rightarrow \frac{\overline{EF}}{2\text{ cm}} = \frac{7\text{ cm}}{4\text{ cm}} \Rightarrow \overline{EF} = \frac{14\text{ cm}}{4} = 3\frac{1}{2}\text{ cm, Choice C.}$$

Tip: When you're going to solve a proportion for a missing element, write the proportion so that the missing element is in the numerator of the first ratio.

6. A. Analyze the problem. The measure of an inscribed angle is half the measure of its intercepted arc. Thus, the measure of the inscribed angle $= \frac{1}{2}(100^\circ) = 50^\circ$, Choice A.

Measurement

This chapter provides a review of the key ideas and formulas of measurement that are most important for you to know for the Praxis Middle School Mathematics test. Multiple-choice sample exercises, comparable to what might be presented on the Praxis Middle School Mathematics test, are given at the end of the chapter. The answer explanations for the sample exercises are provided immediately following.

Precision, Accuracy, and Approximate Error

In the physical world, measurement of continuous quantities is always approximate. The precision and accuracy of the measurement relate to the worthiness of the approximation.

Precision refers to the degree to which a measurement is repeatable and reliable; that is, consistently getting the same data each time the measurement is taken. The precision of a measurement depends on the magnitude of the smallest measuring unit used to obtain the measurement (for example, to the nearest meter, to the nearest centimeter, to the nearest millimeter, and so on). In theory, the smaller the measurement unit used, the more precise the measurement.

Accuracy refers to the degree to which a measurement is true or correct. A measurement can be precise without being accurate. This can occur, for example, when a measuring instrument needs adjustment, so that the measurements obtained, no matter how precisely measured, are inaccurate.

The amount of error involved in a physical measurement is the **approximate error** of the measurement. The **maximum possible error** of a measurement is half the magnitude of the smallest measurement unit used to obtain the measurement. For example, if the smallest measurement unit is 1 inch, the maximum possible error is 0.5 inch. The most accurate way of expressing a measurement is as a **tolerance interval.** For instance, a measurement of 10 inches, to the nearest inch, should be reported as 10 inches ± 0.5 inches. In other words, the true measurement lies between 9.5 inches and 10.5 inches. Closer approximations can be obtained by refining the measurement to a higher degree of precision (for example, by measuring to the nearest half-inch.)

When you do calculations with measurements that are reported as tolerance intervals, you need to consider the amount of error that will ensue. The results of such calculations should be reported as tolerance intervals that indicate the potential minimum and maximum error. To determine these tolerance intervals for the different arithmetic operations, use the guidelines in the following table.

Determining Total Minimum or Maximum Error		
Operation	**Guideline**	**Example**
Addition	Add the minimum/maximum values of the measurement, respectively.	(12 in ± 0.2 in) + (10 in ± 0.5 in) ⇨ (12 in − 0.2 in) + (10 in − 0.5 in) ≤ sum ≤ (12 in + 0.2in) + (10 in + 0.5 in) = 11.8 in + 9.5 in ≤ sum ≤ 12.2 in + 10.5 in = 21.3 in ≤ sum ≤ 22.7 in.
Subtraction	The minimum error is the difference between the *least* possible first number and the *greatest* possible second number, and the maximum error is the difference between the *greatest* possible first number and the *least* possible second number.	(12 in ± 0.2 in) − (10 in ± 0.5 in) ⇨ (12 in − 0.2 in) − (10 in + 0.5 in) ≤ difference ≤ (12 in + 0.2 in) − (10 in − 0.5 in) = 11.8 in − 10.5in ≤ difference ≤ 12.2 in − 9.5 in = 1.3 in ≤ difference ≤ 2.7 in.

(continued)

Determining Total Minimum or Maximum Error *(continued)*

Operation	Guideline	Example
Multiplication	Multiply the minimum/maximum values of the measurement, respectively.	(12 in $\pm$ 0.2 in)(10 in $\pm$ 0.5 in) $\Rightarrow$ (12 in $-$ 0.2 in) (10 in $-$ 0.5 in) $\leq$ product $\leq$ (12 in + 0.2 in)(10 in + 0.5 in) = (11.8 in)(9.5 in) $\leq$ product $\leq$ (12.2 in)(10.5 in) = 112.1 in^2 $\leq$ product $\leq$ 128.1 in^2.
Division	The minimum error is the quotient of the *least* possible first number and the *greatest* possible second number, and the maximum error is the quotient of the *greatest* possible first number and the *least* possible second number.	(12 in $\pm$ 0.2 in) $\div$ (10 in $\pm$ 0.5 in) $\Rightarrow$ (12 in $-$ 0.2 in) $\div$ (10 in + 0.5 in) $\leq$ quotient $\leq$ (12 in + 0.2 in) $\div$ (10 in $-$ 0.5 in) = 11.8 in $\div$ 10.5 in $\leq$ quotient $\leq$ 12.2 in $\div$ 9.5 in = 1.1. $\leq$ quotient $\leq$ 1.3 (rounded to nearest tenth).

Here is an example.

> The length of a rectangular field is 100 ft $\pm$ 1 ft, and the width is 50 ft $\pm$ 1 ft. Determine a tolerance interval for the area of the field.

Since the area of the field equals length times width, the tolerance interval for the area is (100 ft. $\pm$ 1 ft)(50 ft. $\pm$ 1 ft) $\Rightarrow$ (99 ft)(49 ft) $\leq$ area $\leq$ (101 ft)(51 ft) = 4851 ft^2 $\leq$ area $\leq$ 5151 ft^2.

Two ways of conveying the magnitude of error in a measurement are absolute error and relative error (which can be expressed as a decimal or a percent). The **absolute error** of the measurement is the amount of physical error in the measurement, and the **relative error** of the measurement is the ratio of the absolute error to the correct value, or, if the correct value is unknown, to the measurement taken. The formula for relative error is given by $\frac{\text{absolute error}}{\text{correct value}}$ or $\frac{\text{absolute error}}{\text{measured value}}$ (if the correct value is unknown). When relative error is expressed as a percent, it is called **percent error.**

Here are examples.

> If a protractor is used to measure the sum of the angles of a triangle yielding a measurement of 178.2°, what is the absolute error, relative error, and percent error of the measurement?

The absolute error is the difference between the correct value 180° and the measured value 178.2°. That is, the absolute error = 180° $-$ 178.2° = 1.8°. The relative error is $\frac{1.8°}{180°}$ = 0.01, and the percent error is 1%.

Find the percent error of the measurement 25 ft. $\pm$ 0.5 ft. Since the correct value is unknown, the absolute error is 0.5 ft, and the percent error is $\frac{0.5 \text{ ft}}{25 \text{ ft}}$ = 2%.

> **Tip:** Notice that the absolute error has the same units as the units of the measurement, while the relative error and percent error have no units.

Results of calculations with approximate measurements should not be reported with a degree of precision that would be misleading, that is, suggesting a degree of accuracy greater than the actual accuracy that could be obtained using the approximate measurements. Generally, such calculations should be rounded, *after* all calculations have been made, to have the same precision as the measurement with least precision in the calculation. *Caution:* Rounding before final calculations can compound error.

Dimensional Analysis

On the Praxis Middle School Mathematics test, you have to demonstrate your knowledge of measurement using the U.S. customary system and the metric system. See Appendix C, "Measurement Units and Conversions," for some common conversion facts you are expected to know.

You can convert from one measurement unit to another by using an appropriate "conversion fraction." You make conversion fractions by using a conversion fact, such as 1 gallon = 4 quarts. For each conversion fact, you can write *two* conversion fractions. For example, for the conversion fact given, you have $\dfrac{1 \text{ gal}}{4 \text{ qt}}$ and $\dfrac{4 \text{ qt}}{1 \text{ gal}}$ as your two conversion fractions.

Every conversion fraction is equivalent to the number 1 because the numerator and denominator are different names for measures of the same quantity. Therefore, if you multiply a quantity by a conversion fraction, you will not change the value of the quantity.

When you need to change one measurement unit to another unit, multiply by the conversion fraction whose *denominator is the same as the units of the quantity to be converted*. This strategy falls under **dimensional analysis** (or unit analysis), a powerful tool used by scientists (including mathematicians) and engineers to analyze units and to guide or check equations and calculations. When you do the multiplication, the units you started out with will "cancel" (divide) out, and you will be left with the desired new units. If this doesn't happen, then you used the wrong conversion fraction, so do it over again with the other conversion fraction.

Additionally, for some conversions you might need to make a "chain" of conversion fractions to obtain your desired units.

Here is an example.

> Convert 3 gallons to cups. The conversion tables in Appendix C do not have a fact that shows the equivalency between gallons and cups. You have 1 pint = 2 cups, 1 quart = 2 pints, and 1 gallon = 4 quarts. These facts yield 6 conversion fractions, respectively: $\dfrac{1 \text{ pt}}{2 \text{ c}}$ and $\dfrac{2 \text{ c}}{1 \text{ pt}}$, $\dfrac{1 \text{ qt}}{2 \text{ pt}}$ and $\dfrac{2 \text{ pt}}{1 \text{ qt}}$, $\dfrac{1 \text{ gal}}{4 \text{ qt}}$ and $\dfrac{4 \text{ qt}}{1 \text{ gal}}$. Start with your quantity to be converted and keep multiplying by conversion fractions until you obtain your desired units.

$$3 \text{ gal} \times \frac{4 \text{ qt}}{1 \text{ gal}} \times \frac{2 \text{ pt}}{1 \text{ qt}} \times \frac{2 \text{ c}}{1 \text{ pt}} = 48 \text{ c}$$

> **Tip:** It is a good idea to assess your final answer to see whether it makes sense. When you are converting from a larger unit to a smaller unit, you should expect that it will take more of the smaller units to equal the same amount. When you are converting from a smaller unit to a larger unit, you should expect that it will take less of the larger units to equal the same amount.

As seen in conversion of units, in calculations involving measured quantities that have units, the units are carried along as part of the completed defined measure and must undergo the same mathematical operations. You can add or subtract like units, but not unlike units. You can multiply or divide whether you have like or unlike units, provided the product or quotient has meaning.

Perimeter, Area, and Volume

For the Praxis Middle School Mathematics test, you are expected to know how to compute perimeter and area of triangles, quadrilaterals, circles, and regions that are combinations of these figures; to compute the surface area and volume of right prisms, cones, cylinders, spheres, and solids that are combinations of these figures. You will *not* be given a formula sheet with the test. According to the *Praxis Series Study Guide: Middle School Test,* a publication of the testing company, "infrequently used" applicable formulas are provided in particular test questions. Therefore, you can conclude that you need to commit to memory formulas that are commonly used. Here are the most important formulas for perimeter, area, surface area, and volume that you should know for the Praxis Middle School Mathematics test.

Triangle: height h, base b

area $= \dfrac{1}{2} bh$

Triangle: sides a, b, and c

perimeter $= a + b + c$

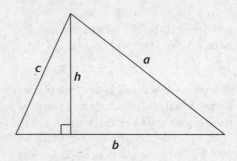

Square: side s

area $= s^2$

perimeter $= 4s$

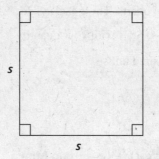

Rectangle: length l, width w

area $= lw$

perimeter $= 2l + 2w$

Parallelogram: height h, base b

area $= bh$

perimeter $= 2b + 2a$

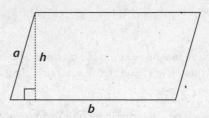

Circle: radius r, diameter d

area $= \pi r^2$

circumference $= 2\pi r = \pi d$

diameter $d = 2r$

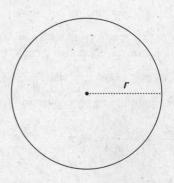

Trapezoid: height h, bases a, b

area $= \dfrac{1}{2} h(a + b)$

perimeter $= a + b + c + d$

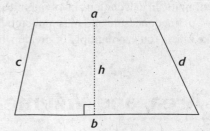

Sphere: radius r

volume $= \frac{4}{3}\pi r^3$

lateral surface area $= 4\pi r^2$

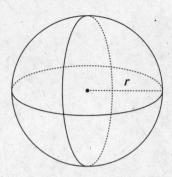

Right prism: height h, area of base B

volume $= Bh$

total surface area $= 2B +$ sum of areas of rectangular sides

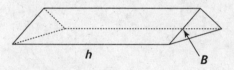

Rectangular prism: length l, width w, height h

volume $= lwh$

total surface area $= 2hl + 2hw + 2lw$

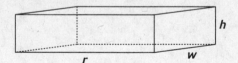

Cube: edge s

volume $= s^3$

total surface area $= 6s^2$

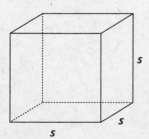

Right circular cylinder: height h, radius of base r

volume $= \pi r^2 h$

lateral surface area $= 2\pi rh$

total surface area $= 2\pi rh + 2\pi r^2$

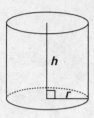

Pyramid: height h, area of base B

volume $= \frac{1}{3}Bh$

total surface area $= B +$ sum of areas of triangular sides

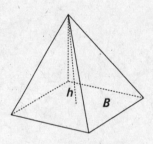

Right circular cone: height h, radius of base r

volume $= \frac{1}{3}\pi r^2 h$

lateral surface area $= \pi r\sqrt{r^2 + h^2} = \pi rs$, where s is the slant height $= \sqrt{r^2 + h^2}$

total surface area $= \pi r\sqrt{r^2 + h^2} + \pi r^2 = \pi rs + \pi r^2$

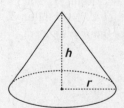

Here are additional formulas that you might need to know for the Praxis Middle School Mathematics test.

Triangle: sides *a*, *b*, and *c*

area = $\sqrt{s(s-a)(s-b)(s-c)}$

where $s = \dfrac{a+b+c}{2}$

perimeter = $a + b + c$

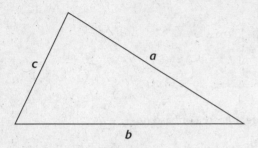

Isosceles triangle: sides *a*, *a*, and *b*

area = $\dfrac{1}{2}b\sqrt{a^2 - \dfrac{b^2}{4}}$

Perimeter = $2a + b$

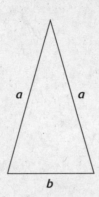

Equilateral triangle: side *s*

area = $\dfrac{\sqrt{3}}{4}s^2$

Perimeter = $3s$

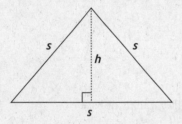

Sector of circle: radius *r*, θ measure of subtended central angle in radians

area = $\dfrac{\theta r^2}{2}$

arc length = $s = r\theta$

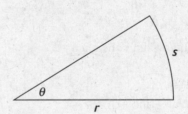

Perimeter and Circumference

The **perimeter** of a figure is the distance around it. You measure perimeter in units of length, such as inches, feet, yards, miles, kilometers, meters, centimeters, and millimeters. To find the perimeter of a closed figure that is made up of line segments, add up the lengths of the line segments.

Here is an example.

Find the perimeter of the figure shown.

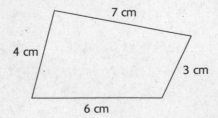

To find the perimeter, add the lengths of the four sides. Perimeter = 6 cm + 3 cm + 7 cm + 4 cm = 20 cm.

The perimeter of a circle is called its **circumference.** The formula for the circumference of a circle is $C = \pi d = 2\pi r$, where d and r are the diameter and radius of the circle, respectively.

Here is an example of finding the circumference of a circle.

Find the circumference of the circle in the diagram. Round your answer to the nearest inch.

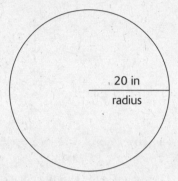

From the diagram, you can see that the radius of the circle is 20 in. Plug into the formula: $C = 2\pi r = 2\pi(20 \text{ in}) = 126$ in (to nearest inch).

Tip: Use the π key when doing calculations involving π.

Here is an example of finding the perimeter of a figure that is a combination of figures.

The figure shown consists of a semicircle of radius r and a rectangle whose longer side is $2r$ and whose shorter side is r. What is the perimeter of the figure in terms of r?

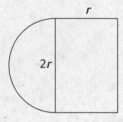

The perimeter = circumference of the semicircle + 2 times shorter side and 1 times the longer side of the rectangle =
$\frac{1}{2}(2\pi r) + 2 \cdot r + 2r = \pi r + 4r.$

Area

The **area** of a plane figure is the amount of surface enclosed by the boundary of the figure. You measure area in square units, such as square inches (in^2), square feet (ft^2), square miles (mi^2), square meters (m^2), square kilometers (km^2), square centimeters (cm^2), and square millimeters (mm^2). The area is always described in terms of square units, regardless of the shape of the figure.

The boundary measurements of a figure are measured in two dimensions (for example, length and width, base and height). The units for the boundary measurements are linear units (for example, inches, feet, miles, meters, and so on). You obtain the square units needed to describe area when you multiply the unit by itself. For example, 1 in × 1 in = $1 \text{ in}^2 = 1$ square inch.

Here is an example of finding the area of a rectangle.

What is the area of a rectangle that is 4 cm by 3 cm?

Sketch a diagram and label it.

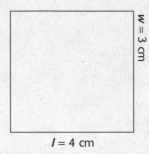

The formula for the area of a rectangle is $A = lw$, where l is the **length** and w is the **width.** Plug into the formula: $A = lw =$ (4 cm)(3 cm) $= 12$ cm^2. The rectangle has an area of 12 cm^2.

To find the area of a triangle, you must know the measure of the triangle's **base** and **height.** The base can be any of the three sides of the triangle. The height for the base is a line drawn from the opposite vertex that meets the base at a right angle. A **vertex** of a triangle is the point where two sides meet. The formula for the area of a triangle is $A = \frac{1}{2}bh$, where b is the length of a base of the triangle, and h is the height for that base. When you are finding the area of a triangle, you can pick any convenient side of the triangle to serve as the base in the formula.

Here is an example of finding the area of a triangle.

Find the area of the triangle in the diagram.

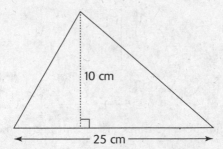

From the diagram, you can see that $b = 25$ cm and $h = 10$ cm. Plug into the formula: $A = \frac{1}{2}bh = A = \frac{1}{2}(25 \text{ cm})(10 \text{ cm}) = \frac{(25 \text{ cm})(10 \text{ cm})}{2} = 125$ cm^2.

The formula for the area of a circle is $A = \pi r^2$, where r is the radius of the circle.

Here is an example of finding the area of a circle.

Find the area of the circle in the diagram. Round your answer to the nearest in^2.

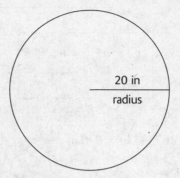

From the diagram, you can see that the radius is 20 in. Plug into the formula: $A = \pi r^2 = \pi(20\text{in})^2 = \pi(400 \text{ in}^2) = 1257 \text{ in}^2$.

Surface Area

When you have a solid figure such as a rectangular prism (a box), a cylinder, or a pyramid, you can find the area of every face (surface) and add the areas together. The sum is called the **surface area** of the solid figure.

Here is an example of finding the surface area of a rectangular box.

What is the surface area of the box shown?

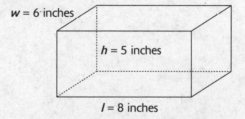

The box is composed of six **faces,** all of which are rectangles. Use the length and height to find the areas of the front and back faces. Use the length and width to find the areas of the top and bottom faces. Use the width and height to find the areas of the two side faces.

Surface Area = 2(8 in)(5 in) + 2(8 in)(6 in) + 2(6 in)(5 in) = 80 in^2 + 96 in^2 + 60 in^2 = 236 in^2

Volume

The **volume** of a solid figure is the amount of space inside the solid. Solid figures have three dimensions (for example, length, width, and height of a box). When you use the dimensions of a solid to find its volume, the units for the volume are cubic units, such as cubic inches (in^3), cubic feet (ft^3), cubic miles (mi^3), cubic meters (m^3), cubic kilometers (km^3), cubic centimeters (cm^3), and cubic millimeters (mm^3).

Here is an example of finding the volume of a right prism.

A **right prism** is a prism whose bases are perpendicular to its sides. The formula for the volume of a right prism is $V = Bh$, where B = the area of the **Base** of the prism. For a rectangular prism, $B = lw$. Thus, the formula for the volume of a rectangular prism is $V = lwh$, where l is the **length,** w is the **width,** and h is the **height.**

Here is an example of finding the volume of a rectangular prism.

What is the volume of the box shown?

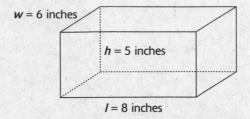

$w = 6$ inches

$h = 5$ inches

$l = 8$ inches

Plug into the formula: $V = Bh = lwh = (8 \text{ in})(6 \text{ in})(5 \text{ in}) = 240 \text{ in}^3$.

Tip: Notice that the units for the volume of the box are in^3 = cubic inches. Cubic units are obtained when a unit is used as a factor in a product three times as in the following: $(\text{in})(\text{in})(\text{in}) = \text{in}^3$.

Sample Exercises

1. A pharmacist measures the mass of a medical substance and uses the appropriate number of significant figures to record the mass as 7 grams, to the nearest gram. Which of the following ways most accurately expresses the range of possible values of the mass of the substance?

   A. 7 grams ± 1.0 grams
   B. 7 grams ± 0.5 grams
   C. 7 grams ± 0.1 grams
   D. 7 grams

2. Using a protractor, a student measures the sum of the interior angles in a triangle and obtains 174.6°. To the nearest tenth of a percent, what is the percent error of this measurement?

   A. 0.03%
   B. 3%
   C. 3.1%
   D. 5.4%

3. For disaster relief in a hurricane-damaged area, \$2.5 billion is needed. This amount of money is approximately equivalent to spending one dollar per second for

   A. 10 years
   B. 40 years
   C. 80 years
   D. 1000 years

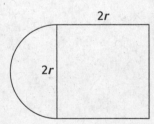

4. The figure shown consists of a semicircle of radius r and a square whose side is $2r$. What is the perimeter of the figure in terms of r?

   A. $\pi r + 4r$
   B. $\pi r + 8r$
   C. $2\pi r + 6r$
   D. $\pi r + 6r$

5. The exterior of a spherical tank with radius 12 feet is to be painted with one coat of paint. The paint sells for \$22.40 per gallon and can be purchased in one-gallon cans only. If a can of paint will cover approximately 400 square feet, what is the cost of the paint needed to paint the exterior of the tank?

   A. \$22.40
   B. \$44.80
   C. \$101.36
   D. \$112.00

Answer Explanations for Sample Exercises

1. **B.** The maximum possible error of a measurement is half the magnitude of the smallest measurement unit used to obtain the measurement. The most accurate way of expressing the measurement is as a tolerance interval. Thus, a measurement of 7 grams, to the nearest gram, should be reported as 7 grams ± 0.5 grams, Choice B.

2. **B.** The absolute error is $180° - 174.6° = 5.4°$. The percent error $= \dfrac{5.4°}{180°} = 0.03 = 3\%$, Choice B.

3. **C.** Analyze the problem. You need to determine how many years it would take to spend $2.5 billion per second. Devise a plan. The best way to determine the answer is to convert $2.5 billion into seconds and then convert the results into years. Write $2.5 billion as a fraction with denominator 1 and let dimensional analysis tell you which conversion fractions to multiply by, keeping in mind that you want

   years as your final answer. $\dfrac{\$2,500,000,000}{1} \cdot \dfrac{1\ \$}{\$1} \cdot \dfrac{1\ \text{min}}{60\ \$} \cdot \dfrac{1\ h}{60\ \text{min}} \cdot \dfrac{1\ d}{24\ h} \cdot \dfrac{1\ \text{yr}}{365\ d} = 79.2744$ or approximately 80 years, Choice C.

4. **D.** Analyze the problem. The perimeter = circumference of the semicircle + 3 times the length of the side of the square $= \dfrac{1}{2}(2\pi r) + 3 \cdot 2r = \pi r + 6r$, Choice D.

5. **D.** Analyze the problem. You want to find the cost of the paint needed to cover the surface area of the sphere. Devise a plan. To determine the cost of the paint will take three steps. First, find the surface area of the sphere; next, find the number of gallons of paint needed; and then find the cost of the paint.

   Step 1. Find the surface area (*SA*) of the sphere with $r = 12$ ft.

   $SA = 4\pi r^2 = 4\pi(12\ \text{ft})^2 = 1809.5575 \ldots \text{ft}^2$ (*Tip:* Don't round this answer.)

   Step 2. Find the number of gallons needed.

   $1809.5575 \ldots \text{ft}^2 \div \dfrac{400\ \text{ft}^2}{1\ \text{gal}} = 4.5238 \ldots$ gallons, so 5 gallons will need to be purchased (since the paint is sold in gallon containers only).

   Step 3. Find the cost of 5 gallons of paint.

   $5\ \text{gallons} \times \dfrac{\$22.40}{1\ \text{gal}} = \$112.00$, Choice D.

Functions, Relations, and Their Graphs

This chapter provides a review of the key ideas and definitions for functions, relations, and their graphs that are most important for you to know for the Praxis Middle School Mathematics test. Multiple-choice sample exercises, comparable to what might be presented on the Praxis Middle School Mathematics test, are given at the end of the chapter. The answer explanations for the sample exercises are provided immediately following.

Relations and the Cartesian Coordinate Plane

An **ordered pair** of numbers, denoted (x, y), is a pair of numbers expressed in a specific order so that one number is written first in the ordered pair, and the other number is written second. In the ordered pair (x, y), x is the **first component,** and y is the **second component.** Two ordered pairs are equal if and only if they have *exactly* the same coordinates; that is, $(x_1, y_1) = (x_2, y_2)$ if and only if $x_1 = x_2$, and $y_1 = y_2$. The set consisting of all possible ordered pairs of real numbers is denoted $R \times R$, or simply R^2. A **relation** $\Re$ in R^2 is any subset of R^2. The set consisting of all the first components in the ordered pairs contained in $\Re$ is the domain of $\Re$, and the set of all second components is the range of R.

Graphically, R^2 is represented by the **Cartesian coordinate plane.** Here is an illustration.

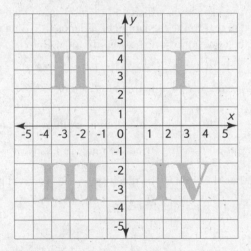

Two intersecting real number lines form the **axes** of the Cartesian coordinate plane. The **horizontal axis** with positive direction to the right is commonly designated the **x–axis,** and the **vertical axis** with positive direction upward is commonly designated the **y–axis.** Their point of intersection is the **origin.** The axes divide the coordinate plane into four **quadrants.** The Roman numerals **I, II, III,** and **IV** name the quadrants. The numbering process starts in the upper right quadrant and proceeds counterclockwise. The location of every point in the coordinate plane is given by an **ordered pair,** (x, y), of real numbers. The numbers x and y are the **coordinates** of the point.

Properties of Functions

A **function** is a set of ordered pairs for which each first component is paired with *one and only one* second component. In other words, a function is a relation in which no two ordered pairs have the same first component but different second components, that is, if (x, y_1) and (x, y_2) are ordered pairs in the function, then $y_1 = y_2$. Thus, the sets of ordered pairs $\{(1, 2), (2, 3)\}$ is a function; but the set of ordered pairs $\{(1, 2), (1, 3)\}$ is *not* a function.

Single letters, such as f and g, are commonly used as names for functions. For the function f, the ordered pairs are written $(x, f(x))$ or (x, y), where $y = f(x)$. You read the function notation $f(x)$ as "f of x." In the function defined by $y = f(x)$, x is the **independent variable,** and y is the **dependent variable.** The variable y is "dependent" on x in the sense that you substitute a value of x, called an **argument** of f, into $y = f(x)$ to find y, the **value** of f at x (also called the **image** of x under f). On the Praxis Middle School Mathematics test, unless a problem clearly indicates otherwise, the functions on the test are real-valued functions. This means that both the domain and range of the functions consist of real numbers. Two functions f and g are **equal**, written $f = g$, if and only if their domains are equal and $f(x) = g(x)$ for all x in their common domain.

Various ways are used to define functions. If a function consists of a *finite* number of ordered pairs, you can define the function by listing or showing its ordered pairs in a **set**, in a **table**, as an **arrow diagram**, or as a **graph** in a coordinate plane. You also might define the function by giving a **rule** or an **equation**. When the number of ordered pairs is *infinite*, more often than not the function is defined by either an **equation** or a **graph**. *Note*: In this book equations that define functions will use only real numbers as coefficients or constants.

When a function f is defined by an equation $y = f(x)$ and no domain is specified, the **domain of f**, denoted D_f, is the largest possible subset of the real numbers for which each x value gives a corresponding y value that is a *real* number. To determine the domain, start with the set of real numbers and exclude all values for x, if any, that would make the equation undefined over the real numbers. If $y = f(x)$ contains a rational expression, to avoid division by zero, exclude values for x, if any, which would make a denominator zero. If $y = f(x)$ contains a radical with an *even* index, to avoid even roots of negative numbers exclude all values for x, if any, that would cause the expression under the radical to be negative.

Division by zero and even roots of negative numbers are the two types of domain problems that you are most likely to encounter on the Praxis Middle School Mathematics test; however, you should be aware that other problems can arise. For instance, the domain for the logarithm function, which will be discussed in a later section in this chapter, cannot include 0 or negative values for x. You can determine the **range of f**, denoted R_f, in a manner similar to that used to find the domain of f if you can first solve the equation $y = f(x)$ explicitly for x. Here is an example of finding D_f and R_f for a function f.

Find the domain, D_f, and the range, R_f, for the function f defined by $y = \dfrac{1}{x-3}$.

For every real number x, except 3, the quantity $\dfrac{1}{x-3}$ is a real number; thus, the domain of f consists of all real numbers except 3, written $D_f = \{x \mid x \text{ is a real number, } x \neq 3\}$. To find the range of f, solve $y = \dfrac{1}{x-3}$ explicitly for x to obtain $x = \dfrac{1+3y}{y}$. Since for every real number y, except 0, the quantity $\dfrac{1+3y}{y}$ is a real number, the range of f consists of all real numbers except 0, written $R_f = \{y \mid y \text{ is a real number, } y \neq 0\}$.

Tip: You might want to determine the domain and range of f by using your graphing calculator to look at its graph. When using your graphing calculator to explore a function, use trial and error and the ZOOM feature to find a good viewing window; otherwise, you might be misled by the graph displayed.

The **graph** of a function f is the set of all ordered pairs (x, y) for which x is in the domain of f and $y = f(x)$; in other words, the graph of a function is a visual representation of its solutions, the set of ordered pairs that make the statement $y = f(x)$ true. The points (or point), if any, at which the graph of f intersects the x-axis are the **x-intercepts** of the graph. A graph can have many x-intercepts, or it might not have any. The x-intercepts, if any, are the real **zeros** of f. The zeros are determined by finding all points x, if any, for which $f(x) = 0$. You can describe a real **zero** of a function f as one of the following: an **x-intercept** for the graph of $y = f(x)$, an **x-value** for which $f(x) = 0$, or a real **root** of the equation $f(x) = 0$. See the section "Polynomial Functions" in this chapter for an illustration of the zeros of a function.

If zero is in the domain of f, then $f(0)$ is the **y-intercept** of the graph of f. A function f cannot have more than one y-intercept because, by definition, each x value in the domain of f is paired with *exactly one* y value in the range.

Moreover, if any vertical line can be drawn so that it cuts the graph of a relation in more than one point, the relation is *not* a function. Therefore, you have the **vertical line test:** Any vertical line in the plane will intersect the graph of a function *f* in no more than one point. Here is an example of a relation that does *not* pass the vertical line test, so it is *not* a function. There are two points on the graph that correspond to *x* = 2, namely (2, 2,) and (2, –2).

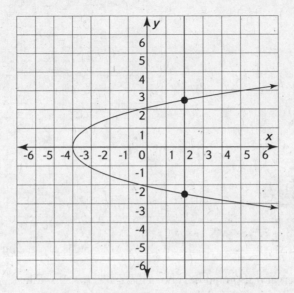

A function *f* is **one-to-one** if and only if $f(a) = f(b)$ implies that $a = b$; that is, if (a, c) and (b, c) are elements of *f*, then $a = b$. In a one-to-one function each first component is paired with *exactly one* second component *and* each second component is paired with *exactly one* first component. Therefore, you have the **horizontal line test:** A function is one-to-one if any horizontal line in the plane intersects the graph of the function in no more than one point. Here is an example of a function that does *not* pass the horizontal line test, so it is *not* a one-to-one function.

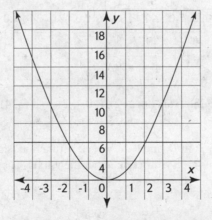

A function *f* is **increasing** on an interval if it moves upward, from left to right, as *x* assumes values from left to right in the interval; that is, whenever $x_1 < x_2, f(x_1) < f(x_2)$. A function is **decreasing** on an interval if it moves downward, from left to right, as *x* assumes values from left to right in the interval; that is, whenever $x_1 < x_2, f(x_1) > f(x_2)$. A function is **constant** in an interval if $f(x_1) = f(x_2)$ for every value of *x* in the interval. A function is **monotonic** if, on its entire domain, the function is either only increasing or only decreasing. A monotonic increasing or decreasing function is one-to-one. Here are examples.

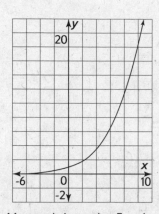

Monotonic Increasing Function

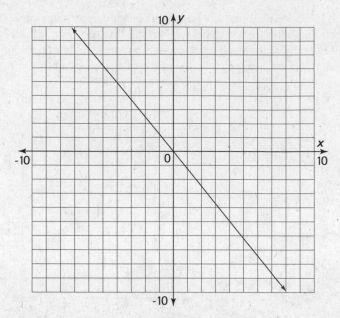

Monotonic Decreasing Function

A function f is **positive** on an interval if its graph lies above the x-axis for all x-values in the interval; similarly, a function f is **negative** on an interval if its graph lies below the x-axis for all x-values in the interval. Here is an example.

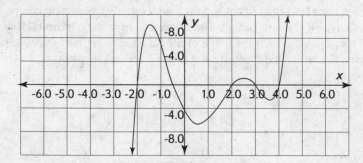

For the function P shown, $P(x) < 0$ in the intervals $(-\infty, -2)$, $(-0.4, 2)$, and $(3, 4)$; and $P(x) > 0$ in the intervals $(-2, -0.4)$, $(2, 3)$, and $(4, \infty)$.

A function is **even** if for every x in D_f, $-x$ is in D_f and $f(-x) = f(x)$. A function is **odd**, if for every x in D_f, $-x$ is in D_f and $f(-x) = -f(x)$. The graphs of even functions are **symmetric** about the **y-axis.** The graphs of odd functions are **symmetric** about the **origin.** Here are examples.

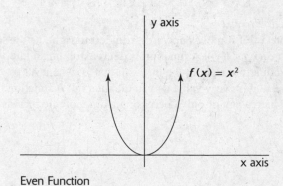

Even Function

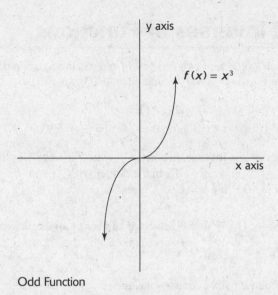

Odd Function

A line $x = k$ is a **vertical asymptote** if as x draws close to k from the left or right, the graph goes toward $-\infty$ or ∞. A line $y = h$ is a **horizontal asymptote** if the function draws close to h as x gets infinitely large or small. A function $y = g(x)$ is an **oblique asymptote** (or **slant asymptote**) if the graph of the function approaches $y = g(x)$ as x gets infinitely large or small. Here are examples.

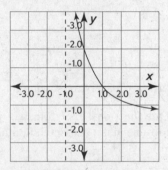

Vertical Asymptote $x = -1$;

Horizontal Asymptote $y = -2$

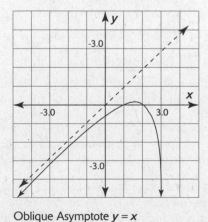

Oblique Asymptote $y = x$

Tip: The graph of a function can *never* intersect a vertical asymptote of the function. However, the graph of a function may cross a line that is a horizontal or oblique asymptote as long as the graph eventually draws asymptotically close to the line.

Composition and Inverses of Functions

The **composition,** denoted $f \circ g$ (read "f of g"), of two functions f and g is the function defined by $(f \circ g)(x) = f(g(x))$ where $Rg \subseteq Df$. In general, composition of functions is *not* commutative; that is, $(f \circ g)(x) \neq (g \circ f)(x)$. Here is an example.

> Given $f(x) = 3x$ and $g(x) = x^2$, find, $(f \circ g)(x)$ and $(g \circ f)(x)$.
> $(f \circ g)(x) = f(g(x)) = 3(g(x)) = 3x^2$; $(g \circ f)(x) = g(f(x)) = (f(x))^2 = (3x)^2 = 9x^2$.

If the function f is a one-to-one function, its **inverse,** denoted f^{-1} (read "f inverse"), is the function such that $(f^{-1} \circ f)(x) = x$ for all x in the domain of f and $(f \circ f^{-1})(x) = x$ for all x in the domain of f^{-1}, and $R_{f^{-1}} = D_f$ and $R_f = D_{f^{-1}}$. Graphically, f^{-1} is a reflection of f over the line $y = x$.

> **Tip:** Do not interpret f^{-1} to mean $\dfrac{1}{f}$. The $^{-1}$ that is attached to f is *not* an exponent; it is a notation that is used to denote the inverse of a function.

If a function f defined by a set of ordered pairs is one-to-one, then f^{-1} may be found by interchanging x and y in each of the ordered pairs of f. For instance, if $f = \{(-1, 2), (3, 5), (6, -1)\}$, then $f^{-1} = \{(2, -1), (5, 3), (-1, 6)\}$. When a one-to-one function f is defined by an equation, two ways you can find the equation of f^{-1} are the following:

> Method 1. Solve $(f \circ f^{-1})(x) = x$ for $f^{-1}(x)$.
>
> Method 2. First, in $y = f(x)$ replace x with y and y with x, and then solve $x = f(y)$, for y.

Here is an example.

> Given $y = f(x) = 3x$, find $f^{-1}(x)$.
>
> Method 1. $(f \circ f^{-1})(x) = x \rightarrow f(f^{-1}(x)) = x \rightarrow 3f^{-1}(x) = x \rightarrow f^{-1}(x) = \dfrac{x}{3}$.
>
> Method 2. First, interchanging x and y gives $x = 3y$. Next, solving for y gives $\dfrac{x}{3} = y$ or $y = \dfrac{x}{3}$.

Only one-to-one functions have inverses that are functions. Therefore, when a function f is not one-to-one, it might be possible to restrict its domain so that f is one-to-one in the **restricted domain.** Then, f will have an inverse function in the restricted domain.

Linear Functions

Linear functions are defined by equations that can be written in the form $y = f(x) = mx + b$. The domain and range are both R, the set of real numbers. The zeros are the roots of the equation $mx + b = 0$. Thus, $x = \dfrac{-b}{m}$ is the only zero.

The graph crosses the x-axis at the point $(\dfrac{-b}{m}, 0)$. The graph is a straight line with slope m and y-intercept b. This is the slope-intercept form of a line. Every linear equation $Ax + By = C$ $(B \neq 0)$ determines a linear function. (See the section "Equations for Lines" in this chapter for an additional discussion of linear equations.)

The **identity function** is the linear function defined by equations that can written as $y = x$ $(m = 1, b = 0)$. It is called the identity function because it matches each x–value with an identical y-value. The domain and range are both R, the set of real numbers. The graph passes through the origin, so the x- and y–intercepts are both zero. The only zero is $x = 0$.

Constant functions are linear functions defined by equations that can be written in the form $y = f(x) = b$ $(m = 0)$. The domain is the set R of real numbers, and the range is the set $\{b\}$ containing the single element b. Constant functions either have no zeros or infinitely many zeros according to the following guideline: If $b \neq 0$, it has no zeros; if $b = 0$, every real number x is a zero. The graph is a horizontal line that is $|b|$ units above or below the x-axis when $b \neq 0$ and coincident with the real axis when $b = 0$.

Proportional functions are linear functions defined by equations that can written as $y = kx$ $(m = k \neq 0, b = 0)$, where k is the **constant of proportionality.** The domain and range are both R, the set of real numbers. The graph passes through the origin, so the x- and y–intercepts are both zero. The only zero is $x = 0$.

Here are examples of linear functions.

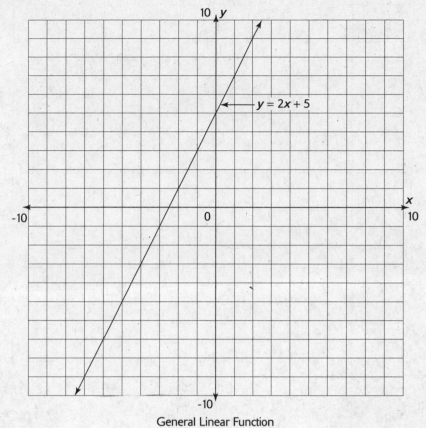

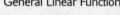

General Linear Function

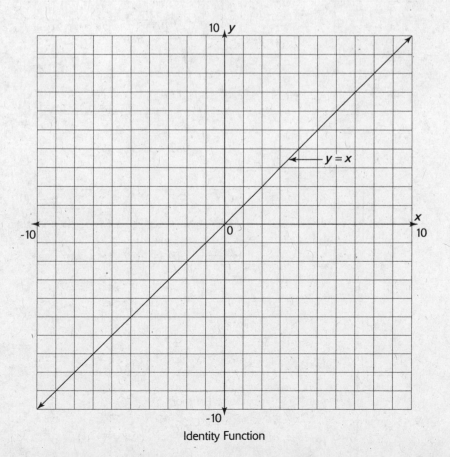

Identity Function

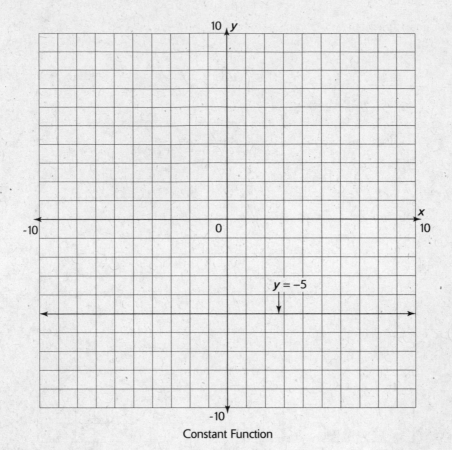

$y = -5$

Constant Function

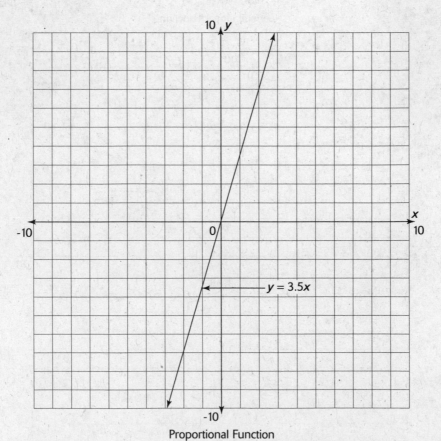

$y = 3.5x$

Proportional Function

Quadratic Functions

Quadratic functions are defined by equations of the form $y = f(x) = ax^2 + bx + c$, $(a \neq 0)$. The domain is the set R of real numbers, and the range is a subset of R. The zeros are the roots of the quadratic equation $ax^2 + bx + c = 0$. The quantity $b^2 - 4ac$, called the **discriminant** of the quadratic equation, determines three cases for the roots of the quadratic function: If $b^2 - 4ac > 0$, the quadratic function has two real *unequal* zeros; if $b^2 - 4ac = 0$, the quadratic function has one real zero (double root); and if $b^2 - 4ac < 0$, the quadratic function has no real zeros.

The graphs of quadratic functions defined by equations of the form $f(x) = ax^2 + bx + c$ are **parabolas.** If $a > 0$, the parabola opens **upward** and has a **minimum value** at its vertex. If $a < 0,$ the parabola opens **downward** and has a **maximum value** at its vertex. The parabola is **symmetric** about its **axis of symmetry,** a vertical line through its vertex that is parallel to the y-axis. Depending on the solution set of $ax^2 + bx + c = 0$, the graph of a quadratic function might or might not intersect the x-axis. Three cases occur: If there are *two* real *unequal* roots, the parabola will intersect the x-axis at those *two* points; if there is exactly *one* real root, the parabola will intersect the x-axis at only that *one* point; and if there are no real roots, the parabola will *not* intersect the x-axis. Here are examples of quadratic functions when $a > 0$ in the equation $f(x) = ax^2 + bx + c$ that defines the quadratic function.

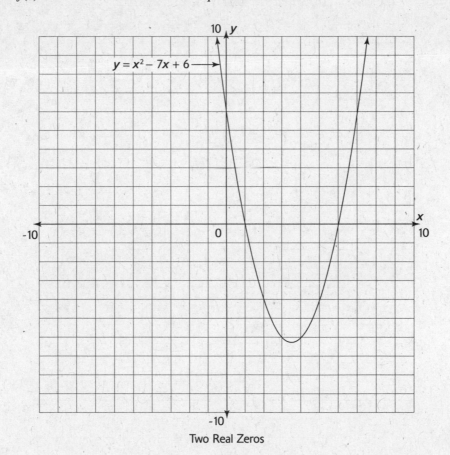

Two Real Zeros

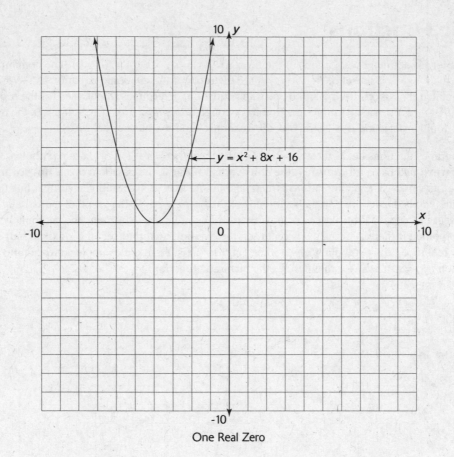

$y = x^2 + 8x + 16$

One Real Zero

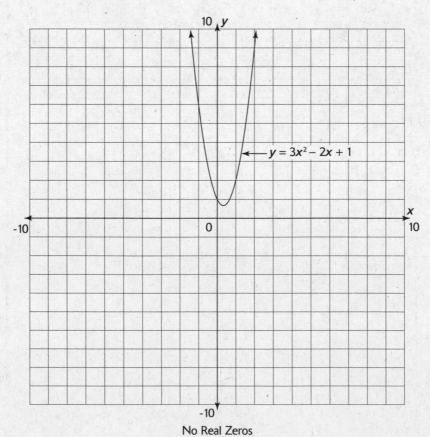

$y = 3x^2 - 2x + 1$

No Real Zeros

The **standard form** for the equation of a parabola that opens upward or downward is $y = a(x - h)^2 + k$ $(a \neq 0)$ with vertex (h, k). Any quadratic function can be put in standard form by using the process of **completing the square**. (See the section "Solving Quadratic Equations" in the chapter "Basic Algebra" for a discussion on completing the square. See the section "Graphs of Conic Relations" in this chapter for a discussion of parabolas that are relations, but not functions.)

Polynomial Functions

Polynomial functions are defined by equations of the form $y = P(x) = a_n x^n + a_{n-1} x^{n-1} + a_{n-2} x^{n-2} + \ldots + a_1 x^1 + a_0$, where $a_n \neq 0$ and the degree of the polynomial is n, a nonnegative integer. The domain for a polynomial function is the set R of real numbers. If n is odd, the polynomial function has range R. If n is even, the range is a subset of R. Linear and quadratic functions are particular types of polynomial functions. The zeros, if any, of a polynomial function are the solutions of the equation $P(x) = 0$. A number r is a zero of a polynomial function P defined by $y = P(x)$ if it is a root of the equation $P(r) = 0$. If r is a real number, the graph of P intersects the x-axis at r. The graph has y-intercept $P(0)$. Here is a graph of the polynomial function defined by $y = P(x) = 0.2(x + 2)(x + 0.4)(x - 2)$ $(x - 3)(x - 4)$, which has five real zeros.

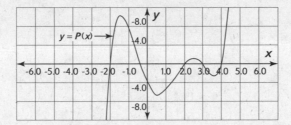

The zeros are $x = -2, -0.4, 2, 3$, and 4. These values also are the five roots of the polynomial equation $P(x) = 0$. The graph for P has y-intercept $= -3.84$ because it crosses the y-axis at $P(0) = 0.2(0 + 2)(0 + 0.4)(0 - 2)$ $(0 - 3)(0 - 4) = 0.2(2)(0.4)(-2)$ $(-3)(-4) = -3.84$.

A useful theorem to know is that if a and b are real numbers such that $P(a)$ and $P(b)$ have opposite signs, then P has at least one zero between a and b. Additional theorems that are helpful to know are the following:

The **Fundamental Theorem of Algebra** states that, over the complex numbers, every polynomial of degree $n \geq 1$ has at least one root. Using this theorem, you can show that, if you allow complex roots and count a root again each time it occurs more than once, every polynomial of degree n has exactly n roots. Thus, every linear function (except for constant functions) has exactly one root, every quadratic function has exactly two roots, and so on.

The **Factor Theorem** states that $P(r) = 0$ if and only if $x - r$ is a factor of the polynomial $P(x)$. For instance, for the cubic equation $P(x) = x^3 - 2x^2 - x + 2$, you have $P(-1) = (-1)^3 - 2(-1)^2 - (-1) + 2 = -1 - 2 + 1 + 2 = 0$, $P(1) = (1)^3 - 2(1)^2 - (1) + 2 = 1 - 2 - 1 + 2 = 0$, and $P(2) = (2)^3 - 2(2)^2 - (2) + 2 = 8 - 8 - 2 + 2 = 0$; Thus, by the Factor Theorem, you know that $x - (-1) = x + 1$, $x - 1$, and $x - 2$ are factors of $P(x) = x^3 - 2x^2 - x + 2$.

The **Remainder Theorem** states that if a polynomial $P(x)$ is divided by $x - a$, the remainder is $P(a)$. For example, you can use synthetic division to show that when $5x^3 - 2x + 3$ is divided by $x - 2$, the remainder is 39 (see Appendix B for an explanation of synthetic division); thus, by the Remainder Theorem, you know that $P(2) = 39$.

Rational Functions

Rational functions are defined by equations of the form $y = f(x) = \dfrac{P(x)}{Q(x)}$, where $P(x)$ and $Q(x)$ are polynomials in x and $Q(x) \neq 0$. The domain is the set $\{x \mid x$ is a real number for which $Q(x) \neq 0\}$. The range is a subset of R. The zeros, if any, occur at x values for which $f(x) = 0$. Graphing rational functions normally proceeds by determining asymptotes of the function. The vertical asymptotes, if any, will be the values for x (if any) for which $Q(x)$ equals zero. The following guidelines will help you identify any horizontal asymptotes: If the degree of $P(x)$ is less than the degree of $Q(x)$, then the x-axis is a horizontal asymptote of $y = \dfrac{P(x)}{Q(x)}$; if the degree of $P(x)$ equals the degree of $Q(x)$, then $y = \dfrac{P(x)}{Q(x)}$, will have a horizontal asymptote at $y = \dfrac{a_n}{b_n}$, where a_n is the leading coefficient of $P(x)$ and b_n is the leading coefficient of $Q(x)$; and if the degree of $P(x)$ exceed the degree of $Q(x)$, $y = \dfrac{P(x)}{Q(x)}$, will *not* have a horizontal asymptote.

Finally, if the degree of $P(x)$ exceed the degree of $Q(x)$ by exactly 1, then $y = \dfrac{P(x)}{Q(x)}$, will have an oblique asymptote. Here are examples of rational functions.

$$y = \frac{x^2 + 3x + 2}{x^2 - 16}$$

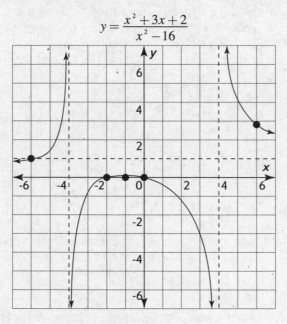

Zeros: -2, -1; Vertical Asymptotes: $x = 4$, -4; Horizontal Asymptote: $y = 1$

$$y = \frac{x^2 - 4}{x - 1}$$

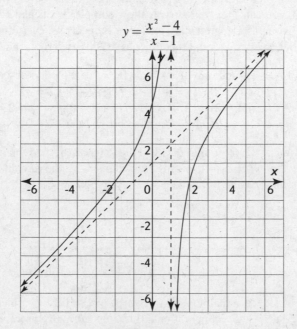

Zeros: 2, -2; Vertical Asymptote: $x = 1$; Oblique Asymptote: $y = x + 1$

Tip: You might want to use your graphing calculator to determine asymptotes of a rational function. When using your graphing calculator to determine asymptotes, enter the function using parentheses around both the numerator and denominator polynomials. Be sure to use trial and error and the ZOOM feature to find a good viewing window; otherwise, you might be misled by the graph displayed.

Square Root Functions

Square root functions are defined by equations of the form $y = f(x) = \sqrt{ax + b}$. The domain is the set $\{x \mid x$ is a real number for which $ax + b \geq 0\}$. The range is the set $\{y \mid y$ is a real number, $y \geq 0\}$. There is one zero at $x = -\dfrac{b}{a}$. The graph is nonnegative. Here is an example of a square root function.

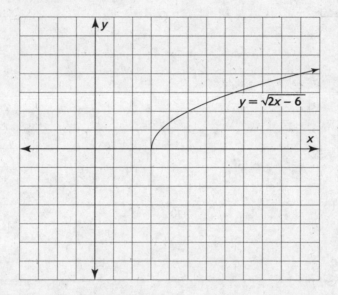

$$y = \sqrt{2x - 6}$$

Absolute Value Functions

Absolute value functions are defined by equations of the form $y = f(x) = |ax + b|$. The domain is the set R of real numbers, and the range is the set $\{y \mid y$ is a real number, $y \geq 0\}$. There is one zero at $x = -\dfrac{b}{a}$, and the y-intercept is at $|b|$. Technically, the absolute value function is a **piecewise function** because you can write it as

$$f(x) = \begin{cases} ax + b \text{ if } x \geq -\dfrac{b}{a} \\ -(ax + b) \text{ if } x < -\dfrac{b}{a} \end{cases}.$$

Here is an example of an absolute value function.

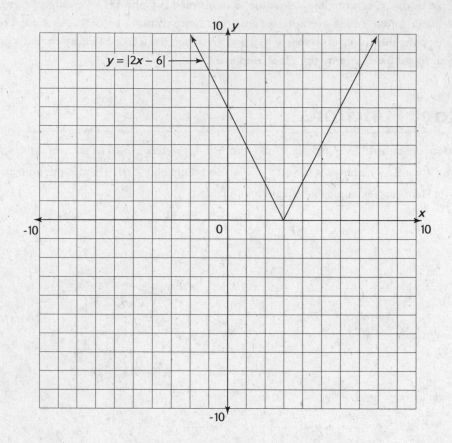

$y = |2x - 6|$

Step Functions

Two examples of step functions are the greatest integer function and the ceiling function.

The **greatest integer function** (or **floor function**) is defined by $y = f(x) = [x]$, where the brackets denote to find the greatest integer less than or equal to x. The domain is the set R of real numbers, and the range is the set of integers. The zeros lie in the interval $[0, 1)$.

The **ceiling function** is defined by $y = f(x) =$ the least integer greater than or equal to x. The domain is the set R of real numbers, and the range is the set of integers. The zeros lie in the interval $(-1, 0]$.

Here are examples of step functions.

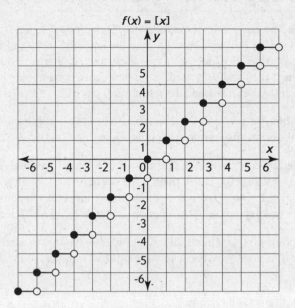

Greatest Integer Function

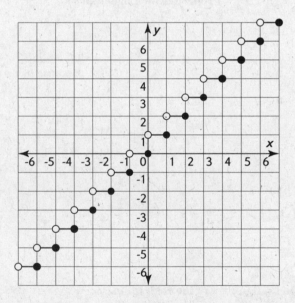

Ceiling Function

Exponential and Logarithm Functions

Exponential functions are defined by equations of the form $y = f(x) = b^x$ $(b \neq 1, b > 0)$, where b is the **base** of the exponential function. The domain is the set R of real numbers, and the range is the set $\{y \mid y > 0\}$, which is to say: $b^x > 0$ for every real number x. The graph of the function does not cross the x-axis, so there are no zeros. The graph of $y = f(x) = b^x$ passes through the points $(0, 1)$ and $(1, b)$ and is located in the first and second quadrants only. The x-axis is a horizontal asymptote. The function is increasing if $b > 1$ and decreasing if $0 < b < 1$.

Two important exponential functions are $y = f(x) = 10^x$, with base 10; and $y = f(x) = e^x$, the **natural exponential function,** with base e, the irrational number whose rational decimal approximation is 2.718281828 (to nine digits).

Logarithmic functions are defined by equations of the form $y = f(x) = \log_b x$ if and only if $b^y = x$ $(x > 0)$, where b is the base of the logarithmic function, $(b \neq 1, b > 0)$. The domain is the set $\{x \mid x > 0\}$, and the range is R, the set of real numbers. The function has one zero at $x = 1$. The graph passes through $(1, 0)$ and $(b, 1)$ and is located in the first and fourth quadrants only. The y-axis is a vertical asymptote. The function is increasing if $b > 1$ and is decreasing if $0 < b < 1$.

Logarithms are ways to write exponents. If $y = \log_b x$, then y is the *exponent* that is used on b to get x; that is, $b^y = x$. Notice that the restriction that $x > 0$ is necessary because b is a positive number, so there is no exponent y for which b^y is not positive.

The following properties for logarithms hold:

Properties for Logarithms

For real numbers b $(b \neq 1, b > 0)$, u, v, w, and p:

$\log_b b^x = x$	$b^{\log_b x} = x$	$\log_b b = 1$ (because $b^1 = b$)	$\log_b 1 = 0$ (because $b^0 = 1$)
If $\log_b u = \log_b v$, then $u = v$	$\log_b \dfrac{1}{u} = -\log_b u$	$\log_b uv = \log_b u + \log_b v$	$\log_b \dfrac{u}{v} = \log_b u - \log_b v$	$\log_b u^p = p\log_b u$

Here are examples using base 2.

$$\log_2(8(4) = \log_2 8 + \log_2 4 = \log_2 2^3 + \log_2 2^2 = 3 + 2 = 5$$

$$\log_2\left(\frac{32}{8}\right) = \log_2 32 - \log_2 8 = \log_2 2^5 - \log_2 2^3 = 5 - 3 = 2$$

$$\log_2(8^4) = 4\log_2 8 = 4 \cdot 3 = 12$$

> **Tip: Since logarithms are exponents, think about the rules for exponents when working with logarithms.**

For a given base, the logarithmic function is the **inverse** of the corresponding exponential function, and reciprocally. (See the section "Composition and Inverses of Functions" in this chapter for a discussion of inverses of functions.). The logarithm function $y = f(x) = \log_{10} x$ (**common logarithmic function**) is the inverse of the exponential function $y = f(x) = 10^x$. The logarithm function $y = f(x) = \log_e x$ ln$x$ (**natural logarithmic function**) is the inverse of the exponential function $y = f(x) = e^x$. Here is an example of their graphs.

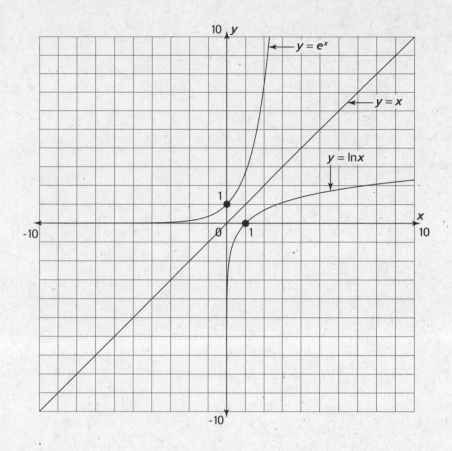

Transformations

Adding or subtracting a positive constant k to $f(x)$ is a **vertical shift.** Adding or subtracting a positive constant h to x is a **horizontal shift.** Vertical and horizontal shifts are summarized in the following table:

Vertical and Horizontal Shifts	
Type of change	*Effect on $y = f(x)$*
(h, k both positive)	
$y = f(x) + k$	Vertical shift: k units up
$y = f(x) - k$	Vertical shift: k units down
$y = f(x + h)$	Horizontal shift: h units to left
$y = f(x - h)$	Horizontal shift: h units to right

Multiplying $f(x)$ by $k > 1$ enlarges or **stretches** the graph of f. Multiplying $f(x)$ by $0 < k < 1$ reduces or **shrinks** the graph of f. The graph of $y = -f(x)$ is a **reflection** of $y = f(x)$ in the x-axis. Here are illustrations using the quadratic function $y = x^2$.

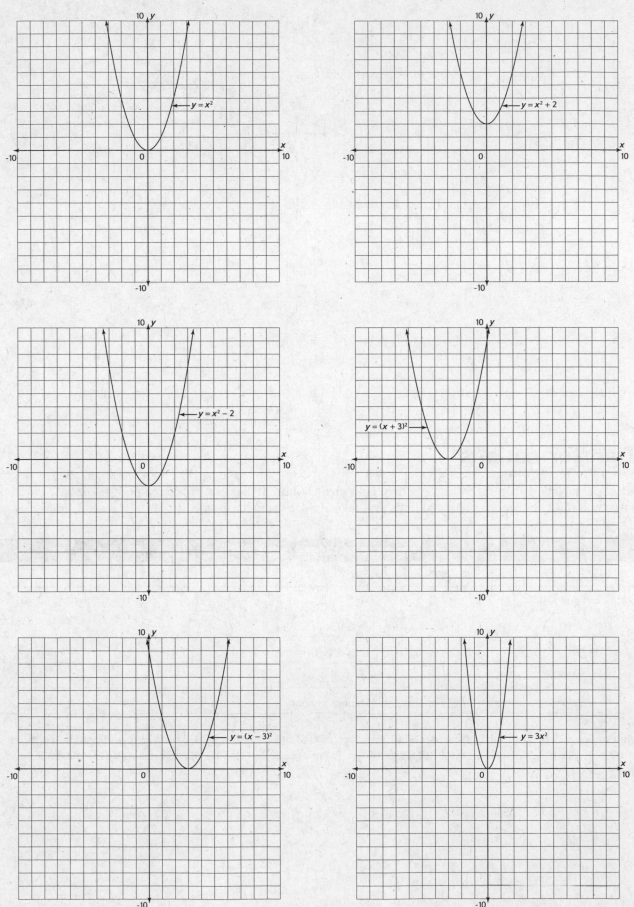

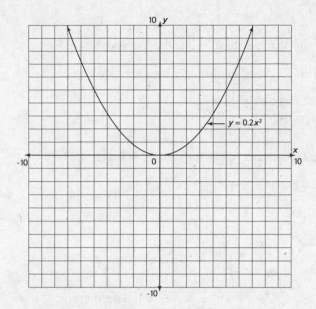

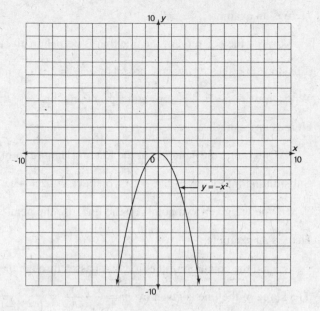

Functions as Mathematical Models

Families of functions (for example, the families of linear functions, quadratic functions, exponential functions, step-functions, and so on) are used to model phenomena in the real world.

Linear functions model processes in which the rate of change is constant. For instance, in science a linear function can be used to model the distance a moving object travels at a constant rate of speed as a function of time or to model the volume occupied by a sample of gas at a constant pressure as a function of its absolute temperature.

Quadratic functions model processes that involve a maximum or a minimum value. For instance, in business a quadratic function can be used to model the profit or revenue of a company as a function of the number of units sold.

Step functions model processes that increase or decrease in increments but remain constant over fixed intervals. For instance, a step function can be used to model the cost of postage for a letter or package as a function of the weight of the letter or package.

Exponential functions model processes that grow or decline rapidly. For instance, they are used to model physical phenomena such as population growth and population decay as a function of time. This family of functions is also used in business for determining the growth of money as a function of time when interest is compounded at a fixed rate.

Equations of Lines

If (x_1, y_1) and (x_2, y_2) are the coordinates of any two points on a line, the **slope** of the line is given by

$m = \dfrac{y_2 - y_1}{x_2 - x_1}$ $(x_1 \neq x_2)$. When a line slopes *upward* to the right, its slope is *positive* and when a line slopes *downward* to the right, its slope is *negative*. If two lines are **parallel** their slopes are equal; and if two lines are **perpendicular,** their slopes are negative reciprocals of each other.

The **standard form** for a linear equation is $Ax + By = C$ (A and B not both zero). However, for the Praxis Middle School test, it is usually more convenient to determine the **equation of a line** using one of the following:

- The **slope-intercept form:** $y = mx + b$, where the line determined by the equation has slope $= m$ and y-intercept $= b$; or

- The **point-slope form:** $y - y_1 = m(x - x_1)$, where m is the slope of the line and (x_1, y_1) is a point on the line.

When you are given the slope (or can obtain it relatively easily) and the y-intercept, use the slope-intercept form.

Here is an example.

Write the equation of the line that is perpendicular to the line that has slope $-\frac{1}{2}$ and y-intercept 5.

The slope m = the negative reciprocal of $-\frac{1}{2} = 2$. The y-intercept $b = 5$. Substituting into $y = mx + b$, you have $y = 2x + 5$.

When you are given the slope and a point on a line, use the point-slope form.

Here is an example.

Determine the equation of the line in standard form with slope –3 that passes through the point (1, 2).

Substituting into $y - y_1 = m(x - x_1)$, you have $y - 2 = -3(x - 1) \rightarrow y - 2 = -3x + 3 \rightarrow 3x + y = 5$.

When you are given two points on the line, use the point-slope form.

Here is an example.

Find the equation of the line that passes through the points (–3, 4) and (–5, 2).

The **slope** of the line is given by $m = \dfrac{y_2 - y_1}{x_2 - x_1} = \dfrac{2 - 4}{(-5) - (-3)} = \dfrac{2 - 4}{-5 + 3} = \dfrac{-2}{-5 + 3} = \dfrac{-2}{-2} = 1$. Selecting (–3, 4) from the two points and substituting into $y - y_1 = m(x - x_1)$, you have $(y - 4) = 1(x - (-3)) \rightarrow y - 4 = x + 3 \rightarrow y = x + 7$.

Tip: Enclose negative values in parentheses when substituting into formulas to avoid making a sign error.

Two special cases of linear equations are the equations for horizontal and vertical lines. **Horizontal lines** have equations of the form y = k (m = 0). **Vertical lines** have equations of the form $x = h$ (undefined slope).

The following table summarizes linear equations.

Linear Equations	
Slope-intercept form (functional form)	$y = mx + b$
Point-slope form	$y - y_1 = m(x - x_1)$
Standard form	$Ax + By = C$ (A and B not both zero)
Horizontal line	$y = k$ for any constant k
Vertical line (not a function)	$x = h$ for any constant h

Tip: Not all authorities agree on the form of the standard form. Some write the standard form as $Ax + By + C = 0$; others, designate $y = mx + b$ as the standard form. We do not anticipate that your correct responses on the Praxis Middle School test will be jeopardized by this discrepancy.

Graphs of Linear Inequality Relations

To graph linear inequality relations such as $3x + y \leq 5$, $y \geq x + 7$, $2x - y < 5$ and $y > 2$, use the following guidelines:

1. Graph the corresponding linear equation. To indicate that the graph that represents the equation <u>is</u> included in the solution set, use a solid line for the graph if the inequality is $\leq$ or $\geq$. To indicate that the graph that represents the equation is *not* included in the solution set, use a dashed line if the inequality is < or >. This line separates the coordinate plane into two half-planes.

2. Select a point in either half-plane that is NOT on the line (the origin is a convenient choice unless the line passes through it). Test whether the coordinates of the point make the inequality a true statement. If so, then shade the half-plane that contains the point. If not, then shade the opposite half-plane.

Here is an example.

Graph $3x + y \leq 5$.

1. Graph $3x + y = 5$. For convenience, rewrite the equation as $y = -3x + 5$. Two points that satisfy this equation are $(0, 5)$ and $(1, 2)$. Draw the line between these two points. Make the line a solid line to indicate that all points that satisfy $3x + y = 5$ are in the solution set.

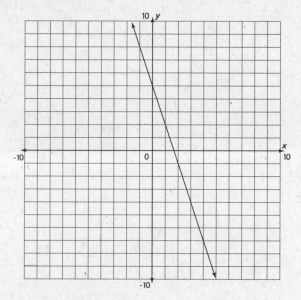

2. Test the origin. Substituting into $3x + y \leq 5$, you have $0 + 0 \leq 5$, which is true; so shade the half-plane containing $(0, 0)$.

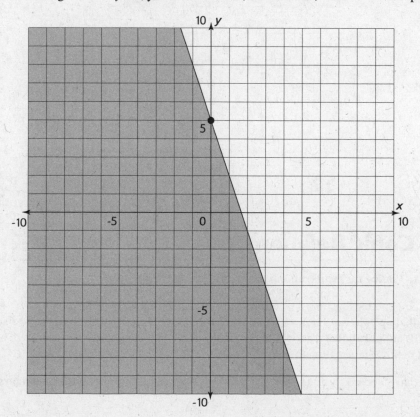

$3x + y \leq 5$

Here are other examples.

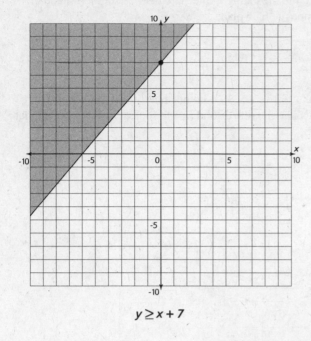

$$y \geq x + 7$$

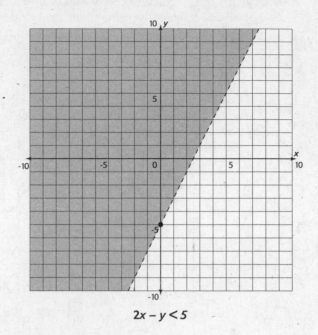

$$2x - y < 5$$

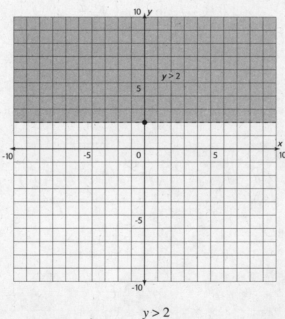

$$y > 2$$

Graphs of Conic Relations

The four basic kinds of **conics** are the **parabola, circle, ellipse,** and **hyperbola.**

The section "Quadratic Functions" in this chapter presents quadratic functions defined by $y = ax^2 + bx + c$ $(a \neq 0)$ whose graphs are parabolas that open upward if $a > 0$ and downward if $a < 0$. Similarly, the graphs of relations defined by $x = ay^2 + by + c$, $(a \neq 0)$ are **parabolas** that open to the right if $a > 0$ and open to the left if $a < 0$. These parabolas have standard form: $x = a(y - k)^2 + h$ $(a \neq 0)$ with vertex (h, k).

The graph of a **circle** has standard form: $(x - h)^2 + (y - k)^2 = r^2$, where (h, k) is the **center** and the **radius** is $|r|$ units.

The graph of an **ellipse** has standard form: $\dfrac{(x-h)^2}{a^2} + \dfrac{(y-k)^2}{b^2} = 1$, with **center** at (h, k). The ellipse has **vertices** $(h-a, k)$, $(h+a, k)$, $(h, k-b)$, and $(h, k+b)$. The line segment joining the vertices $(h-a, k)$ and $(h+a, k)$ is a **horizontal axis** of symmetry and the line segment joining the vertices $(h, k-b)$ and $(h, k+b)$ is a **vertical axis** of symmetry. The longer axis is called the **major axis** and the shorter axis is called the **minor axis.** The lengths of the two axes are $2|a|$ and $2|b|$.

The graph of a **hyperbola** has two standard forms:

Form (1) $\dfrac{(x-h)^2}{a^2} - \dfrac{(y-k)^2}{b^2} = 1$, with center at (h, k). It opens left and right along the line $y = k$, and it passes through the **vertices** $(h-a, k)$ and $(h+a, k)$. It has the intersecting lines $y = k + \dfrac{b}{a}(x-h)$ and $y = k - \dfrac{b}{a}(x-h)$ as (slanting) **asymptotes.** The asymptotes are the diagonals of a rectangle with dimensions $2|a|$ by $2|b|$ centered at (h, k).

Form (2) $\dfrac{(y-k)^2}{b^2} - \dfrac{(x-h)^2}{a^2} = 1$, with center at (h, k). It opens up and down along the line $x = h$, and it passes through the **vertices** $(h, k-b)$, and $(h, k+b)$. As in Form (1), Form (2) has the intersecting lines $y = k + (x-h)$ and $y = k - (x-h)$ as (slanting) **asymptotes.** The asymptotes are the diagonals of a rectangle with dimensions $2|a|$ by $2|b|$ centered at (h, k).

Here are examples of the four types of conics.

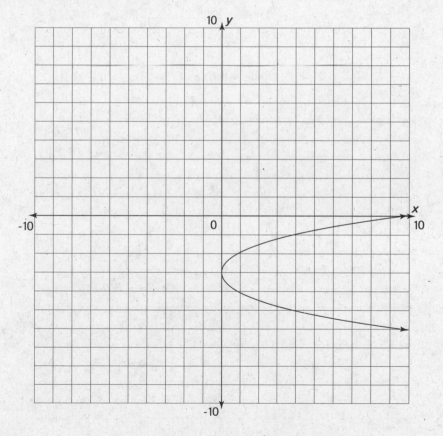

Parabola with vertex $(0, -3)$

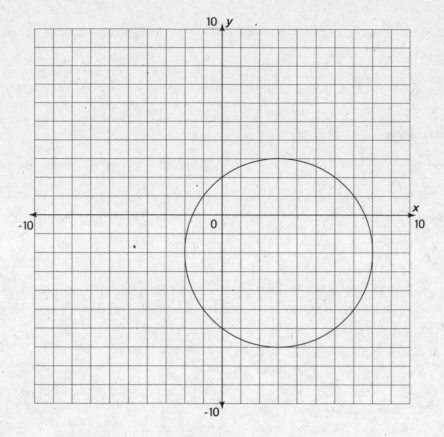

Circle with Center (3, –2)

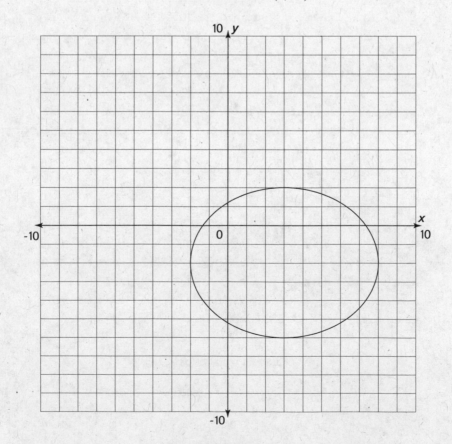

Ellipse with Center (3, –2)

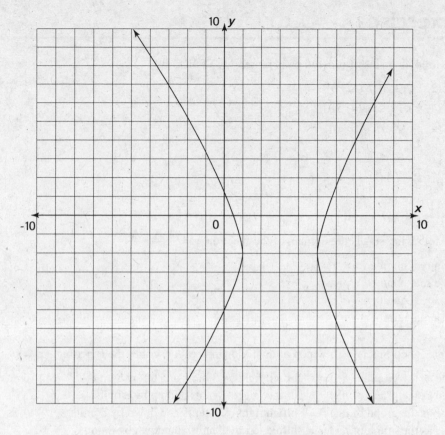

Hyperbola with Center (3, –2)

Sample Exercises

1. Which of the following sets of ordered pairs represents a function?

   I. $\{(4, 5), (2, 1), (2, 10), (-2, 0)\}$
   II. $\{(4, 5), (4, 5^2), (4, 5^3), (4, 5^4)\}$
   III. $\{(2, 3), (4, 3), (8, 3), (16, 3)]$

   A.   II only
   B.   III only
   C.   II and III only
   D.   I, II, and III

2. Which of the following sets is the domain of the function $y = \dfrac{x-5}{x^2 - 6x + 9}$?

   A. $\{x \mid x$ is a real number, $x \neq 5\}$
   B. $\{x \mid x$ is a real number, $x \neq -3\}$
   C. $\{x \mid x$ is a real number, $x \neq 3\}$
   D. $\{x \mid x$ is a real number$\}$

3. Given the cubic function $f(x) = x^3$, which of the following best describes the function $g(x) = (x - 3)^3 + 8$?

   A.   the same as the graph of $f(x) = x^3$ shifted right by 3 units and up by 8 units
   B.   the same as the graph of $f(x) = x^3$ shifted left by 3 units and up by 8 units
   C.   the same as the graph of $f(x) = x^3$ shifted right by 3 units and down by 8 units
   D.   the same as the graph of $f(x) = x^3$ shifted left by 3 units and down by 8 units

4. Which of the following functions is the polynomial of lowest degree that has zeros at $-6, -3, 2,$ and 4?

   A. $P(x) = x(x + 6)(x + 3)(x - 2)(x - 4)$
   B. $P(x) = (x - 6)(x - 3)(x + 2)(x + 4)$
   C. $P(x) = (x + 6)(x + 3)(x - 2)(x - 4)$
   D.   It cannot be determined from the information given.

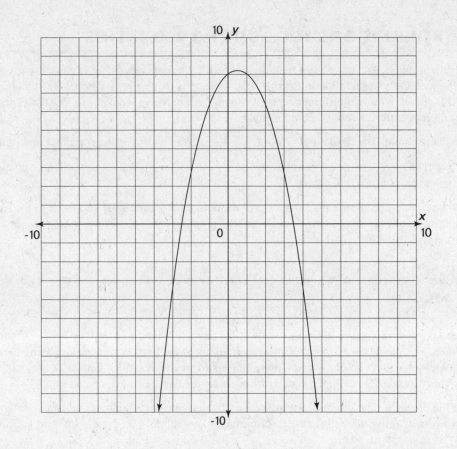

5. A quadratic function $y = ax^2 + bx + c$ has the graph shown. Which of the statements about the discriminant of the function is true?

   A. $b^2 - 4ac < 0$.

   B. $b^2 - 4ac = 0$.

   C. $b^2 - 4ac > 0$.

   D. $b^2 - 4ac$ is undefined.

Answer Explanations for Sample Exercises

1. **B.** Analyze the problem. A function is a relation in which each first component is paired with *one and only one* second component. Only the relation in Roman III satisfies this requirement, Choice B. In Roman I, the first component 2 is paired with two different second components, namely, 1 and 10. In Roman II, the first component 4 is paired with four different second components.

2. **C.** Analyze the problem. The domain of $y = \dfrac{x-5}{x^2-6x+9}$ excludes any value for x that makes the denominator equal zero. Set $x^2 - 6x + 9 = 0$ and solve for x: $x^2 - 6x + 9 = 0 \Rightarrow (x-3)^2 = 0 \Rightarrow x = 3$. Thus, the domain is the set R of real numbers excluding $x = 3$, Choice C.

3. **A.** Analyze the problem. Subtracting 3 from x will result in a horizontal shift of 3 units to the right. Adding 8 to $f(x)$ will result in a vertical shift of 8 units up. Thus, the graph of $g(x) = (x-3)^3 + 8$ is the same as the graph of $f(x) = x^3$ shifted right by 3 units and up by 8 units, Choice A.

> **Tip:** If you are unsure whether the shift is to the right or left or up or down, graph the two functions on your graphing calculator to check.

4. **C.** Analyze the problem. You are given the zeros of the desired polynomial. By the Factor Theorem if r is a zero of a polynomial, $P(x)$, then $x - r$ is a factor of $P(x)$. Looking at the answer choices and using the previous statement, you can see that choices A and C have the desired zeros; however, Choice A also has an additional factor of x. Thus, Choice C is the polynomial of lowest degree that has the given zeros.

5. **C.** Analyze the problem. The graph of the quadratic function intersects the real axis at two points, indicating the function has two real zeros. Therefore, the discriminant, $b^2 - 4ac$, must be greater than zero, Choice C.

Probability

This chapter provides a review of the key ideas and formulas of probability that are most important for you to know for the Praxis Middle School Mathematics test. Multiple-choice sample exercises, comparable to what might be presented on the Praxis Middle School Mathematics test, are given at the end of the chapter. The answer explanations for the sample exercises are provided immediately after the exercises at the end of the chapter.

Sample Spaces and Probability Distributions

A **sample space, S,** is the set of all possible outcomes of an experiment. Each member of S is called an **outcome** (or simple event, sample point, or elementary outcome).

Note: A sample space can be finite or infinite. For the Praxis Middle School Mathematics test, only finite sample spaces are considered.

An **event, E,** is a collection of outcomes from S; that is, an event E is a subset of the sample space S. An event E is said to **occur** if a member of E occurs when the experiment is performed. For example, if the sample space is the set of outcomes from the experiment of drawing one tile (without looking) from a box containing five small wooden square tiles (assume the tiles are identical in size), numbered 1 through 5, and E is the event that the tile drawn shows an odd number; then $S = \{1, 2, 3, 4, 5\}$ and $E = \{1, 3, 5\}$, where "1" represents the outcome "the tile drawn shows a 1," "2" represents the outcome "the tile drawn shows a 2," and so on.

Note: By convention, capital letters are used to designate events, with the word *event* being omitted in cases where the meaning is clear.

A **probability measure** on a sample space, S, is a function that assigns to each outcome in S a real number between 0 and 1, inclusive, so that the values assigned to the outcomes in S sum to 1. The value assigned to an outcome in S is called the **probability** of that outcome. For instance, for $S = \{1, 2, 3, 4, 5\}$, the sample space for the tile-drawing experiment, the probability of each outcome in S is $\frac{1}{5}$. (Since the tiles are physically identical, each has a 1 in 5 chance of being drawn.) The sum of the probabilities of the outcomes in S is $P(1) + P(2) + P(3) + P(4) + P(5) =$ $\frac{1}{5} + \frac{1}{5} + \frac{1}{5} + \frac{1}{5} + \frac{1}{5} = \frac{5}{5} = 1$.

The **probability of an event E,** denoted $P(E)$, is the sum of the probabilities of the individual outcomes that are members of the event E. The probability of an event is a numerical value between 0 and 1, inclusive, that quantifies the chance or likelihood that the event will occur.

Here is an example.

Given the sample space $S = \{1, 2, 3, 4, 5\}$, the set of outcomes from the tile-drawing experiment, and $E = \{1, 3, 5\}$, the event that the tile drawn shows an odd number, then $P(E) = P(1) + P(3) + P(5) = \frac{1}{5} + \frac{1}{5} + \frac{1}{5} = \frac{3}{5}$.

Outcomes are **equally likely** if each outcome is as likely to occur as any other outcome.

If all outcomes in the sample space are equally likely, the probability of an event E is given by:

$$P(E) = \frac{\text{Number of outcomes favorable to } E}{\text{Total number of outcomes in the sample space}}.$$

For example, if the sample space is $S = \{1, 2, 3, 4, 5\}$, the set of outcomes from the tile-drawing experiment, and E is the event that the tile drawn shows an odd number, then $P(E) = \frac{\text{Number of outcomes favorable to } E}{\text{Total number of outcomes in the sample space}} = \frac{3}{5}$.

Probabilities can be expressed as fractions, decimals, or percents. In the example given, the probability of drawing an odd-numbered tile can be expressed as $\frac{3}{5}$, 0.6, or 60 percent.

Keep in mind that the formula for probability in which the outcomes are equally likely will *not* apply to sample spaces in which the events are not equally likely. For instance, the sample space for spinning the spinner shown is $S = \{\text{red, yellow, green}\}$.

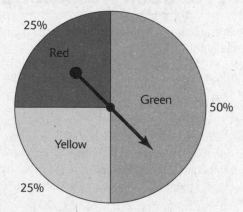

The probabilities for the different outcomes are the following: $P(\text{red}) = \frac{1}{4}$, $P(\text{yellow}) = \frac{1}{4}$, and $P(\text{green}) = \frac{1}{2}$.

An event is **certain** to occur if and only if the probability of the event is 1. An event is **impossible** if and only if the probability of the event is 0. The probability of any event is a number between 0 and 1, inclusive. For example, suppose that the sample space is $S = \{1, 2, 3, 4, 5\}$, the set of outcomes from the tile-drawing experiment; W is the event that the tile drawn shows a whole number; and Z is the event that the tile drawn shows the number 6. Then $P(W) = 1$ and $P(Z) = 0$.

Thus, the lowest probability you can have is 0, and the highest probability you can have is 1. All other probabilities fall between 0 and 1. You can express this relationship symbolically this way: $0 \leq P(X) \leq 1$, for any event X. The closer the probability of an event is to 1, the more likely is the event to occur; and the closer the probability of an event is to zero, the less likely is the event to occur.

Determining the outcomes in a sample space is a critical step in solving a probability problem. For simple experiments, counting techniques such as making a **tree diagram** or an **organized chart** are two useful ways to generate a list of the outcomes. More sophisticated techniques, which include the **fundamental counting principle, permutations,** and **combinations,** are needed for problems that are less straightforward. See the topic "Counting Techniques" in the chapter "Discrete Mathematics" for a discussion of these methods.

Here is an example of using a tree diagram to determine the outcomes in a sample space.

Find the sample space for the experiment of recording the up faces when a fair coin is tossed, and then a fair six-sided die is rolled. The tree starts with the possibilities for the coin toss and then branches to the possibilities for the roll of the die as shown, where "H" stands for "heads appears on the up face of the coin," "T" stands for "tails appears on the up face of the coin," "1" stands for "the number 1 appears on the up face of the die," "2" stands for "the number 2 appears on the up face of the die," and so on.

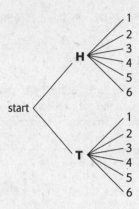

By following the different paths, you can determine that the sample space is {H1, H2, H3, H4, H5, H6, T1, T2, T3, T4, T5, T6} and that there are 12 total possible (equally likely) outcomes for the experiment.

Here is an example of using an organized chart to determine the outcomes of a sample space.

   Find the sample space for tossing a coin three times.

The table is constructed using the labels 1st toss, 2nd toss, and 3rd toss as headings and then listing all possibilities under the headings.

1st Toss	2nd Toss	3rd Toss
H	H	H
H	H	T
H	T	H
H	T	T
T	H	H
T	H	T
T	T	H
T	T	T

From the table, you can determine that the sample space is {HHH, HHT, HTH, HTT, THH, THT, TTH, TTT} and that there are eight total possible (equally likely) outcomes for the experiment.

Conditional Probability and Independent and Dependent Events

A **compound event** is any event combining two or more given events.

The **complement of an event A,** denoted $\overline{A}$ (or A^c), is the event that A does not occur. The probability of the complement of an event A is given by $P(\overline{A}) = 1 - P(A)$. For example, if $P(A) = 0.06$, then $P(\overline{A}) = 1 - P(A) = 1 - 0.06 = 0.94$.

In probability, the word *or* is used in the inclusive sense. Thus, **$P(A$ or $B)$** is the probability that event A occurs or event B occurs or that both events occur simultaneously on one trial of an experiment.

The **Addition Rule** states that $P(A \text{ or } B) = P(A) + P(B) - P(A \text{ and } B \text{ occur simultaneously})$. This rule applies to *one* trial of an experiment.

Here is an example.

A standard deck of 52 playing cards consists of four suits: clubs (♣), spades (♠), hearts (♥), and diamonds (♦). Clubs and spades are black-colored suits; hearts and diamonds are red-colored suits. Each suit has 13 cards consisting of three face cards (king, queen, and jack) and number cards from one (ace) to ten as shown here.

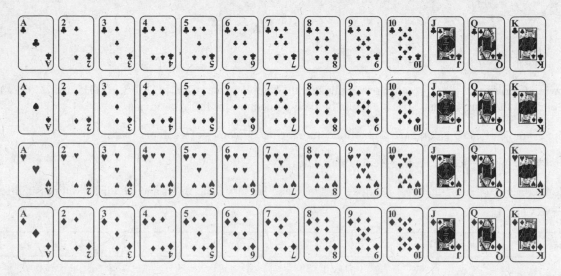

Suppose that a card is drawn at random from a standard deck of 52 playing cards; find the probability that the card is a face card or a diamond.

There are 12 face cards so $P(\text{face card}) = \frac{12}{52}$. There are 13 diamonds, so $P(\text{diamond}) = \frac{13}{52}$. There are 3 diamond face cards, so $P(\text{face card and diamond occur simultaneously}) = \frac{3}{52}$. Thus, $P(\text{face card or diamond}) = P(\text{face card}) + P(\text{diamond}) - P(\text{face card and diamond occur simultaneously}) = \frac{12}{52} + \frac{13}{52} - \frac{3}{52} = \frac{22}{52} = \frac{11}{26}$.

Usually the most efficient and straightforward way to find $P(A \text{ or } B)$ is to sum the number of ways that event A can occur and the number of ways that event B can occur, *being sure to add in such a way that no outcome is counted twice*, and then divide by the total number of outcomes in the sample space.

Applying this strategy for the example given, you have the following.

There are 12 face cards. There are 10 diamonds that are *not* face cards. Thus, there are $12 + 10 = 22$ distinct cards favorable to the event "face card or diamond." Therefore, $P(\text{face card or diamond}) = \frac{12+10}{52} = \frac{22}{52} = \frac{11}{26}$.

Two events are **mutually exclusive** if they cannot occur at the same time; that is, they have no outcomes in common. For example, suppose that you draw one card from a deck of cards, the event of drawing a red card and the event of drawing a club are mutually exclusive.

Two events A and B are **independent** if the occurrence of one does not affect the probability of the occurrence of the other. For instance, the event of obtaining a head on the up face when a fair coin is tossed and the event of obtaining a five on the up face when a fair die is rolled are independent. If events A and B are not independent, they are said to be **dependent.** For example, if a box contains 6 red marbles and 4 blue marbles, the event of drawing a red marble without replacement on the first draw and the event of drawing a blue marble on the second draw are dependent.

The probability of an event B, given that an event A has occurred, is called a **conditional probability** and is denoted $P(B \mid A)$. In other words, you compute the probability of event B by taking into account that the event A has already occurred.

Here are examples.

Suppose that you draw two marbles from a box containing 6 red marbles and 4 blue marbles, find the probability of drawing a blue marble on the second draw given that (a) a red marble was drawn without replacement on the first draw and (b) a red marble was drawn with replacement on the first draw.

(a) After the red marble is drawn without replacement, there are 5 red marbles and 4 blue marbles in the box. Therefore, $P(\text{blue} \mid \text{red drawn without replacement}) = \frac{4}{9}$.

(b) After the red marble is drawn with replacement, there are 6 red marbles and 4 blue marbles in the box. Therefore, $P(\text{blue} \mid \text{red drawn with replacement}) = \frac{4}{10} = \frac{2}{5}$.

The table shows the gender and type of residence of the 2000 senior students at a university.

Gender and Type of Residence of Senior Students ($n = 2000$)		
	Females	*Males*
Apartment	229	180
Dorm	203	118
House	200	272
With Parent(s)	258	201
Sorority/Fraternity House	241	98

What is the probability that a senior selected at random (a) lives in a dorm given that the senior is female? (b) is a female senior given that the senior lives in a dorm?

(a) The total number of female seniors is $229 + 203 + 200 + 258 + 241 = 1131$. Of that total, 203 live in a dorm. Thus, $P(\text{Dorm} \mid \text{Female}) = \frac{203}{1131}$.

(b) The total number of seniors living in a dorm is $203 + 118 = 321$. Of that total, 203 are female. Thus, $P(\text{Female} \mid \text{Dorm}) = \frac{203}{321}$.

The **Multiplication Rule** states that $P(A \text{ and } B) = P(A)\, P(B \mid A)$. This rule applies when *two* trials are performed.

Here is an example.

> Two cards are drawn at random without replacement from a standard deck of 52 playing cards. What is the probability of drawing a jack on the first draw and a king on the second draw.

There are 4 jacks in the deck of 52 cards, so the probability of a jack on the first draw is $\frac{4}{52}$. After the jack is drawn without replacement, there are 4 kings in the remaining deck of 51 cards. Therefore, P(jack on 1st draw and king on 2nd draw) = P(jack on 1st draw) P(king on 2nd draw $\mid$ jack on 1st draw) = $\frac{4}{52} \cdot \frac{4}{51} = \frac{1}{13} \cdot \frac{4}{51} = \frac{4}{13 \cdot 51}$.

Note: On the Praxis Middle School Mathematics test, sometimes the computations are indicated as in this example.

If, $P(A \text{ and } B) = P(A)\, P(B)$, then the events A and B are independent.

Here is an example.

> Two cards are drawn at random with replacement from a standard deck of 52 playing cards. What is the probability of drawing a club on the first draw and a king on the second draw?

There are 13 clubs in the deck of 52 cards, so the probability of a club on the first draw is $\frac{13}{52}$. After the club is drawn and replaced in the deck, there are 4 kings in the deck of 52 cards. Therefore, P(club on 1st draw and king on 2nd draw) = P(club on 1st draw) P(king on 2nd draw | club on 1st draw) = $\frac{13}{52} \cdot \frac{4}{52} = \frac{1}{52}$.

Notice that in this case, that P(club on 1st draw and king on 2nd draw) = $\frac{13}{52} \cdot \frac{4}{52} = P$(club) P(king), so the event of drawing a club on the first draw with replacement and the event of drawing a king on the second draw are independent.

> **Tip:** For the Praxis Middle School Mathematics test, to find the probability that event *A* occurs on the first trial and event *B* occurs on the second trial, multiply the probability of event *A* times the probability of event *B*, where you have determined the probability of *B* by taking into account that the event *A* has already occurred.

To find the probability that **at least one** of something occurs, use the rule of complements as follows: P(at least one) = $1 - P$(none).

Here is an example.

A fair coin is tossed three times. Find the probability that at least one head occurs. The sample space is {HHH, HHT, HTH, HTT, THH, THT, TTH, TTT}, where "H" indicates "heads" and "T" indicates "tails." Thus, P(at least one head) = $1 - P$(no heads) = $1 - P$(TTT) = $1 - \frac{1}{8} = \frac{7}{8}$. By looking at the sample space, you can see that this answer is correct because there are seven outcomes in which a head occurs. In fact, you could have worked the problem directly as follows: P(at least one head) = $\frac{7}{8}$. With larger sample spaces, it is often more convenient to determine the probability of at least one by using $1 - P$(none).

The **odds in favor** of an event A are given by $\frac{P(A)}{1 - P(A)}$, usually expressed in the form $p : q$ (or p to q), where p and q are integers with no common factors and $\frac{P(A)}{1 - P(A)} = \frac{p}{q}$. The **odds against** an event A are given by $\frac{1 - P(A)}{P(A)}$, usually expressed in the form $q : p$ (or q to p), where p and q are integers with no common factors and $\frac{1 - P(A)}{P(A)} = \frac{q}{p}$.

Here is an example.

Find the odds in favor of and the odds against getting a five on the up face when a fair die is rolled one time.

P(five) = $\frac{1}{6}$. Thus, the odds in favor of getting a five is given by $\frac{\frac{1}{6}}{1 - \frac{1}{6}} = \frac{\frac{1}{6}}{\frac{5}{6}} = \frac{1}{5}$ or 1 to 5, and the odds against getting a five is 5 to 1.

Empirical Probability

In **empirical probability,** the probability of an event E is defined by conducting the experiment a large number of times, called **trials,** and counting the number of times that event E actually occurred. Based on these results, the probability of E is *estimated* as follows:

Empirical Probability of E = $P(E)$ = $\frac{\text{Number of times } E \text{ occurred}}{\text{Total number of trials}}$.

As the numbers of trials increases, the empirical probability approaches the true probability of the event. The empirical probability of an event is also called its **relative frequency probability** or **experimental probability.**

Here is an example.

> Out of 100 light bulbs tested at Company X, 2 are defective. What is the empirical probability that a Company X light bulb is defective?
>
> Empirical P(Company X light bulb is defective.) $= \dfrac{2}{100} = 0.02 = 2\%$.

In some situations, empirical probability is the only feasible way to assign a probability to an event. For instance, insurance companies set premiums based on empirical probabilities.

Geometric Probability

Geometric probability involves determining probabilities associated with geometric objects.

Here is an example.

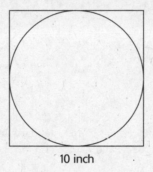

10 inch

> The figure shown is a circle inscribed in a 10-inch square. A point is randomly selected within the square. What is the probability that the point will be inside the circle as well? Round your answer to three decimal places.

To calculate the probability that the point will be inside the circle, you calculate the ratio of the area of the circle to the area of the square.

> P(Point is inside circle.) $= \dfrac{\text{area of circle}}{\text{area of square}} = \dfrac{\pi \left(5 \text{ in}\right)^2}{\left(10 \text{ in}\right)^2} = \dfrac{25\pi}{100} = 0.785$.

Sample Exercises

1. Given a bag of 25 colored tiles containing 10 blue, 7 red, 5 green, and 3 yellow. If a person picks out a single tile from the bag without looking, what is the probability that it will be a green tile? (Assume the tiles are identical except for color.)

   A. $\frac{3}{25}$

   B. $\frac{7}{25}$

   C. $\frac{1}{5}$

   D. $\frac{2}{5}$

2. Two cards are drawn at random without replacement from a standard deck of 52 playing cards. What is the probability of drawing a queen on the second draw, if the first card, drawn without replacement, was a jack?

   A. $\frac{3}{51}$

   B. $\frac{4}{51}$

   C. $\frac{3}{52}$

   D. $\frac{4}{52}$

3. Two cards are drawn at random with replacement from a standard deck of 52 playing cards. What is the probability of drawing a jack on the first draw and a queen on the second draw?

   A. $\frac{1}{13 \cdot 13}$

   B. $\frac{3}{13 \cdot 51}$

   C. $\frac{4}{13 \cdot 51}$

   D. $\frac{16}{51 \cdot 51}$

4. Each of the two triangles in the figure shown has an area of 12 cm². The dimensions of the rectangle in the middle of the figure are 10 cm by 4 cm. If a point is selected at random inside the figure, what is the probability that the point will be inside the rectangle as well. Round your answer to three decimal places.

   A. 0.375
   B. 0.400
   C. 0.600
   D. 0.625

Answer Explanations for Sample Exercises

1. **C.** Analyze the problem. There are 25 total possible outcomes. Each outcome is equally likely. There are five favorable outcomes. The probability of drawing a green tile is

$$P(\text{green}) = \frac{\text{number of favorable outcomes}}{\text{total number of outcomes possible}} = \frac{\text{number of green tiles}}{\text{total number of tiles}} = \frac{5}{25} = \frac{1}{5}, \text{ Choice C.}$$

Tip: Problems of this type might not state that the objects are physically identical as was given in this problem. Nevertheless, you will have to make that assumption to work the problem.

2. **B.** Analyze the problem. After the jack is drawn, there are 51 cards left, 4 of which are queens. Therefore,

$$P(\text{queen} \mid \text{jack drawn without replacement}) = \frac{4}{51}, \text{ Choice B.}$$

3. **A.** Analyze the problem. There are 4 jacks in the deck of 52 cards, so the probability of a jack on the first draw is $\frac{4}{52}$. After the jack is drawn and replaced in the deck, there are 4 queens in the deck of 52 cards. Therefore,

$P(\text{jack on 1st draw and queen on 2nd draw}) = P(\text{jack on 1st draw}) \, P(\text{queen on 2nd draw} \mid \text{jack on 1st draw}) =$

$\frac{4}{52} \cdot \frac{4}{52} = \frac{1}{13 \cdot 13}$, Choice A.

4. **D.** Analyze the problem. The total area of the figure equals the sum of the areas of the two triangles plus the area of the rectangle $= 2(12 \text{ cm}^2) + (10 \text{ cm})(4 \text{ cm}) = 24 \text{ cm}^2 + 40 \text{ cm}^2 = 64 \text{ cm}^2$.

$$P(\text{Point is inside rectangle.}) = \frac{\text{area of rectangle}}{\text{total area of figure}} = \frac{40 \text{ cm}^2}{64 \text{ cm}^2} = 0.625, \text{ Choice D.}$$

Data Analysis and Basic Statistical Concepts

This chapter provides a review of the key ideas of data analysis and basic statistical concepts that are most important for you to know for the Praxis Middle School Mathematics test. Multiple-choice sample exercises, comparable to what might be presented on the Praxis Middle School Mathematics test, are given at the end of the chapter. The answer explanations for the sample exercises are provided immediately following.

Organizing Data

There are several ways to record, organize, and present data. For the Praxis Middle School Mathematics test, you should be able to perform data analysis by reading and interpreting information from **charts** and **tables, pictographs, circle graphs, line graphs, dotplots, stem-and-leaf plots, bar graphs, histograms,** and **scatterplots.**

Charts and **tables** organize information as entries in rows and columns. Row and column labels explain the data recorded in the chart or table. A **frequency table** is a tabular representation of data that shows the frequency of each value in the data set. A **relative frequency table** shows the frequency of each value as a proportion or percentage of the whole data set. The total of all relative frequencies should be 1.00 or 100 percent, but instead might be very close to 1.00 or 100 percent, due to round-off error. Here is an example.

Grade Distribution for Test 1		
Grade	*Frequency*	*Relative Frequency*
A	5	0.20
B	8	0.32
C	9	0.36
D	2	0.08
F	1	0.04
Total	**25**	**1.00**

Pictographs use symbols or pictures to represent numbers. Each symbol stands for a definite number of a specific item. This information should be stated on the graph. To read a pictograph, you count the number of symbols shown and then multiply by the number it represents. Fractional portions of symbols are approximated and used accordingly. Here is an example.

Responses of 15 Dog Owners to the Question: "Do You Own a Cat?"	
🐕 = 1 dog owner	
Yes	🐕 🐕 🐕 🐕
No	🐕 🐕 🐕 🐕 🐕 🐕 🐕 🐕 🐕 🐕 🐕

A **circle graph,** or **pie chart,** is a graph in the shape of a circle. Circle graphs are used to visually display the relative contribution of each category of data within a set of data to the whole set. It is also called a "pie" chart because it looks like a pie cut into slices. The slices are labeled to show the categories for the graph. Usually the portion of the graph that corresponds to each category is shown as a percent. The total amount of percentage on the graph is 100 percent. The graph is made by dividing the 360 degrees of the circle into portions that correspond to the percentages for each category. You read a circle graph by reading the percents displayed on the graph for the different categories. Here is an example.

Grade Distribution of 25 Students for Test 1

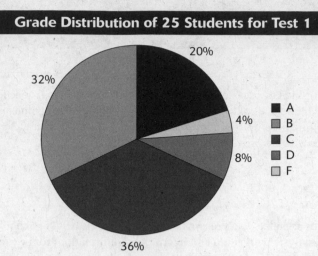

Line graphs use connected line segments to show information from a data set. The data values are plotted as ordered pairs on a grid that has a horizontal and vertical scale. Consecutive points are connected by line segments. The slants of the line segments between points show trends in the data. Upward slants indicate increasing data values; downward slants indicate decreasing data values; and line segments with no slant (horizontal line) indicate that the data values are remaining constant. Line graphs are particularly suitable for showing change over time. Two or more sets of data can be plotted on the same graph, which facilitates comparisons between the data sets. Here is an example of a line graph.

Fahrenheit Temperature: 8 A.M. – 8 P.M.

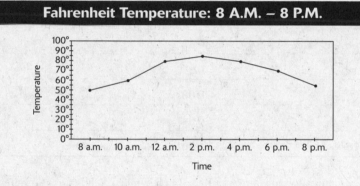

A dotplot (or line plot) is a graph in which the possible values of the data are indicated along the horizontal axis, and dots (or other similar symbols) are placed above each value to indicate the number of times that particular value occurs in the data set. Here is an example.

Minutes Waited in Line by 14 Customers at a Fast Food Restaurant

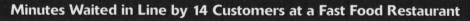

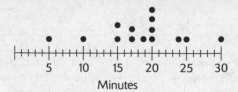

A **stem-and-leaf plot** is a graphical display of data in which each data value is separated into two parts: a stem (such as the leftmost digit for data consisting of two-digit numbers) and a leaf (such as the rightmost digit for data consisting of two-digit numbers). Usually, the stems are listed vertically (from smallest to largest), and the corresponding leaves for the data values are listed horizontally (from smallest to largest) beside the appropriate stem. Here is an example.

Ages of 39 U.S. Presidents at Death	
Stem	*Leaf*
4	6 9
5	3 6 7 7 8
6	0 0 3 3 4 4 5 6 7 7 7 8
7	0 1 1 1 2 3 7 8 8 9
8	0 1 3 5 8
9	0 0 3 3

A **bar graph** uses rectangular bars of the same width to show the frequency, relative frequency, or amount of different categories of a data set. Labels at the base of the bars specify the categories. The bars are equally spaced from each other and may be displayed vertically or horizontally. The length or height of the bar indicates the frequency, relative frequency, or amount for the category represented by that particular bar. A scale, marked in intervals, for measuring the height (or length) of the bars will be shown on the graph. To read a bar graph, examine the scale to determine the units and the amount corresponding to each interval. Then determine where the heights or lengths of the bars fall relative to the scale.

Here is an example.

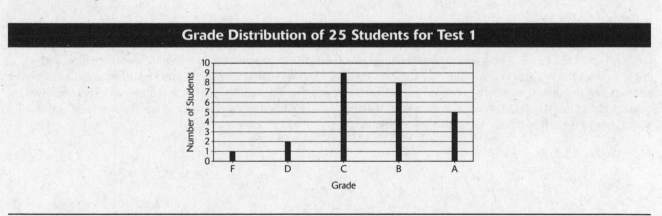

Grade Distribution of 25 Students for Test 1

Two or more sets of data can be displayed on the same graph to facilitate comparison of the data sets to each other. Here is an example.

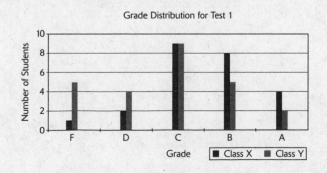

Grade Distribution for Test 1

A **histogram** is a special type of bar graph that summarizes data by displaying frequencies or relative frequencies of the data within specified intervals, called **class intervals.** Class intervals are of equal width and cover from the lowest to the highest data value. The left and right endpoints for the class intervals are selected so that each data value clearly falls within one and only one class interval. The frequency or relative frequency of occurrence of the data values within a class interval is represented by a rectangular (or vertical) column. The height (or length) of the column is proportional to the frequency or relative frequency of data values within that interval. Unlike the bars in other bar graphs, the bars in a histogram are side-by-side with no space in between. In a **frequency histogram,** the scale for measuring the height (or length) of the bars is marked with actual frequencies (or counts). In a **relative frequency histogram,** the scale is marked with relative frequencies instead of actual frequencies. The total of the relative frequencies corresponding to the class intervals should be 1.00 or 100 percent, but might instead be very close to 1.00 or 100 percent due to round-off error.

Here is an example of a frequency histogram.

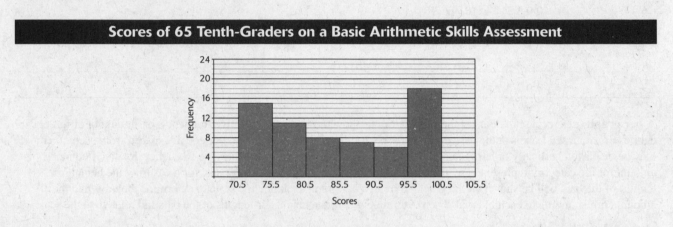

Scores of 65 Tenth-Graders on a Basic Arithmetic Skills Assessment

A **scatterplot** is a graph of **bivariate data,** paired values of data from two variables, plotted on a coordinate grid. The data are paired in a way that matches each value from one variable with a corresponding value from the other variable. The pattern of the plot can be useful in determining whether there is a relationship between the two variables; and, if there is, the nature of that relationship. For the Praxis Middle School Mathematics test, you should be able to examine scatterplots and distinguish between those indicating linear and those indicating nonlinear relationships between two variables. For linear relationships, a scatterplot that slants to the right indicates a positive linear relationship, and one that slants to the left indicates a negative linear relationship.

Here are examples.

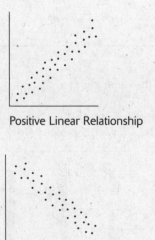

Positive Linear Relationship

Negative Linear Relationship

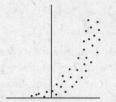

Nonlinear Exponential Relationship

Nonlinear Quadratic Relationship

Drawing valid conclusions from graphical representations of data requires that you have read the graph accurately and analyzed the graphical information correctly. Sometimes a graphical representation will distort the data in some way, leading you to draw an invalid conclusion. Here is an example.

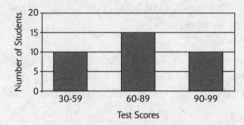

At first glance, the data for this graph look evenly distributed. Upon closer examination, you can see that each of the first two intervals covers a 29-point spread, but the last interval covers only a 19-point spread, making it difficult to draw conclusions from the graph.

When you interpret graphical information on the Praxis Middle School Mathematics test, follow these suggestions:

- Make sure that you understand the title of the graph.
- Read the labels on the parts of the graph to understand what is being represented.
- Make sure that you know what each symbol in a pictograph represents.
- Examine carefully the scale of bar graphs, line graphs, histograms, and scatterplots.
- Look for trends such as rising values (upward slanting line segments), falling values (downward slanting line segments), and periods of inactivity (horizontal line segments) in line graphs.
- Look for concentrations of data values and note the general shape for dotplots, stem-and-leaf plots, bar graphs, histograms, and scatterplots.
- Mark or draw on the graphs.
- Be ready to do simple arithmetic computations.
- Make sure that the numbers add up correctly.
- Use only the information in the graph. Do not answer based on your personal knowledge or opinion.

Measures of Central Tendency

A **measure of central tendency** is a numerical value that describes a data set by attempting to provide a "central" or "typical" value of the data set. Three common measures of central tendency are the **mean, median,** and **mode.** Each of these measures is a way to describe a central value of a set of data. Measures of central tendency should have the same units as those of the data values from which they are determined. If no units are specified for the data values, no units are specified for the measures of central tendency.

The **mean** of a data set is another name for the arithmetic average of the data values. Thus, the
mean = $\dfrac{\text{sum of the data values}}{\text{number of data values}}$.

Here is an example.

Find the mean of the following data set: 21, 35, 34, 30, 32, 36, 24, 35, 28, 35.

Mean = $\dfrac{\text{sum of the data values}}{\text{number of data values}} = \dfrac{21+24+28+30+32+34+35+35+35+36}{10} = \dfrac{310}{10} = 31$.

> **Tip:** Using the statistical features of your graphing calculator is the most efficient way to calculate the mean of a data set. For the TI-83, press **2nd STAT** to access the **LIST** menu. Select **MATH,** then press **3 to choose** 3:mean(. Enter the data inside braces and close the parentheses as shown here: mean({21, 35, 34, 30, 32, 36, 24, 35, 28, 35}). **Press ENTER. The display will show the mean, which in this case is** 31.

A **weighted mean** is a mean computed by assigning weights to the data values. To find a weighted mean, do the following: First, multiple each data value by its assigned weight and then sum the results. Next, divide the sum obtained by the sum of the weights. Thus, for data values $x_1, x_2, \ldots, x_n$ with respective assigned weights $w_1, w_2, \ldots, w_n$, weighted average = $\dfrac{\sum w_i x_i}{\sum w_i}$. Here is an example.

A student scores 80, 60, and 50 on three exams. Find the weighted mean of the student's three scores, where the score of 80 counts 20 percent, the score of 60 counts 20 percent, and the score of 50 counts 60 percent.

weighted mean = $\dfrac{\sum w_i x_i}{\sum w_i} = \dfrac{20\%(80)+20\%(60)+60\%(50)}{20\%+20\%+60\%} = \dfrac{16+16+30}{1} = \dfrac{62}{1} = 62$.

The **median** is the middle value or the mean of the two middle values in an *ordered* set of data. You can determine the median of a data set using a two-step process: First, put the data values in order from least to greatest (or greatest to least). Next, find the middle data value. If there is no single middle data value, find the mean of the two middle data values. Here is an example.

Find the median of the following data set: 21, 35, 34, 30, 32, 36, 24, 35, 28, 35.

Step 1. Put the data values in order: 21, 24, 28, 30, 32, 34, 35, 35, 35, 36.

Step 2. Find the mean of the two middle values: $\dfrac{32+34}{2} = 33$. Thus, the median is 33.

> **Tip:** Using the statistical features of your graphing calculator is the most efficient way to calculate the median of a data set. For the TI-83, press **2nd STAT** to access the **LIST** menu. Select **MATH,** then press **4 to choose** 4:median(. Enter the data inside braces and close the parentheses as shown here: median({21, 35, 34, 30, 32, 36, 24, 35, 28, 35}). **Press ENTER. The display will show the median, which in this case is** 33.

The **mode** is the data value or values that occur with the highest frequency in a data set; a data set can have one mode, more than one mode, or no mode. When a data set has two or more values that occur with the highest frequency, each of those values is a mode. A data set in which each data value occurs the same number of times has no mode. Here is an example.

> Find the mode of the following data set: 21, 35, 34, 30, 32, 36, 24, 35, 28, 35.

The value 35 occurs three times, which is the highest frequency of occurrence for any one value in the data set. Thus, the mode is 35.

The mean, median, and mode are ways to describe a central value of a data set. To know which of these measures of central tendency you should use to describe a data set, consider their characteristics.

The **mean** has several important characteristics.

- Even though the mean represents a central value of a data set, the mean does not necessarily have the same value as one of the values in the data set.
- The mean is calculated from the actual data values in the data set. If any one value is changed, the value of the mean also will change.
- A disadvantage of the mean is that it is influenced by outliers, especially in a small data set. An **outlier** is a data value that is extremely high or extremely low in comparison to most of the other data values. For a data set that has one or more high outliers, the mean is misleadingly high. Similarly, for a data set that has one or more low outliers, the mean is misleadingly low.

The **median** is the most useful alternative to the mean as a measure of central tendency.

- Like the mean, the median does not necessarily have the same value as one of the values in the data set. If the data set contains an odd number of data values, the median is the same as the middle value; however, for an even number of data values, the median is the mean of the two middle values.
- The median is not influenced by outliers.
- A disadvantage of the median is that its determination is based on the relative size of the data values in the data set rather than on their actual values.

The **mode** is the simplest measure of central tendency to determine.

- If a data set has a mode, the mode (or modes) is the same as one of the data values.
- The mode is the only appropriate measure of central tendency for data that are strictly nonnumeric (for example, eye color).
- A disadvantage of the mode is that its determination is based on relative frequency rather than on the actual values in the data set.

When you are summarizing data, you might want to report more than one measure of central tendency, if appropriate. For numeric data if you select only one measure, the mean is preferred for data sets in which outliers are not present. The median is the preferred measure when outliers are present. The mode is the preferred measure for nonnumeric categorical data.

Measures of Dispersions

A **measure of dispersion** is a value that describes the variability of a data set. The interpretation of measures of central tendency of a data set is enhanced when the variability about the central value is known. For the Praxis Middle School Mathematics test, measures of dispersion you need to know are the **range, standard deviation,** and **variance.**

The **range** for a data set is the difference between the **maximum value** (the greatest value) and the **minimum value** (least value) in the data set: range = maximum value - minimum value. The range should have the same units as those of the data values from which it is computed. If no units are specified, then the range will not specify units. Here is an example.

> Find the range of the following data set: 21, 35, 34, 30, 32, 36, 24, 35, 28, 35.
>
> Range = maximum value - minimum value = 36- 21 = 15.

The range gives an indication of the spread of the values in a data set, but its value is determined by only two of the data values. A measure of dispersion that is based on all the data values in a data set is the standard deviation. The **standard deviation** is a measure of the variability of a set of data values about the mean of the data set. If there is no variability in a data set, each data value equals the mean, so the standard deviation is zero. The more the data values vary from the mean, the greater the standard deviation, which means the data set has more spread. The standard deviation should have the same units as those of the data values from which it is computed. If no units are specified, then the standard deviation will not specify units. The **variance** of a data set is the square of its standard deviation.

Tip: Based on the list of topics covered under Content Category IV Data, Probability, and Statistical Concepts in the *Middle School Mathematics (0069) Test at a Glance* (www.ets.org/Media/Tests/PRAXIS/pdf/0069.pdf), it appears (currently, in 2008) that you will not have to calculate a standard deviation or variance when taking the Praxis Middle School Mathematics test.

You can use your understanding of standard deviation to assess a data value based on its location relative to the mean. The **z-score** for a data value is its distance in standard deviations from the mean of the data values. Computing a z-score is given by the formula: $\dfrac{\text{data value} - \text{mean}}{\text{standard deviation}}$

If the z-score is positive, the data value is greater than the mean; if the z-score is negative, the data value is less than the mean. If the z-score is zero, the data value and the mean are equal. Here is an example.

Suppose a student scored 80 on a chemistry test and 90 on a biology test. The mean and standard deviations of the scores on the two tests are shown in the following table:

Course	Mean	Standard Deviation
Chemistry	70	5
Biology	84	6

On which test did the student perform better relative to the mean performance of the class on the test?

The student's z-score for the chemistry test is $\dfrac{\text{score} - \text{mean}}{\text{standard deviation}} = \dfrac{80 - 70}{5} = 2$; thus, the student scored two standard deviations above the mean on the chemistry test. The student's z-score for the biology test is $\dfrac{\text{score} - \text{mean}}{\text{standard deviation}} = \dfrac{90 - 84}{6} = 1$; thus, the student scored one standard deviation above the mean on the biology test. Therefore, relative to the mean performance of the class, the student performed better on the chemistry test.

Additional Descriptive Measures

Other measures that are used to describe a data set are percentiles and quartiles. The Pth **percentile** is a value at or below which P percent of the data fall. For example, the median is the 50th percentile because 50 percent of the data fall below the median. **Quartiles** are values that divide an ordered data set into four portions, each of which contains approximately one-fourth of the data. Twenty-five percent of the data values are below the **first quartile** (also called the **25th percentile**); 50 percent of the data values are below the **second quartile** (also called the **50th percentile),** which is the same as the median; and 75 percent of the data values are below the **third quartile** (also called the **75th percentile**).

For a set of data, the **5-number summary** consists of the minimum value (Min), the first quartile (Q_1), the median, the third quartile (Q_3), and the maximum value (Max) of the data set. A **box-and-whiskers plot** is a graphical representation of the 5-number summary for a data set.

Here is an example.

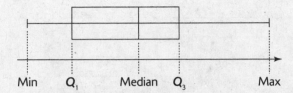

A data set can be described in terms of the skewness of its distribution. **Skewness** describes the "lopsidedness" of the distribution. A distribution that is **symmetric** has no skew. A distribution that has a longer tail to the right is **positively skewed.** A distribution that has a longer tail to the left is **negatively skewed.** In a positively skewed distribution, the mean lies to the right of the median. In a negatively skewed distribution, the mean lies to the left of the median. The mean and median coincide for a symmetric distribution (no skew).

Here are examples.

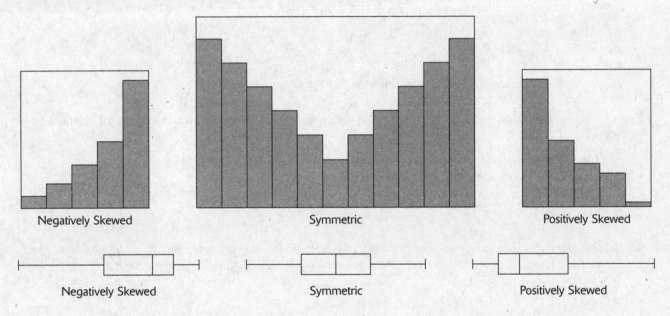

Sample Exercises

Scores of 65 Tenth-Graders on a Basic Arithmetic Skills Assessment

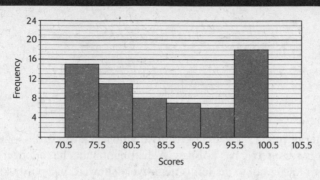

1. The histogram shows the distribution of scores of 65 tenth-graders on a basic arithmetic assessment. Assuming the scores on the assessment are recorded as whole numbers, what percent of the tenth-graders scored below 80.5?

   A. 26%
   B. 40%
   C. 60%
   D. It cannot be determined from the information given in the graph.

2. For which of the following data sets is the median clearly preferred over the mean as a measure of central tendency?

   A. The data set contains outliers.
   B. The data set has a somewhat symmetrical distribution.
   C. The data values are numerical.
   D. The data set has no outliers.

3. Jude has participated in eight track meets so far this season. His running times for the 400-meter race have been 73, 63, 68, 64, 69, 61, 66, and 64 seconds. What is Jude's mean running time for the eight meets?

   A. 64 seconds
   B. 65 seconds
   C. 66 seconds
   D. 66.5 seconds

	Exam 1	Exam 2	Exam 3	Exam 4
Student's Grade	65	87	92	70
Class Mean	55	88	86	60
Class Standard Deviation	5	2	4	10

4. The data in the table show a student's scores on four exams in a college economics class along with the means and standard deviations of the 50 scores for all the students in the class? On which of the exams did the student perform best relative to the mean performance of the class?

    A. Exam 1

    B. Exam 2

    C. Exam 3

    D. Exam 4

5. Loy scored at the 84th percentile on a multiple-choice statistics exam. The best interpretation of this information is that

    A. Loy answered 84 percent of the questions on the test correctly.

    B. Only 16 percent of the other students did worse on the test than did Loy.

    C. Loy answered 84 questions correctly.

    D. Loy did as well or better than 84 percent of the students who took the exam.

Answer Explanations for Sample Exercises

1. **B.** Analyze the problem. The graph shows the number of students who scored in each interval. Devise a plan. To find the percent of students who scored below 80.5 will take two steps. First, find the number of students who scored below 80.5. Next, divide the result by 65, the total number of students, expressing the quotient as a percent. Carry out the plan.

   Step 1. Looking at the histogram, you see that $15 + 11 = 26$ students scored below 80.5.

   Step 2. $\frac{26}{65} = 0.4 = 40\ \%$, Choice B.

2. **A.** When a data set contains outliers, the median, which is not influenced by outliers, is the preferred alternative to the mean, Choice A. For the data sets in choices B and D, the mean is the preferred measure of central tendency. Not enough information is provided in Choice C to "clearly" prefer the median over the mean.

3. **C.** Method 1. The most efficient way to work this problem is to use the statistical features of your graphing calculator. For the TI-83, press **2nd STAT** to access the **LIST** menu. Select **MATH**, then press **3** to choose **3: mean (**. Enter the data inside braces and close the parentheses as shown here: **mean({73, 63, 68, 64, 69, 61, 66, 64})**. Press **ENTER**. The display will show 66, which is the mean, Choice C.

> **Tip: You should plan to use a graphing calculator when taking the test. However, make sure you practice using it so that you can access the features smoothly and efficiently.**

   Method 2. mean $= \dfrac{\text{the sum of the running times}}{\text{number of running times}} = \dfrac{73 + 63 + 68 + 64 + 69 + 61 + 66 + 64}{8} = \dfrac{528}{8} = 66$, Choice C.

4. **A.** Analyze the problem. The table shows the student's scores and the means and standard deviations of all the scores for the four exams. This information can be used to calculate z-scores. Devise a plan. A good way to compare the student's performance on the four exams relative to the mean performance of the class is to compute the student's z-score for each of the four exams. Carry out the plan.

   Exam 1: z-score $= \dfrac{\text{score} - \text{mean}}{\text{standard deviation}} = \dfrac{65 - 55}{5} = 2$. Therefore, the student scored 2 standard deviations above the class mean on Exam 1.

   Exam 2: z-score $= \dfrac{\text{score} - \text{mean}}{\text{standard deviation}} = \dfrac{87 - 88}{2} = -0.5$. Therefore, the student scored 0.5 standard deviation below the class mean on Exam 2.

   Exam 3: z-score $= \dfrac{\text{score} - \text{mean}}{\text{standard deviation}} = \dfrac{92 - 86}{4} = 1.5$. Therefore, the student scored 1.5 standard deviations above the class mean on Exam 3.

   Exam 4: z-score $= \dfrac{\text{score} - \text{mean}}{\text{standard deviation}} = \dfrac{70 - 60}{10} = 1$. Therefore, the student scored 1 standard deviation above the class mean on Exam 4.

   Since the student's z-score for Exam 1 is greater than any of the z-scores for the other exams, the student's best performance relative to the mean performance of the class was on Exam 1, Choice A.

5. **D.** The 84th percentile is a value at or below which 84 percent of the data fall. Therefore, the best interpretation of Loy's score is that she did as well or better than 84 percent of the students who took the exam, Choice D.

Discrete Mathematics

This chapter provides a review of the key ideas and formulas for discrete mathematics that are most important for you to know for the Praxis Middle School Mathematics test. Multiple-choice sample exercises, comparable to what might be presented on the Praxis Middle School Mathematics test, are given at the end of the chapter. The answer explanations for the sample exercises are provided immediately following.

Set Terminology

A **set** is a collection of items or objects. Uppercase letters, such as A and B, are used to name sets. The items in a set A are its **elements** or **members.** To show that x is an element of A, you write $x \in A$ (read "x is an element of set A"). If y is *not* an element of A, you write $y \notin A$. (Note that a diagonal slash through a symbol negates the original meaning of the symbol.) A set is defined by means of braces in which you describe the members of the set by a list, a verbal description, or mathematical symbolism. For instance, the set D of digits used in the base-ten place value system can be defined in the following ways: $D = \{0, 1, 2, 3, 4, 5, 6, 7, 8, 9\}$, $D = \{$digits used in the base-ten place value system$\}$, or $D = \{x \mid x$ is a whole number $< 10\}$. The third way is read "The set of all x such that x is a whole number less than 10." The vertical line, $\mid$, is read "such that." This latter way of describing a set is called **set builder notation.** The set that contains no items is called the **empty set** and is designated by the symbol $\varnothing$.

Sets need to be **well-defined.** This term means that if you are given a set, you can tell which objects belong in the set and which objects do not belong in the set. For instance, the set $I = \{$important people$\}$ is *not* well-defined because you are not given enough information to know who qualifies as an "important person;" on the other hand, the set $P = \{$Presidents of the United States who were elected before 2008$\}$ is well-defined because you can decide whether a given individual does or does not belong in P.

Two sets A and B are **equal,** written $A = B$, if and only if they contain *exactly* the same elements, without regard to the order in which the elements are listed in the two sets or whether elements are repeated. For instance, $\{1, 4, 8\} = \{1, 8, 4\} = \{4, 1, 8\} = \{4, 8, 1\} = \{8, 1, 4\} = \{8, 4, 1\}$ and $\{1, 4, 8\} = \{1, 1, 4, 4, 8, 8\}$.

A set A is a **subset** of set B, denoted $A \subseteq B$, if every element of A is an element of B. For example, $\{1, 4\} \subseteq \{1, 4, 8\}$. Additionally, if B contains at least one element that is not in A, then A is a **proper subset** of B, denoted $A \subset B$. Thus, $\{1, 4\} \subset \{1, 4, 8\}$. You can show two sets A and B are equal by showing that $A \subseteq B$ and $B \subseteq A$. Also, we will state without proof that the empty set is a subset of every set.

> **Tip:** Do not confuse the relationship "is an element of" with the relationship "is a subset of." For instance, $4 \in \{1, 4, 8\}$, but $\{4\} \notin \{1, 4, 8\}$; on the other hand, $\{4\} \subseteq \{1, 4, 8\}$, but $4 \not\subseteq \{1, 4, 8\}$.

The **cardinality** (or **cardinal number**) of a set A is the number of distinct elements in A. The cardinality of a set can be **finite,** meaning the set has a definite number of elements that can be counted, or **infinite,** meaning the set has an unlimited number of elements. Throughout this book, the cardinality of a finite set A will be denoted $n(A)$. For instance, if $A = \{1, 4, 8\}$, $n(A) = 3$. Note that you do not include duplications when listing the elements of a set.

Basic Set Operations and Venn Diagrams

If in a discussion all the sets under consideration are subsets of a given set U, then U is the **universal set of discourse,** or simply, **the universal set.** In this section assume that all sets under consideration are subsets of a given universal set U.

The three basic operations for sets are union, intersection, and complement.

The **union** of two sets A and B, denoted, $A \cup B$, is the set of all elements that are in A or in B or in both. In set-builder notation, $A \cup B = \{x \mid x \in A \text{ or } x \in B\}$. For instance, if $A = \{2, 4, 6, 8\}$ and $B = \{1, 2, 4, 5, 6\}$, then $A \cup B = \{1, 2, 4, 5, 6, 8\}$. Notice that when you form the union of two sets, you do not list an element more than once because it is unnecessary to do so. Note also that the word *or* is used in the *inclusive* sense; that is, *or* means "one or the other, or possibly both at the same time."

The **intersection** of two sets A and B, denoted, $A \cap B$, is the set of all elements that are both in A and in B; that is, the elements that are common to both sets. In set-builder notation, $A \cap B = \{x \mid x \in A \text{ and } x \in B\}$. For instance, if $A = \{2, 4, 6, 8\}$ and $B = \{1, 2, 4, 5, 6\}$, then $A \cap B = \{2, 4, 6\}$. When two sets have no elements in common, their intersection is the empty set, and the sets are said to be **disjoint.** For instance, for $A = \{2, 4, 6, 8\}$ and $C = \{1, 3, 5\}$, $A \cap C = \varnothing$, and A and C are disjoint.

The **complement** of a set A, denoted $\overline{A}$ (or A^C), is the set of all elements in the universal set U that are *not* in A. In set-builder notation, $\overline{A} = \{x \mid x \in U, x \notin A\}$. For example, If $U = \{x \mid x \text{ is a counting number} \leq 10\}$ and $A = \{2, 4, 6, 8\}$, then $\overline{A} = \{1, 3, 5, 7, 9, 10\}$.

A **Venn diagram** is a visual depiction of a set operation or relationship. In a Venn diagram the universal set is usually represented by a rectangular region, which encloses everything else in the diagram. The sets in U are represented by circles. Shading is used to depict the results of a set operation. Here are examples of Venn diagrams.

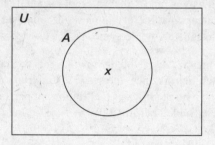

$x \in A$

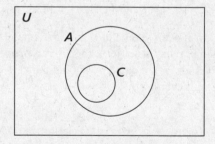

$C \subset A$

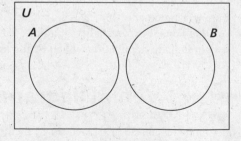

$A \cap B = \varnothing$

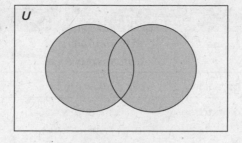

$$A \cup B = \varnothing$$

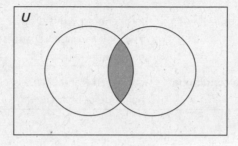

$$A \cap B$$

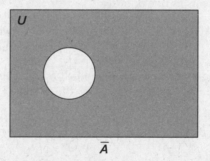

$$\overline{A}$$

Basic Concepts of Logic

A **statement** (or **proposition**) is a declarative sentence that meaningfully can be assigned a **truth value** of either true or false. For instance, "The sum of 1 and 2 is 3" is a statement whose truth value is true, but "The sum of 1 and 2 is 5" is a statement whose truth value is false. Other examples of statements are "It is raining," "The moon is made of green cheese," and "The number $\frac{1}{2}$ is a fraction." The following examples are *not* statements because their truth values cannot be determined without further specification: "She is married," "The number x is irrational," and "The set A is a subset of the set B." Sentences that are questions (for example, "What is your name?) or commands (for example, Come here.") are *not* statements because they cannot be classified as either true or false. Commonly, single letters (either lower- or uppercase) are used to designate statements.

Simple statements are statements that are simple declarative sentences. Five basic **logical connectives** can be used to construct **compound statements** from simple statements. The resulting compound statements have special names. Given the simple statements P and Q, the following table summarizes compound statements constructed from P and Q.

Compound Statements				
Logical Connective	**Compound Statement**	**Name**	**This compound statement is true . . .**	**This compound statement is false . . .**
not	not P	**negation**	if and only if P is false.	if and only if P is true.
or	P or Q	**disjunction**	if either P is true, or Q is true, or both are true.	only if both P and Q are false.
and	P and Q	**conjunction**	only if both P and Q are true.	if either P is false, or Q is false, or both are false.
If . . . , then . . .	If P, then Q	**conditional**	if either both P and Q are true, or if P is false (regardless of the truth value of Q)	only when P is true and Q is false.
if and only if	P if and only Q	**biconditional**	only when P and Q are either both true or both false.	only when P and Q have opposite truth values.

Here are examples.

> Given P = "1 + 2 = 3," Q = "4 is an even number," R = "1 + 2 = 5," and S = "4 is an odd number," classify each of the following compound statements as true or false.

(1) P and Q. Answer: P is true, and Q is true, so "P and Q" is true.

(2) not R. Answer: R is false, so "not R" is true.

(3) P or S. Answer: P is true, and S is false, so "P or S" is true.

(4) If R then Q. Answer: R is false, so "If R, then Q" is true.

(5) R or S. Answer: R is false, and S is false, so R or S is false.

(6) If P then S. Answer: P is true, and S is false, so "If P, then S" is false.

(7) P and S. Answer: P is true, and S is false, so "P and S" is false.

(8) (not P) or Q. Answer: "not P" is false, and Q is true, so "(not P) or Q" is true.

A **tautology** is a compound statement that is always true regardless of the truth value combinations of the simple statements from which it is constructed. A **contradiction** is a compound statement that is always false regardless of the truth value combinations of the simple statements from which it is constructed. For example, the statement, "P or not P" is a tautology; but the statement, "P and not P" is a contradiction.

Tautologies that are biconditional statements are **logical equivalences.** That is to say, when a biconditional statement is a tautology, the statement on the left of "if and only if" is **logically equivalent** to the statement on the right of "if and only if." In other words, from a logical standpoint, the two statements have exactly the same meaning.

Statements Associated with a Conditional Statement

Associated with any conditional statement, "**If P, then Q,**" are three other conditional statements: the converse, the inverse, and the contrapositive. The **converse** is the statement, "**If Q, then P.**" The **inverse** is the statement, "**If not P, then not Q.**" The **contrapositive** is the statement, "**If not Q, then not P.**" A conditional statement is *not* logically equivalent to either its converse or to its inverse; however, **a conditional statement and its contrapositive are logically equivalent.** In other words, a contrapositive and the conditional from which it is derived have exactly the same meaning.

Here is an example of a conditional statement and its converse, inverse, and contrapositive, along with an explanation of the truth value of each.

Conditional: If a geometric shape is a square, then it is a polygon. True, because all squares are polygons.

Converse: If a geometric shape is a polygon, then it is a square. False, because the shape could be a polygon that is not a square such as a trapezoid, hexagon, or so on.

Inverse: If a geometric shape is not a square, then it is not a polygon. False, because there are geometric shapes (for example, triangles) that are not squares but are polygons.

Contrapositive: If a geometric shape is not a polygon, then it is not a square. True, because there are no squares that are not polygons.

Conditional statements are used extensively in mathematics. Some ways you can express that the statement, "If P, then Q" is true are the following:

"If P is true, then Q is also true;" "Q is true, if P is true;" "P is true implies Q is true;" "Q is true whenever P is true;" "P is true only if Q is also true;" "For Q to be true, it is sufficient that P is true;" "For P to be true, it is necessary that Q is true."

Quantifiers and Negation

Quantifiers are phrases that include words such as *all, every, no, some, at least one, there exists,* and *there is at least one.* Quantifiers are used in statements to clarify the generality or existence of the objects in the statements relative to the universe of discourse. For example, suppose that the universe of discourse is the set of polygons, P, then the quantifier, *All,* in the statement, "All squares are rectangles," signifies that, for the statement to be true, it must be true for each and every square $\in P$, no exceptions. In contrast, the quantifier, *Some,* in the statement, "Some rectangles are squares," signifies that, for the statement to be true, there must be at least one rectangle $\in P$ that is a square.

When a quantifier signals that for a statement to be true, *all* objects in the universe of discourse must make the statement true, the quantifier is a **universal quantifier,** symbolized by $\forall$. When a quantifier signals that for a statement to be true, there must *exist at least one* object in the universe of discourse that makes the statement true, the quantifier is an **existential quantifier,** symbolized by $\exists$.

> **Tip:** To help you remember the symbols for the quantifiers, notice that the symbol $\forall$ looks like an inverted uppercase A (for *all*), and the symbol $\exists$ looks like a backward uppercase E (for *exists*).

The following table classifies common phrases as universal or existential quantifiers.

Quantifiers	
Universal Quantifiers, symbolized by $\forall$	*Existential Quantifiers, symbolized by $\exists$*
all, for all, every, for every, each, for each, everything, no, nothing, not any, not all, none of these	some, for some, at least one, there exists at least one, there is at least one, there is, there are, something

Here are examples.

All flowers are plants. (universal)

Some flowers are roses. (existential)

You should be aware that it is common for statements to omit quantifiers when the meaning is clear and the universal set is obvious. For instance, the statement, "Triangles are polygons," means "All triangles are polygons." Also, a quantifier might be disguised as another phrase. For instance, the phrases, "If x" and "whenever x" are denoted symbolically as: $\forall x$. Be on the alert for such hidden quantifiers.

Negating statements involving quantifiers can be a challenge. Use the following convention:

> To negate a statement that involves a universal quantifier, use an existential quantifier in a statement that contradicts the original statement.

> To negate a statement that involves an existential quantifier, use a universal quantifier in a statement that contradicts the original statement.

Four important forms involving quantifiers that you should be able to negate with an example of each are shown here.

Important Statement Forms			
Statement Form	*Negation of Statement Form*	*Example Statement*	*Negation of Example Statement*
All As are Bs.	Some As are not Bs.	All polygons are squares.	Some polygons are not squares.
Some As are Bs.	No As are Bs.	Some triangles are right triangles.	No triangles are right triangles.
No As are Bs.	Some As are Bs	No real numbers are rational.	Some real numbers are rational.
Some As are not Bs.	All As are Bs.	Some primes are not odd.	All primes are odd.

The four statement forms are illustrated in the following Venn diagrams.

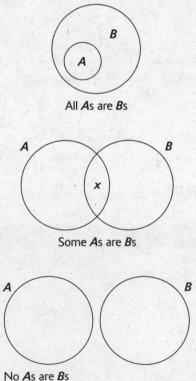

All As are Bs

Some As are Bs

No As are Bs

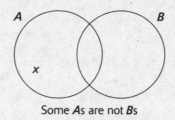

Some *A*s are not *B*s

Counting Techniques

The **Fundamental Counting Principle** states that if one event can occur in any one of *m* ways, and, after it has occurred, a second event can occur in any one of *n* ways, then the first event *and* the second event can both occur, in the order given, in *m* · *n* ways. This principle can be extended to any number of events. Note that *this counting technique produces results in which order determines different outcomes.* Here are examples.

How many different 10-digit telephone numbers begin with area code 936 and prefix 569?

Four additional digits are needed to complete telephone numbers that begin (936) 569-. Therefore, in this problem, there are four events, namely, determining each of the four digits. You can think of each of the positions of the four digits as a slot to fill. In this example, you make your selection for each slot from the same set, the digits zero to nine. Since digits in a telephone number can repeat, we say that "repetitions are allowed." There are 10 ways to fill the first slot, 10 ways to fill the second slot, 10 ways to fill the third slot, and 10 ways to fill the fourth slot; so, the total number of different telephone numbers that begin (936) 569- is 10 · 10 · 10 · 10 = 10,000.

In how many possible ways can a president, vice-president, secretary, and membership chairperson be selected from 25 members of a club if all members are eligible for each position and no member can hold more than one office?

In this problem, there are four events, namely, selecting each of the four officers. You can think of each of the officer positions as a slot to fill. Since the officers must all be different, repetitions are not allowed in the selection process. There are 25 ways to fill the president's slot; after that, there are 24 ways remaining to fill the vice-president's slot; after that, there are 23 ways remaining to fill the secretary's slot; and, finally, there are 22 ways remaining to fill the membership chairperson's slot. Thus, there are 25 · 24 · 23 · 22 = 303,600 possible ways to select a president, vice-president, secretary, and membership chairperson from the 25 members of the club.

The **Addition Principle** states that if one task can be done in any one of *m* ways and a second task can be done in any one of *n* ways and if the two tasks *cannot* be done at the same time, then the number of ways to do the first *or* the second task is *m* + *n* ways. This principle can be extended to more than one task. Here is an example.

A student must select one elective from a list of 3 art classes, 10 kinesiology classes, and 2 music classes. How many possible classes are there to choose from?

The student can choose an elective from the art classes in 3 ways, from the kinesiology classes in 10 ways, and from the music classes in 2 ways. Therefore, there are 3 + 10 + 2 = 15 classes from which to choose.

The Addition Principle can be modified in the following way for situations in which two tasks overlap; that is, when the two tasks can be done at the same time: If one task can be done in any one of *m* ways and a second task can be done in any one of *n* ways and if the two tasks *can* be done at the same time, then the number of ways to do the first or the second task is *m* + *n* − (the number of ways the two tasks can be done at the same time). Here is an example.

A person selects one card at random from a standard deck of 52 playing cards. In how many ways can a king or a diamond be selected? (See the section "Conditional Probability and Independent and Dependent Events" in the chapter titled "Probability" for a display of a standard deck of 52 playing cards.)

There are 4 ways to select a king, 13 ways to select a diamond, and 1 way to select a king and a diamond at the same time (the king of diamonds). Therefore, there are $4 + 13 - 1 = 16$ ways to select a king or a diamond.

A **permutation** is an ordered arrangement of a set of distinct items. That is, when the order in which you make a selection for an arrangement of items determines different outcomes, the arrangement is a permutation of the items. The number of permutations of n distinct items is $n! = n \cdot (n-1) \cdot (n-2) \cdot \cdots \cdot 3 \cdot 2 \cdot 1$. Note: The notation $n!$ is read "n factorial." By definition $0! = 1$. Here is an example.

In how many different ways can five people be seated in a row of five seats?

You can work this problem using the Fundamental Counting Principle, or you can recognize that the seating arrangement is the permutation of five distinct items (persons). Thus, there are $5! = 5 \cdot 4 \cdot 3 \cdot 2 \cdot 1 = 120$ ways for the people to be seated.

Tip: For the TI-83, the factorial function is item 4 under PRB in the MATH menu.

The number of permutations of r items selected from n distinct items is ${}_nP_r = \dfrac{n!}{(n-r)!}$. It is important when you apply the formula ${}_nP_r$, that you make sure the following conditions are met: the n items must be n *distinct* items, the r items must be selected *without repetition* from the same set, and you must count different orderings of the same items as *different* outcomes. Here is an example.

In how many possible ways can a president, vice-president, secretary, and membership chairperson be selected from 25 members of a club if all members are eligible for each position and no member can hold more than one office?

You can work this problem using the Fundamental Counting Principle, or you can recognize that this problem satisfies the conditions for a permutation; that is, the 25 members of the club are distinct, the four officers are selected without repetition from the same set of 25 members, and different orderings of the same people are counted as a different slate of officers. Thus, the number of permutations of 4 items selected from 25 items is ${}_{25}P_4 = \dfrac{25!}{(25-4)!} = \dfrac{25!}{(21)!} =$

$\dfrac{25 \cdot 24 \cdot 23 \cdot 22 \cdot 21!}{21!} = 25 \cdot 24 \cdot 23 \cdot 22 = 303{,}600$ possible ways to select a president, vice-president, secretary, and

membership chairperson from the 25 members of the club.

Tip: You can use your graphing calculator to compute ${}_nP_r$. For the TI-83, the ${}_nP_r$ function is item 2 under PRB in the MATH menu.

A **combination** is an arrangement of a set of distinct items in which different orderings of the same items are considered to be the same. That is, when the order in which you make a selection for an arrangement of items does *not* determine different outcomes, the arrangement is a combination of the items. The number of combinations of r items selected from n distinct items is ${}_nC_r = \dfrac{n!}{r!(n-r)!}$. *Note:* The notation ${}_nC_r$ is also written $\begin{pmatrix} n \\ r \end{pmatrix}$. It is important when you apply the formula ${}_nC_r$ that you make sure the following conditions are met: the n items must be n *different* items; the r items must be selected *without repetition* from the same set; and you must consider different orderings of the same items to be *the same*. Here is an example.

How many ways can a four-member committee be formed from the 25 members of a club?

Since the order in which committee members are selected does not change the makeup of the committee, you would *not* try to work this problem using the Fundamental Counting Principle because it produces results in which order determines different outcomes. This example satisfies the conditions for a combination; that is, the 25 members of the club are distinct, the four committee members are selected without repetition from the same set of 25 members, and different orderings of the same people are counted as the same committee. Thus, the number of combinations of 4 items selected from 25 items is $_{25}C_4 = \dfrac{25!}{4!(25-4)!} = \dfrac{25!}{4!(21)!} = \dfrac{25 \cdot 24 \cdot 23 \cdot 22 \cdot 21!}{4!21!} = \dfrac{25 \cdot 24 \cdot 23 \cdot 22}{4 \cdot 3 \cdot 2 \cdot 1} = 12{,}650$ possible ways to form a four-member committee from the 25 members of the club.

> **Tip:** You can use your graphing calculator to compute $_nC_r$. For the TI-83, the $_nC_r$ function is item 3 under PRB in the MATH menu.

As you can see the one important way that combinations and permutations differ is that different orderings of the same items are counted as separate results for permutation problems, but not for combination problems. The following table categorizes some situations as (most likely) indicating either a permutation or combination problem.

Permutations	*Combinations*
creating passwords, license plates, words, or codes; assigning roles; filling positions; making ordered arrangements of things (people, books, colors, and so on), selecting first, second, third place, and such; distributing items among several objects or people; and similar situations.	forming a committee; making a collection of things (coins, books, and so on); counting subsets of a set; dealing hands from a deck of cards; listing the combinations from a set of items; selecting questions from a test; selecting students for groups; and similar situations.

For the Praxis Middle School Mathematics test, you should be able to work most, if not all, the permutation problems you might encounter by using the Fundamental Counting Principle rather than the formula $_nP_r$. For the situations similar to those given for combinations in the table, you will need to use $_nC_r$. You can compute $_nC_r$ by working out the formula, by using your graphing calculator, or by using the method shown in the following section.

Pascal's Triangle and $\begin{pmatrix} n \\ r \end{pmatrix}$

Pascal's triangle is a triangular array of numbers that can be derived from the formula $_nC_r$. Row 0, the top row, of the triangle has one element; Row 1, the next row, has two elements; Row 2 has three elements; Row 3 has four elements; and so on. Each row begins and ends with a one and is symmetric from left to right, including Row 1, whose one element is 1. An element, other than a 1, in a row is the sum of the two elements most directly above it. Here is an example of Pascal's triangle showing Row 0 through Row 8.

```
0:                          1
1:                       1    1
2:                    1    2    1
3:                 1    3    3    1
4:              1    4    6    4    1
5:           1    5   10   10    5    1
6:        1    6   15   20   15    6    1
7:     1    7   21   35   35   21    7    1
8: 1    8   28   56   70   56   28    8    1
```

For any row n in Pascal's triangle, the elements are the numbers $\begin{pmatrix} n \\ r \end{pmatrix}$ for $r = 0, \ldots, n$, in this order. These numbers also are the coefficients, called the **binomial coefficients**, in the expansion of $(x + y)^n$. For instance, the elements in row 3 of Pascal's triangle are $\begin{pmatrix} 3 \\ 0 \end{pmatrix} = 1$, $\begin{pmatrix} 3 \\ 1 \end{pmatrix} = 3$, $\begin{pmatrix} 3 \\ 2 \end{pmatrix} = 3$, and $\begin{pmatrix} 3 \\ 3 \end{pmatrix} = 1$. When you expand $(x + y)^3$, you obtain $x^3 + 3x^2y + 3xy^2 + y^3$, which has coefficients **1, 3, 3, 1**, the same numbers that are in Row 3 of Pascal's triangle.

If you find it convenient, you can use Pascal's triangle to find values of $\begin{pmatrix} n \\ r \end{pmatrix}$, rather than working out the formula or using

a graphing calculator. For instance, if you want to compute $\begin{pmatrix} 6 \\ 2 \end{pmatrix}$, locate the third term in Row 6 of Pascal's triangle, which is 15.

Tip: Keep in mind that for each row in Pascal's triangle, $\begin{pmatrix} n \\ r \end{pmatrix}$ starts at $r = 0$, not 1.

Sequences

A **sequence** is a function whose domain is a subset of the integers, usually the natural numbers $N = \{1, 2, 3, \ldots\}$ or the whole numbers $W = \{0, 1, 2, \ldots\}$. (For this section, sequences are restricted, without loss of generality, to domains equal to N.) The notation a_n denotes the image of the integer n; that is, a_n is the **nth term** (or **element**) of the sequence. The **initial term** of the sequence is denoted a_1. When a_n can be expressed as a formula that can be used to generate any term of the sequence, it is conventional to call a_n the **general term** of the sequence. Even though a sequence is a function (a set of ordered pairs), it is customary to describe a sequence by listing the terms in the order in which they correspond to the natural numbers. For example, the list of terms of the sequence with initial term a_1 is $a_1, a_2, a_3, a_4, \ldots, a_n, \ldots$.

An **arithmetic sequence** (also called **arithmetic progression**) is a sequence of the form $a_1, a_1 + d, a_1 + 2d, \ldots, a_1 + (n - 1)d, \ldots$, where a_1 is the **initial term**, d is the **common difference** between terms, and $a_n = a_1 + (n - 1)d$ is the **general term**. Here is an example.

The arithmetic sequence with initial term $a_1 = -2$ and common difference $= 4$ has general term $-2 + 4(n - 1)$. The list of terms, starting with the term corresponding to $n = 1$ are $-2 + 4(1 - 1), -2 + 4(2 - 1), -2 + 4(3 - 1), -2 + 4(4 - 1), \ldots = -2 + 4(0), -2 + 4(1), -2 + 4(2), -2 + 4(3), \ldots = -2, -2 + 4, -2 + 8, -2 + 12, \ldots = -2, 2, 6, 10, \ldots$.

A **geometric sequence** (also called **geometric progression**) is a sequence of the form $a_1, a_1r, a_1r^2, \ldots, a_1r^{n-1}, \ldots$, where a_1 is the **initial term**, r is the **common ratio** between terms, and $a_n = a_1r^{n-1}$ is the **general term**. Here is an example.

The geometric sequence with initial term $a_1 = -1$ and common ratio $= 2$ has general term $(-1)2^{n-1}$. The list of terms, starting with the term corresponding to $n = 1$ are $(-1)2^{1-1}, (-1)2^{2-1}, (-1)2^{3-1}, (-1)2^{4-1}, \ldots = (-1)2^0, (-1)2^1, (-1)2^2, (-1)2^3, \ldots = -1(1), -1(2), -1(4), -1(8), \ldots = -1, -2, -4, -8, \ldots$.

Some sequences consist of numbers called **figurate numbers** because they can be displayed as geometric shapes. Here is an example of a sequence of **triangular numbers**. The nth term is $1 + 2 + 3 + + (n - 1) + n$.

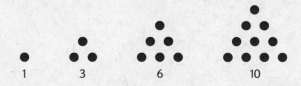

Here is an example of a sequence of **square numbers.** The nth term is n^2.

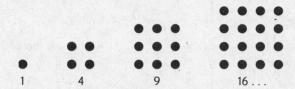

A **recursive definition** for a sequence is a definition that includes the value of one or more initial terms of the sequence and a formula that tells you how to find each term from previous terms. Here is an example.

List the first four terms of the sequence defined as follows: $f(1) = 1, f(n) = 3f(n-1) + 1$ for $n \geq 2$.

For the recursive formula given in the problem, you will need to find the previous term before you can find the next term. You proceed as shown here.

$f(1) = 1; f(2) = 3f(1) + 1 = 3(1) + 1 = 3 + 1 = 4; f(3) = 3f(2) + 1 = 3(4) + 1 = 12 + 1 = 13; f(4) = 3f(3) + 1 = 3(13) + 1 = 39 + 1 = 40$; thus, the first four terms are 1, 4, 13, and 40.

The **Fibonacci sequence** is defined by the recursive definition: $a_1 = 1, a_2 = 1$, and $a_n = a_{n-1} + a_{n-2}, n \geq 3$. A list showing its first seven terms is 1, 1, 2, 3, 5, 8, 13, ...

For the Praxis Middle School Mathematics test, you might be asked to determine the general term or the next term of a sequence when a few terms of the sequence are given. Even though, in reality, the initial terms do not necessarily determine a unique sequence, you will have to assume there is a pattern that continues in the same manner, and then you can make an educated guess about the general term or the next term. Here are some guidelines.

Look for an identifiable pattern such as:

Arithmetic: $a_1 + (n-1)d$ (Is there a common difference?)

Geometric: $a_1 r^{n-1}$ (Is there a common ratio?)

Figurate: n^2 or $1 + 2 + 3 + + (n-1) + \ldots + n$ (Are the terms perfect squares or triangular numbers?)

Quadratic: $n^2 \pm c$ or $kn^2 \pm c$ (Are the terms perfect squares or a multiple of perfect squares plus or minus a constant?)

Cubic: $n^3 \pm c$ or $kn^3 \pm c$ (Are the terms perfect cubes or a multiple of perfect cubes plus or minus a constant?)

Exponential: $2^n \pm c, 3^n \pm c, k2^n \pm c$, or $k3^n \pm c$ (Are the terms powers of 2 or 3 or a multiple of powers of 2 or 3 plus or minus a constant?)

Factorial: $n!$ (Are the terms obtained by multiplying the previous terms in some way?)

Recursive: $a_n = a_{n-1} \pm a_{n-2}$ (Are the terms obtained by adding or subtracting the previous terms in some way?).

Here are examples.

Find the 20th term in the sequence 2, 5, 8, 11, 14, ...

The terms shown have a common difference of 3 with initial term $a_1 = 2$. If this pattern continues in the same manner, the general term is $a_1 + (n-1)d = 2 + 3(n-1)$. Thus, the 20th term is $2 + 3(20-1) = 2 + 3(19) = 59$.

Find the 10th term in the sequence 2, 6, 18, 54, 162, ...

The terms shown have a common ratio of 3 with initial term $a_1 = 2$. If this pattern continues in the same manner, the general term is $a_1 r^{n-1} = 2 \cdot 3^{n-1}$. Thus, the 10th term is $2 \cdot 3^{10-1} = 2 \cdot 3^9 = 39{,}366$.

Find the 8th term in the sequence 2, 5, 10, 17, 26, ...

The terms shown can be rewritten as $1^2 + 1$, $2^2 + 1$, $3^2 + 1$, $4^2 + 1$, $5^2 + 1$, ... If this pattern continues in the same manner, the general term is $n^2 + 1$. Thus, the 8th term is $8^2 + 1 = 64 + 1 = 65$.

Tip: Sometimes it is convenient to begin an arithmetic or geometric sequence at $n = 0$ instead of $n = 1$, so be sure to check for the starting value of n when you work problems involving sequences on the Praxis Middle School Mathematics test.

Graph Terminology

A **graph** (or **vertex-edge graph**) is a discrete structure consisting of a nonempty, finite set of **vertices** and a set of **edges** connecting these vertices. Two vertices are **adjacent** if there is an edge in the graph that connects them. The edge between two vertices is said to be **incident** to the vertices. The **degree of a vertex** is the number of edges that are incident to that vertex. Graphs are commonly used to model and solve problems involving optimal situations for networks, paths, schedules, and relationships among finitely many objects. The following figure is a graph with six vertices and seven edges.

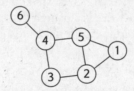

The sum of the degrees of the vertices of a graph that has k edges is the even number $2k$. Therefore, there are no graphs with an odd number of vertices of odd degree.

A **simple graph** is a graph in which each distinct pair of vertices is connected by a single edge (no parallel edges) and no edge connects a vertex to itself (no loops).

A **complete graph** is a simple graph in which every distinct pair of vertices are adjacent; that is, each vertex is connected to every other vertex. Here is an illustration.

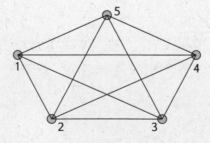

A **path** in a graph is a sequence of vertices such that from each of its vertices there is an edge to the next vertex. A **simple path** is a path in which no edge is repeated.

A graph is **connected** if there is a path between each pair of vertices.

A **circuit** is a path that begins and ends at the same vertex. A **simple circuit** is a circuit in which no edge is repeated.

A **tree** is a connected graph that contains no simple circuits. In a tree with n vertices, there are exactly $n - 1$ edges. Here is an example of a tree graph that has six vertices and five edges.

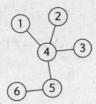

An **adjacency matrix** is a convenient way to specify the information in a graph, provided the graph has no parallel edges (multiple edges). The adjacency matrix is a square $n \times n$ array of numbers, where n is the number of vertices in the graph. There is one column and one row for each vertex. Each entry in the matrix is either a 1 or 0. If vertex v_i and v_j are connected by an edge, a 1 is recorded in the ith row and jth column of the matrix; otherwise a 0 is recorded there. Since the vertices of the graph do not have to be listed in a specific order, the adjacency matrix for a particular graph is not unique.

Here is an example of a graph and an adjacency matrix that represents the graph when the vertices are in the order a, b, c, and d.

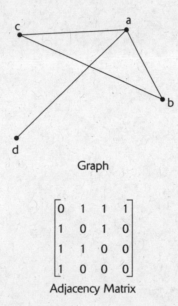

Graph

$$\begin{bmatrix} 0 & 1 & 1 & 1 \\ 1 & 0 & 1 & 0 \\ 1 & 1 & 0 & 0 \\ 1 & 0 & 0 & 0 \end{bmatrix}$$

Adjacency Matrix

Euler and Hamiltonian Paths

An **Euler path** in a graph is a path that uses each edge exactly once. A graph that has only vertices of even degree or a graph that has *exactly* two vertices of odd degree will have an Euler path. When a graph has *exactly* two vertices of odd degree, its Euler path must begin on one of those vertices. Furthermore, there is no Euler path for a graph that has more than two vertices of odd degree. Here are examples of two graphs that have Euler paths. Graph 1 has only vertices of even degree, and Graph 2 has exactly two vertices of odd degree.

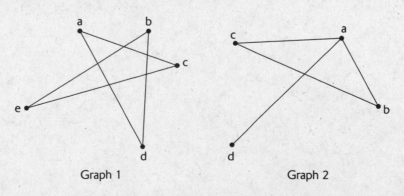

Graph 1   Graph 2

In Graph 1 shown, the path a, d, b, e, c, a is an Euler path. In Graph 2, the path a, b, c, a, d is an Euler path.

A **Hamiltonian path** in a graph is a path that uses each vertex exactly once. It does not have to use every edge of the graph. In a Hamiltonian path each vertex must be incident with at least two edges. In the graph shown, the path a, b, c, d is a Hamiltonian path.

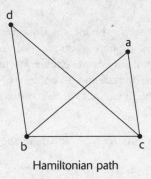

Hamiltonian path

Sample Exercises

1. Let the universal set $U = \{$whole numbers $\leq 10\}$, $A = \{x \in U \mid x$ is odd$\}$, $B = \{x \in U \mid x$ is prime$\}$, find $A \cap B$.

   A. $\{3, 5, 7\}$
   B. $\{2, 3, 5, 7\}$
   C. $\{1, 2, 3, 5, 7\}$
   D. $\{1, 2, 3, 5, 7, 9\}$

2. Which of the following statements is logically equivalent to the statement, "If it is snowing, then the air is cold"?

   A. If the air is cold, then it is snowing.
   B. If it is not snowing, then the air is not cold.
   C. If the air is not cold, then it is not snowing.
   D. The air is not cold, if it is not snowing.

3. What is the negation of the following statement: "All swans are white"?

   A. Some swans are white.
   B. Some swans are not white.
   C. No swan is white.
   D. No swan is not white.

4. How many different passwords for an online account can be made consisting of four letters followed by two digits, if the account login is not case sensitive?

   A. $4 \cdot 2$
   B. $_{26}C_4 \, _{10}C_2$
   C. $26^4 \cdot 10^2$
   D. 36^6

5. A civic club has 250 members. A committee of 3 members is to be selected to attend a national conference. How many different committees could be formed?

   A. $_{250}C_3$
   B. $_{250}P_3$
   C. 250^3
   D. $250!$

6. Given the recursive function defined by $f(1) = 1$ and $f(n) = 2f(n-1) + 1$ for $n \geq 2$, what is the value of $f(4)$?

   A. 3
   B. 7
   C. 15
   D. 31

7. Which of the following characteristics would prevent a graph with exactly six vertices from having an Euler path?

    A. The graph is connected.

    B. The graph has six even vertices.

    C. The graph has four even vertices and two odd vertices.

    D. The graph has two even vertices and four odd vertices.

Answer Explanations for Sample Exercises

1. A. Analyze the problem. The set $U = \{1, 2, 3, \ldots, 10\}$, the set $A = \{1, 3, 5, 7, 9\}$, the set $B = \{2, 3, 5, 7\}$. The intersection of A and B is the set of elements common to both. Thus, $A \cap B = \{3, 5, 7\}$, Choice A.

2. C. Analyze the problem. The given statement, "If it is snowing, then the air is cold," is a conditional statement. Only its contrapositive, "If the air is not cold, then it is not snowing," Choice C, is logically equivalent to the given statement.

3. B. Analyze the problem. The given statement, "All swans are white," contains a universal quantifier. You can eliminate choices C and D because the negation of a universal quantifier must contain an existential quantifier. To contradict that all swans are white, you need only show that there exists at least one swan that is not white. Thus, "Some swans are not white," Choice B, is the negation of the given statement.

4. C. Analyze the problem. Since there are six slots to be filled for a password, you can work this problem by extending the Fundamental Counting Principle to six events. There are 26 possibilities for each of the four letters and 10 possible values for each of the two digits. Thus, the total number of possible passwords is $26 \cdot 26 \cdot 26 \cdot 26 \cdot 10 \cdot 10 = 26^4 \cdot 10^2$, Choice C.

5. A. Since the order in which committee members are chosen does not make a difference as regards the composition of the committee, the number of different committees of size 3 that can be selected from the 250 members is $_{250}C_3$, Choice A.

6. C. For the recursive formula given in the problem, you will need to find $f(2)$ and $f(3)$ before you can find $f(4)$. Since the problem tells you that $f(1) = 1$ and that $f(n) = 2f(n-1) + 1$ for $n \geq 2$, then

$f(2) = 2f(1) + 1 = 2(1) + 1 = 2 + 1 = 3; f(3) = 2f(2) + 1 = 2(3) + 1 = 6 + 1 = 7; f(4) = 2f(3) + 1 = 2(7) + 1 = 14 + 1 = 15$, Choice C.

7. D. Analyze the problem. Since there is no Euler path for a graph that has more than two vertices of odd degree, Choice D is the correct response. None of the characteristics in the other answer choices would prevent the graph from having an Euler path.

Preparing for the Problem-Solving Exercises

The problem-solving exercises on the Praxis Middle Mathematics test consist of three equally-weighted constructed response questions. The purpose of this chapter is to help you prepare for these questions that require a created response. Sample problem-solving exercises, comparable to what might be presented on the Praxis Middle School Mathematics test, are given at the end of the chapter. The answer explanations for the sample problem-solving exercises are provided immediately following.

Achieving a Maximum Score on the Constructed Responses

ETS does not release the exact details of the way the Praxis Middle School Mathematics test is scored. According to *Mathematics: Middle School Mathematics (0069) Test at a Glance* (www.ets.org), the multiple-choice part of the test is weighted 67 percent of the total score, and the short constructed-response part of the test is weighted 33 percent of the total score. Each short constructed response receives a score of 0 to 3. To receive the highest rating of 3, you need to adhere to the following criteria:

- Correctly answer all parts of the question.
- Give a complete and full explanation for your answers.
- Demonstrate a strong understanding of the mathematical content relevant to the question.
- Demonstrate that you completely understand the most important aspects of any stimulus material provided.

According to ETS, a team of trained scorers will be scoring your response. To maximize your score from these individuals who will read your response and judge how well you meet the scoring criteria, you need to present your response in a way that is favorable to you. Here are some tips:

- Present your work in a logical manner that is easy to follow.
- Follow the instructions in the question. For example, if you are told explicitly to use a certain method, do not work the problem another way.
- Show your work. Don't leave out steps—less is NOT more. You want to make sure that the reader understands what you did.
- Use words to explain your work in detail. Don't expect the reader to fill in the blanks.
- When you are given stimulus material, state explicitly what you understand about it.
- Backup your work with explicit mathematical justification.
- Do not make assumptions that are not given in the problem.
- Do not make statements that you cannot justify or explain mathematically.
- When you use variables, state what they represent.
- Make your drawings and graphs as accurate as possible. Label parts. For coordinate grids, label the axes and mark your scales.
- Write or print legibly.
- If you have to erase, erase completely and shake off excess eraser dust. If you have to scratch out (in the interest of time, perhaps), do so neatly and in a way that does not make your work difficult to read.
- For certain problems, to help the readers identify your answers, you might underline or circle your answers in each part of a question that has multiple parts.
- Proofread your work when you finish the solution. Make sure that you don't have any missing words or symbols and that your symbols are written correctly. Double-check that you have answered *all* parts of the question.

Finally, ETS recommends that you plan to spend about 80 minutes on the multiple-choice questions and about 40 minutes on the constructed-response questions. However, the sections are not independently timed, so you can allocate your time as you want. Since the constructed-response section counts 33 percent of the test, you should allocate sufficient time to that section to produce a response for each question. We recommend that you allocate at least 45 minutes for the constructed responses. This strategy means that for the multiple-choice questions, you will have, on average, about $1\frac{7}{8}$ minutes for each multiple-choice question, instead of an average of 2 minutes as recommended by ETS; but it leaves you a full 15 minutes for each of the constructed-response questions.

When you start working on the constructed-response section, read all three of the questions first. You do not have to work the questions in the order presented. Start with the question that seems the easiest for you to answer; then go to the next question with which you are most comfortable; finish with the question that seems the hardest to you.

Tip: Make sure that you have a reliable watch with you, so that you can pace yourself during the test.

Using Reasoning Skills

When you are problem solving, you will use reasoning skills to arrive at answers or conclusions and to develop explanations or arguments for those answers or conclusions. Generally speaking, there are two basic ways of reasoning in problem solving: inductive reasoning and deductive reasoning.

Inductive reasoning moves from specific examples to general ideas. For example, you might use inductive reasoning to ascertain that the general term for a sequence that begins 1, 4, 9, 16, . . . and continues in this manner is n^2, where n is the position of the *nth* term in the sequence. Because inductive reasoning is based on examples, you evaluate your work in terms of its reasonableness and whether your answers or conclusions make sense and are supported by sound analysis of the examples.

Deductive reasoning begins with one or more general assertions or **premises,** which are basic assumptions or widely held principles, and applies these general statements in a logically sound manner to specific cases to arrive at answers or reach conclusions. For instance, if you know that the general term of a sequence is given by n^2, then you can use deductive reasoning to conclude that the 10th term is 10^2 or 100. When you use deductive reasoning, you evaluate your work based on the truth of the premises with which you began and the soundness of the logic you used to arrive at your answer or to reach a conclusion.

In some problem situations, you can find yourself using both types of reasoning. For instance, when you are trying to write an equation to solve a contextual (word) problem, you might use inductive reasoning to help you formulate the equation by looking at several examples using specific values for the unknown element or elements. After you formulate the equation, you could use deductive reasoning to solve it through a step-by-step logical process.

Organizing Problem Solving

For the Praxis Middle School Mathematics test, you will find it helpful to organize your problem solving using the following four-step process:

1. **Analyze the problem.** Read the problem and determine what it's asking. Look for words like *find, determine, what is, how many, how far, how much, write an equation,* and *prove.* Ask yourself: What content area (for example, arithmetic, algebra, geometry, and so forth) is the primary focus of the question? What prior knowledge do I have that relates to the problem? Have I solved a similar problem in the past? What facts do I know that apply to the situation? Is there a formula that I could use? Are measurements units involved, and, if so, can dimensional analysis help me figure out what to do? Would sketching a diagram (or marking on a diagram that's been given) help me better understand the problem?

Tip: Analyzing the problem is the most important step in problem solving. *Never* short-change this step or skip it.

2. **Devise a plan.** Decide how you can use the information you are given to determine a solution. Try to relate the current problem to problems you have solved in the past to help you decide what approach might work best. Some strategies to consider, *depending on the nature of the problem*, are to look for a pattern; make a table or chart; draw a picture or diagram; try one or more simpler versions of the problem and work your way up to the original problem; make a guess, test it to see whether you guessed the solution, and, if not, analyze your results to help you formulate a rule or equation that describes the problem situation; translate the information given into mathematical symbolism and write and solve an equation; and, when applicable, start with a final result and work backward to the beginning. Make sure that your plan will give you a solution that answers the question. In articulating your plan, be sure to include any intermediate steps along the way.

3. **Carry out the plan.** Work out the solution, using the plan you decided upon. Be careful to make sure that you copy all information accurately. Check the order of the numbers if subtraction or division is involved. Check the signs—especially if negative numbers are involved. Key numbers into your calculator carefully. Look at the display after every entry to make sure you entered what you intended to enter.

4. **Check your response.** Did you answer *all parts* of the question? Did you give a complete and full explanation for your answers? Are you confident that you demonstrated a strong understanding of the mathematical content relevant to the question? Are you convinced that you demonstrated that you completely understand the most important aspects of any stimulus material provided?

Here is an example of using the four-step problem-solving process.

A bank offers its customers two different plans for monthly charges on checking accounts. With Plan A, the account holder pays a fee of $0.15 per check processed during the month with no monthly service charge on the account. With Plan B, the account holder pays a $5.00 monthly service charge with a fee of $0.05 per check processed during the month.

(a) Write an equation that represents the monthly cost of the checking account for each plan. Define any variables that you use.

(b) Find the "break-even point" for the number of checks processed per month; that is, find the number of checks processed per month for which the costs of the two plans are equal.

(c) In the xy-coordinate system, graph the monthly cost (on the y-axis) *versus* the number of checks processed per month (on the x-axis) for each equation you wrote in part (a). Write a summary of what you can observe from the graphs about the relative merits of each plan.

Analyze the problem. The question has three parts: First, you must write equations that will model the two plans; next, you must find the break-even point for the two plans; and, finally, you must graph the two equations and discuss your observations. This problem asks you to apply your algebraic knowledge of writing, solving, and graphing equations. Each equation will have two variables: the number of checks processed per month and the monthly cost of the checking account. The break-even point occurs when the costs of the two plans are equal. Graphically, the break-even point is the point of intersection of the graphs of the two equations.

Devise a plan. To complete part (a), let x = the number of checks processed per month and then write an equation for the monthly cost y of each plan in terms of x. To complete part (b), set the costs of the two plans equal, and solve for x. This solution is the x-value for the break-even point. To complete part (c), graph the two equations and then verbally describe the information conveyed in the graph about the two plans.

Carry out the plan.

(a) Let x = the number of checks processed per month, and let y = the monthly cost of the checking account.

For Plan A, the monthly cost $y = \$0.15x$.

For Plan B, the monthly cost $y = \$0.05x + \$5.00$.

(b) To find the break-even point, set the costs of the two plans equal to each other and solve for x.

$0.15x = \$0.05x + \$5.00$

$0.10x = \$5.00$

$x = \dfrac{\$5.00}{\$0.10} = 50$ checks processed per month. The break-even point for the two plans occurs when the number of checks processed per month is 50 checks. Thus, when $x = 50$ checks processed per month, the monthly cost of Plan A equals the monthly cost of Plan B; that is, $y = \$0.15(50) = \$0.05(50) + \$5.00 = \$7.50$.

(c)

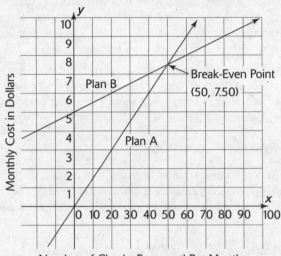

Number of Checks Processed Per Month

At the break-even point, the graphs of the Plan A and Plan B equations intersect. To the left of the break-even point, the graph of the Plan A equation is below the graph of the Plan B equation; and to the right of the break-even point, the graph of the Plan B equation is below the graph of the Plan A equation.

Therefore, if the customer expects to have less than 50 checks processed per month, then it would be more economical to choose Plan A. If the customer expects to have more than 50 checks processed per month, then it would be more economical to choose Plan B. If the customer expects to have exactly 50 checks processed per month, then the total monthly cost of the account would be $7.50 with either plan.

Check your response. Did you answer *all parts* of the question? ✓ Did you give a complete and full explanation for your answers? ✓ Are you confident that you demonstrated a strong understanding of the mathematical content relevant to the question? ✓ Are you convinced that you demonstrated that you completely understand the most important aspects of any stimulus material provided? ✓

Note: Steps 1 through 3 of this four-step problem solving process also will be helpful to you when you are given contextual problems in the multiple-choice section of the Praxis Middle School Mathematics test. For those problems, in Step 4, you should ask: Did I answer the question? Is my answer reasonable? Does my answer make sense? And, if applicable, are my units correct? Of course, for routine problems, after you analyze the problem, you might just work out the solution without going through the steps in a formal manner.

Note: The problem-solving process given in this section is based on a similar process presented in *How to Solve It*, which was written by George Polya in 1945.

Sample Problem-Solving Exercises

1. The **power set** of a set A, denoted $\wp(A)$, is the set containing all possible subsets of A including the empty subset and the set A itself. For example, the power set of the set $A = \{a, b, c\}$ is the set $\wp(A) = \{\varnothing, \{a\}, \{b\}, \{c\}, \{a, b\}, \{a, c\}, \{b, c\}, \{a, b, c\}\}$. Notice that $\wp(A)$ contains 1 set that has cardinality zero, namely, the empty set; 3 sets that have cardinality 1; 3 sets that have cardinality 2; and 1 set that has cardinality 3, namely, the set A itself.

   (a) Given set $B = \{a, b, c, d\}$, use your knowledge of Pascal's triangle to answer the following questions: In $\wp(B)$ how many subsets will have cardinality zero, how many will have cardinality 1, how many will have cardinality 2, how many will have cardinality 3, and how many will have cardinality 4? Show and explain how you arrived at your answers.

   (b) Use your knowledge of Pascal's triangle to answer the following question: For a set C that contains 6 elements, what is the cardinality of the power set $\wp(C)$? Show and explain how you arrived at your answer.

   (c) Use your knowledge of Pascal's triangle to answer the following question: If the cardinality of the power set $\wp(D)$ is 32, how many elements are in set D? Show and explain how you arrived at your answer.

2. Paul leaves his apartment at 7:00 A.M., and drives 315 miles to his parents' house. He stops only once during the trip. His average speed for the first 120 miles of the trip was 60 miles per hour. After driving 120 miles, Paul stops to have breakfast. After his stop, Paul drives an average speed of 65 miles per hour for the rest of the trip.

   (a) What was Paul's average speed for the 315-mile trip if the average speed is calculated *excluding* the time Paul spent having breakfast? Show your work.

   (b) What was Paul's average speed for the 315-mile trip if the average speed is calculated *including* the time Paul spent having breakfast? Show your work.

   (c) What time did Paul arrive at his parents' house? Show your work.

3. In a survey of 200 students, it was determined that 30 students are taking algebra, English, and sociology; 50 are taking algebra and English; 60 are taking algebra and sociology; 44 are taking English and sociology; 10 are taking only algebra; 8 are taking only English; and 12 are taking only sociology. If a student is chosen at random from the 200 students, what is the probability of each of the following?

   (a) The student is not taking any of the three courses. Show your work and explain your reasoning.

   (b) The student is taking both algebra and English, but not sociology. Show your work and explain your reasoning.

   (c) The student is taking algebra, given that the student is taking English. Show your work and explain your reasoning.

Sample Correct Constructed Responses for the Sample Problem-Solving Exercises

1. (a) The set $B = \{a, b, c, d\}$ has 4 elements. Since the order in which the elements are listed in a set does not determine a different set, the number of subsets of cardinality r (where $r = 0, 1, 2, 3,$ and 4) that can be created from a set of cardinality 4 is the number of combinations of r items selected from 4 distinct items, which has the formula $\binom{4}{r}$. Thus, the number of subsets of cardinality zero is $\binom{4}{0}$; the number of subsets of cardinality 1 is $\binom{4}{1}$; the number of subsets of cardinality 2 is $\binom{4}{2}$; the number of subsets of cardinality 3 is $\binom{4}{3}$; and the number of subsets of cardinality 4 is $\binom{4}{4}$.

These quantities can be evaluated using Pascal's triangle because for any row n in Pascal's triangle, the elements are the numbers $\binom{n}{r}$ for $r = 0, \ldots, n$, in this order. Therefore, for row 4, the elements in Pascal's triangle are the numbers $\binom{4}{0}, \binom{4}{1}, \binom{4}{2}, \binom{4}{3},$ and $\binom{4}{4}$.

To arrive at the answers, first create a few rows of Pascal's triangle.

```
0:                        1
1:                      1   1
2:                    1   2   1
3:                  1   3   3   1
4:                1   4   6   4   1
5:              1   5  10  10   5   1
6:            1   6  15  20  15   6   1
7:          1   7  21  35  35  21   7   1
```

The numbers in the fourth row of Pascal's triangle are 1, 4, 6, 4, 1. Therefore, in $\wp(B)$ the number of subsets of cardinality zero is <u>1</u>; the number of subsets of cardinality 1 is <u>4</u>; the number of subsets of cardinality 2 is <u>6</u>; the number of subsets of cardinality 3 is <u>4</u>; and the number of subsets of cardinality 4 is <u>1</u>.

(b) You can use the sixth row of Pascal's triangle to determine that a set C that contains 6 elements will have 1 subset of cardinality zero, 6 subsets of cardinality 1, 15 subsets of cardinality 2, 20 subsets of cardinality 3, 15 subsets of cardinality 4, 6 subsets of cardinality 5, and 1 subset of cardinality 6, for a total of $1 + 6 + 15 + 20 + 15 + 6 + 1 = 64$ subsets. Therefore, the power set $\wp(C)$ will have cardinality <u>64</u>.

(c) Since for any row n in Pascal's triangle, the elements are the numbers $\binom{n}{r}$ for $r = 0, \ldots, n$, in this order, then the sum of these elements is the number of subsets in the power set of a set that has n elements. If the cardinality of the power set $\wp(D)$ is 32, look for a row of Pascal's triangle that sums to 32. Row 5 has elements, 1, 5, 10, 10, 5, and 1. The sum of these elements is $1 + 5 + 10 + 10 + 5 + 1 = 32$. An examination of the first seven rows of Pascal's triangle indicates that the sum of the elements in each row below row 5 is less than 32 and that the sum of the elements in each row above row 5 is greater than 32. Thus, row 5 is the only row whose elements sum to 32. Therefore, the set D must contain <u>5</u> elements.

2. (a) distance = rate × time $\Rightarrow$ rate (speed) = $\dfrac{\text{distance}}{\text{time}}$ $\Rightarrow$ time = $\dfrac{\text{distance}}{\text{rate (speed)}}$

Let R = Paul's average speed for the 315-mile trip excluding the hour spent for breakfast; then

$$R = \frac{315 \text{ miles}}{\text{time for the 315-mile trip excluding the 1 hour stop}}.$$

To find R, first find the time for the 315-mile trip excluding the 1-hour stop.

Let T = the time for the 315-mile trip excluding the 1-hour stop. To find T, first, find the time it took Paul to travel the first 120 miles; next, find the time it took Paul to travel the next part of the trip, which is 315 miles – 120 miles = 195 miles, and then add the two times.

$$T = \frac{120 \text{ mi}}{60 \text{ mi/h}} + \frac{195 \text{ mi}}{65 \text{ mi/h}} = 2\text{ h} + 3\text{ h} = 5\text{ h}$$

Thus, $R = \dfrac{315 \text{ m}}{5 \text{ h}}$ = <u>63 miles per hour</u> = Paul's average speed for the 315-mile trip excluding the 1-hour stop for breakfast.

(b) To determine the average speed when the time spent for breakfast is included makes the total time for the trip one hour longer. Thus, the total time for the trip is 5 h + 1 h = 6 h.

Let R_B = Paul's average speed for the 315-mile trip including the hour spent for breakfast, then $R_B = \dfrac{315 \text{ m}}{6 \text{ h}}$ = <u>52.5 miles per hour</u> = Paul's average speed for the 315-mile trip including the 1-hour stop for breakfast.

(c) Paul's total travel time is 6 hours, so he will arrive at his parents' house at 7:00 A.M. + 6 hours = <u>1 P.M.</u>

3. (a) The probability of an event E is $P(E) = \dfrac{\text{Number of outcomes favorable to } E}{\text{Total number of outcomes in the sample space}}$.

Let $P(\text{None})$ = the probability that a randomly selected student is not taking any of the three courses; then

$$P(\text{None}) = \frac{\text{Number of students not taking any of the three courses}}{200}.$$

To find $P(\text{None})$, you need to find the number of students not taking any of the three courses. Draw a Venn diagram to represent the universal set U of 200 students and the subsets of algebra, English, and sociology students. Label the seven regions inside the circles a, b, c, d, e, f, and g.

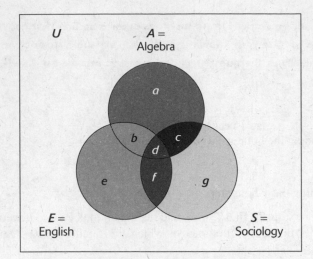 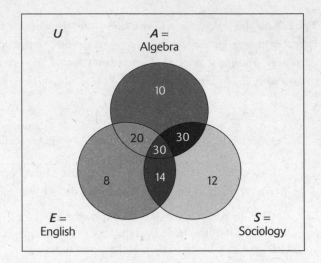

Start with d, the intersection of the three sets. It was given that the $n(A \cap E \cap S) = 30$, so the number of students in region $d = 30$. Next, look at regions b, c, and f. It was given that $n(A \cap E) = 50$, but since 30 belongs in d, then the number of students in region $b = 50 - 30 = 20$. In a similar way, the number of students in region $c = 60 - 30 = 30$, and the number of students in region $f = 44 - 30 = 14$. Next, look at regions a, e, and g. Since region a contains students who are taking only algebra, the number of students in a was given to be 10; similarly, the number of students in region $e = 8$; and the number of students in region $g = 12$. Then add to find the total number of students in regions a, b, c, d, e, f, and g, and, thus, to determine that there are exactly $10 + 20 + 30 + 30 + 8 + 14 + 12 = 124$ students who are taking at least one of the three courses. Thus, there are $200 - 124 = 76$ students who are not taking any of the three courses. Therefore, $P(\text{None}) = \dfrac{76}{200} = \underline{0.38}$.

(b) Let $P(A \cap E$, but not $S) =$ the probability that a randomly selected student is taking both algebra and English, but not sociology, then

$$P(A \cap E, \text{ but not } S) = \frac{\text{Number of students in } A \cap E, \text{ but not } S}{200}.$$

From the Venn diagram, the number of students in $A \cap E$, but not $S =$ the number of students in region $b = 20$ students. Thus,

$$P(A \cap E, \text{ but not } S) = \frac{20}{200} = \underline{0.10}.$$

(c) Let $P(A \mid E) =$ The probability the student is taking algebra, given that the student is taking English. Since it's given that the student is taking English, then the number of students under consideration is limited to the number of students in E. This number is the total number of students in regions b, d, e, and f, which is $20 + 30 + 8 + 14 = 72$ students. Of these 72 students, the number of students who are taking algebra is the number of students in regions b and d, which is $20 + 30 = 50$. Therefore,

$$= P(A \mid E) = \frac{50}{72} = \frac{25}{36} = \underline{0.69} \text{ (approximately)}.$$

Tip: Underlining the answers in each part of these three sample problem-solving exercises was a good idea because doing so made it easier to identify the answers. Use your judgment as to whether underlining might be helpful to the readers for certain problems.

PART II

PRACTICE TESTS

Middle School Mathematics (0069) Practice Test 1 with Answer Explanations

Middle School Mathematics (0069) Practice Test 2 with Answer Explanations

Middle School Mathematics (0069) Practice Test 3 with Answer Explanations

Answer Sheet for Practice Test 1

1 Ⓐ Ⓑ Ⓒ Ⓓ	21 Ⓐ Ⓑ Ⓒ Ⓓ
2 Ⓐ Ⓑ Ⓒ Ⓓ	22 Ⓐ Ⓑ Ⓒ Ⓓ
3 Ⓐ Ⓑ Ⓒ Ⓓ	23 Ⓐ Ⓑ Ⓒ Ⓓ
4 Ⓐ Ⓑ Ⓒ Ⓓ	24 Ⓐ Ⓑ Ⓒ Ⓓ
5 Ⓐ Ⓑ Ⓒ Ⓓ	25 Ⓐ Ⓑ Ⓒ Ⓓ
6 Ⓐ Ⓑ Ⓒ Ⓓ	26 Ⓐ Ⓑ Ⓒ Ⓓ
7 Ⓐ Ⓑ Ⓒ Ⓓ	27 Ⓐ Ⓑ Ⓒ Ⓓ
8 Ⓐ Ⓑ Ⓒ Ⓓ	28 Ⓐ Ⓑ Ⓒ Ⓓ
9 Ⓐ Ⓑ Ⓒ Ⓓ	29 Ⓐ Ⓑ Ⓒ Ⓓ
10 Ⓐ Ⓑ Ⓒ Ⓓ	30 Ⓐ Ⓑ Ⓒ Ⓓ
11 Ⓐ Ⓑ Ⓒ Ⓓ	31 Ⓐ Ⓑ Ⓒ Ⓓ
12 Ⓐ Ⓑ Ⓒ Ⓓ	32 Ⓐ Ⓑ Ⓒ Ⓓ
13 Ⓐ Ⓑ Ⓒ Ⓓ	33 Ⓐ Ⓑ Ⓒ Ⓓ
14 Ⓐ Ⓑ Ⓒ Ⓓ	34 Ⓐ Ⓑ Ⓒ Ⓓ
15 Ⓐ Ⓑ Ⓒ Ⓓ	35 Ⓐ Ⓑ Ⓒ Ⓓ
16 Ⓐ Ⓑ Ⓒ Ⓓ	36 Ⓐ Ⓑ Ⓒ Ⓓ
17 Ⓐ Ⓑ Ⓒ Ⓓ	37 Ⓐ Ⓑ Ⓒ Ⓓ
18 Ⓐ Ⓑ Ⓒ Ⓓ	38 Ⓐ Ⓑ Ⓒ Ⓓ
19 Ⓐ Ⓑ Ⓒ Ⓓ	39 Ⓐ Ⓑ Ⓒ Ⓓ
20 Ⓐ Ⓑ Ⓒ Ⓓ	40 Ⓐ Ⓑ Ⓒ Ⓓ

CUT HERE

Part A

40 Multiple-Choice Questions

(Suggested Time—80 minutes)

Directions: Each of the questions or incomplete statements below is followed by four answer choices (A, B, C, or D). Select the one that is best in each case, and then fill in the corresponding lettered space on the answer sheet.

1. A temperature reading went from 13° to –2°. Which of the following represents the number of degrees of change in temperature?

   A. $|13| - |2|$
   B. $|13 - 2|$
   C. $|13| + |-2|$
   D. $|13| - |-2|$

2. For which of the following expressions is $a - b$ a factor?

   I. $a^2 - b^2$
   II. $a^2 - ab + b^2$
   III. $a^3 - b^3$
   IV. $a^3 - 3a^2b + 3ab^2 - b^3$

   A. I and II only
   B. I, III, and IV only
   C. II and III only
   D. III and IV only

3. A student needs an average of at least 80 on four tests to earn a grade of B in an economics class. The student has grades of 68, 92, and 84 on the first three tests. What is the *lowest* grade the student can make on the fourth test and still receive a B in the economics class?

   A. 99
   B. 82
   C. 80
   D. 76

4. If $xy \neq 0$, then $\dfrac{3}{x} + \dfrac{4}{y} =$

   A. $\dfrac{12}{xy}$
   B. $\dfrac{7}{x+y}$
   C. $\dfrac{7}{xy}$
   D. $\dfrac{4x+3y}{xy}$

5. Which of the following expressions is equivalent to the expression $\left(x^2 + 4\right)^{-\frac{1}{2}}$?

   A. $-\dfrac{x^2+4}{2}$
   B. $-\sqrt{x^2+4}$
   C. $\dfrac{1}{\sqrt{x^2+4}}$
   D. $\dfrac{1}{x+2}$

6. A trip of 204 miles requires 8.5 gallons of gasoline. At this rate, how many gallons of gasoline would be required for a trip of 228 miles?

   A. 9 gal
   B. 9.5 gal
   C. 10 gal
   D. 10.5 gal

7. $4^x + 12^x =$

   A. $4^x(1 + 3^x)$
   B. $4(5^x)$
   C. 16^x
   D. 16^{2x}

GO ON TO THE NEXT PAGE

8. Which property of the complex numbers is illustrated here?

$(2 - 3i) + (5 + 6i) + (1 - 2i) = (7 + 3i) + (1 - 2i) =$
$(2 - 3i) + (6 + 4i) = 8 + i$

   A. the distributive property
   B. the associative property of addition
   C. the commutative property of addition
   D. the existence of an additive inverse

9. The whole number y is exactly three times the whole number x. The whole number z is the sum of x and y. Which of the following CANNOT be the value of z?

   A. 314
   B. 416
   C. 524
   D. 1032

10. $2x^3y(x + 3)(3x - 1) =$

   A. $3x^2 + 8x - 3$
   B. $6x^5y - 16x^4y - 6x^3y$
   C. $6x^5y + 16x^4y - 6x^3y$
   D. $6x^6y + 16x^5y - 6x^3y$

11. Solve $2x(x - 2) = 1$

   A. $x = \dfrac{1}{2}$ or 3
   B. $x = 1 \pm \sqrt{6}$
   C. $x = \dfrac{-2 \pm \sqrt{6}}{2}$
   D. $x = \dfrac{2 \pm \sqrt{6}}{2}$

12. What is the y value of the ordered pair that is a solution to the system $\begin{cases} 2x - 3y = 16 \\ 4x + 5y = 10 \end{cases}$?

   A. -5
   B. -2
   C. 2
   D. 5

13. A pharmacist measures the mass of a medical substance and uses the appropriate number of significant figures to record the mass as 10 grams, to the nearest gram. Which of the following ways most accurately expresses the range of possible values of the mass of the substance?

   A. 10 grams $\pm$ 0.1 grams
   B. 10 grams $\pm$ 0.5 grams
   C. 10 grams $\pm$ 1.0 grams
   D. 10 grams

14. A carpenter needs to drill a hole in a triangular piece of wood so that the hole is equidistant from each side of the triangle. Which of the following constructions should the carpenter do to determine the location of the hole?

   A. Find the intersection of the bisectors of the three angles.
   B. Find the intersection of the three altitudes of the triangle.
   C. Find the intersection of the perpendicular bisectors of the three sides.
   D. Find the intersection of the three medians of the triangle.

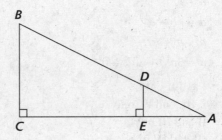

15. In triangle ABC, segment $\overline{CE}$ has length 200 meters and segment $\overline{EA}$ has length 100 meters. In triangle ADE, segment $\overline{DE}$ has length 50 meters. What is the area of triangle ABC?

   A. 7500 m^2
   B. 15,000 m^2
   C. 22,500 m^2
   D. 45,000 m^2

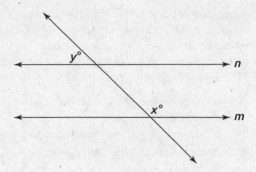

16. In the figure, lines *m* and *n* are parallel and $x = 8y$. What is the value of *x*?

    A. 10
    B. 20
    C. 160
    D. 170

17. A length of cable is attached to the top of a 15-foot pole. The cable is anchored 8 feet from the base of the pole. What is the length of the cable?

    A. 12 feet
    B. 17 feet
    C. 23 feet
    D. 289 feet

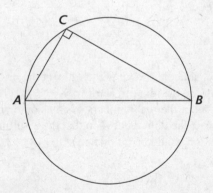

18. In the figure, the circle circumscribed about the right triangle has a radius of 5.5 cm. What is the length of the hypotenuse of the right triangle?

    A. It cannot be determined from the information given.
    B. 11π cm
    C. 5.5π cm
    D. 11 cm

19. A solid cube of silver has edges 4 cm long. A metallurgist melts the cube down and uses all the molten silver to make two smaller identical solid cubes. What is the length of an edge of one of the smaller cubes?

    A. 2 cm
    B. $2\sqrt{2}$ cm
    C. $2\sqrt[3]{2}$ cm
    D. $2\sqrt[3]{4}$ cm

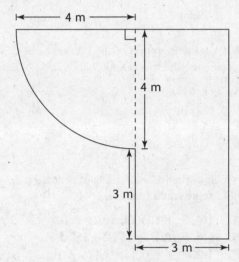

20. The figure in the diagram consists of a fourth of a circle and a rectangle with the dimensions shown. What is the approximate area of the figure?

    A. 21 m^2
    B. 34 m^2
    C. 41 m^2
    D. 64 m^2

21. For disaster relief in a fire-damaged area, $1.6 billion is needed. This amount of money is approximately equivalent to spending one dollar per second for how many years?

    A. 10
    B. 50
    C. 100
    D. 500

GO ON TO THE NEXT PAGE

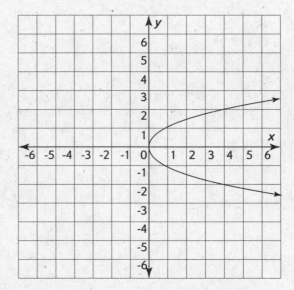

22. What is the midpoint of the line segment connecting the two points R and S shown here?

   A. (1, 6)
   B. (5, 2)
   C. (2.5, 1)
   D. (0.5, 3)

23. Which of the following sets of ordered pairs does NOT represent a function?

   A. {(4, 5), (3, 1), (3, 10), (−2, 0)}
   B. {(5, 5), $(5^2, 5)$, $(5^3, 5^3)$, $(5^4, 5^4)$}
   C. {(2, 3), (4, 3), (8, 3), (16, 3)}
   D. {(0, 0)}

24. The rate for renting a Jet Ski at a popular marina is $20 per hour or portion of an hour. Which of the following types of functions best models the cost of renting a Jet Ski?

   A. linear function
   B. absolute value function
   C. step function
   D. quadratic function

25. Determine the domain D_f and the range R_f of the function $y = \dfrac{x^2 + 40x - 500}{500}$, where x is a real number between 500 and 750.

   A. $D_f = \{x \mid 500 < x < 750\}$;
       $R_f = \{y \mid 539 < y < 1184\}$
   B. $D_f = \{x \mid x \text{ is a real number}\}$;
       $R_f = \{y \mid 539 < y < 1184\}$
   C. $D_f = \{y \mid 539 < y < 1184\}$;
       $R_f = \{x \mid 500 < x < 750\}$
   D. $D_f = \{x \mid 500 < x < 750\}$;
       $R_f = \{y \mid y \text{ is a real number}\}$

26. Using data collected through experimentation, a social scientist develops a function $y = f(x)$ that relates hours of sleep y to age x. In addition to being a relation, which of the following statements MUST be true about the function?

   A. It has a smooth graph with no cusps or jagged edges.
   B. Every y value has one and only one x value.
   C. The graph of the function passes through the origin.
   D. It gives a single value for hours of sleep for each value in the age range.

27. The parabola shown with vertex at the origin is the graph of the relation $R = \{(x, y) \mid y^2 = x\}$. To what subset of the real numbers, if any, could you restrict the domain of R so that the resulting relation would be a function?

   A. $\{x \mid x = 0\}$
   B. $\{x \mid x < 0\}$
   C. $\{x \mid x \geq 0\}$
   D. No such subset of the real numbers exists.

28. A line passes through the point (0, 5) and is perpendicular to the line that has equation $x - 3y = 10$. Which of the following equations represents the line?

   A. $x + 3y = 5$
   B. $x - 3y = 5$
   C. $3x + y = 5$
   D. $-3x + y = 5$

29. Given the cubic function $f(x) = x^3$, which of the following best describes the function $f(x) = (x-2)^3$?

   A. the same as the graph of $f(x) = x^3$ shifted up by 2 units

   B. the same as the graph of $f(x) = x^3$ shifted down by 2 units

   C. the same as the graph of $f(x) = x^3$ shifted right by 2 units

   D. the same as the graph of $f(x) = x^3$ shifted left by 2 units

30. If $f(x) = \dfrac{2x+6}{x+2}$ and $g(x) = x + 2$,

then $\big(g \circ f\big)(x) = g(f(x)) =$

   A. $\dfrac{4x+10}{x+2}$

   B. $\dfrac{2x+10}{x+4}$

   C. $\dfrac{4x+8}{x+2}$

   D. $\dfrac{2x+8}{x+4}$

31. Rose has participated in eight track meets so far this season. Her running times for the 400-meter race have been 73, 63, 68, 64, 69, 61, 66, and 64 seconds. What is Rose's median running time for the eight meets?

   A. 64 seconds

   B. 65 seconds

   C. 66 seconds

   D. 66.5 seconds

Book Genre Preference	
Genre	*Number of Students*
Biography/Historical Nonfiction	44
Historical Fiction	58
Mystery	64
Science/Nature Informational	50
Science Fiction/Fantasy	104
Total	**320**

32. The table shows the results of a poll of young readers regarding what genre of books they read most often. If a pie chart is constructed using the data in the table, what central angle should be used to represent the category science fiction/fantasy?

   A. 32.5°

   B. 52°

   C. 117°

   D. 187.2°

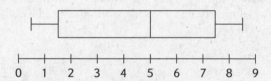

33. In the box and whiskers plot shown, the vertical line at 5 indicates that 5 is which of the following?

   A. the median

   B. the mean

   C. the standard deviation

   D. an outlier

GO ON TO THE NEXT PAGE

	Diagnosis is Positive	Diagnosis is Negative
Smoker	50	10
Non-Smoker	30	310

34. The table shows the diagnosis of 400 subjects consisting of smokers and nonsmokers who were tested for lung cancer in a certain clinic. If one of the 400 subjects tested is randomly selected, what is the probability that the subject was positively diagnosed as having lung cancer, given that the subject is a smoker?

 A. $\dfrac{1}{8}$

 B. $\dfrac{1}{6}$

 C. $\dfrac{5}{8}$

 D. $\dfrac{5}{6}$

35. A meteorologist predicts that there is a 60-percent chance of a thunderstorm and a 10-percent chance that a thunderstorm will produce hail. What is the probability that a thunderstorm that produces hail will occur?

 A. 6%
 B. 10%
 C. 50%
 D. 70%

36. Only one of 20 remote controls in a box is defective. The remote controls are tested one at a time. If the first five remote controls tested are not defective, what is the probability that the sixth remote control tested is defective?

 A. $1 - \left(\dfrac{19}{20}\right)^5$

 B. $\dfrac{1}{15}$

 C. $\dfrac{1}{4}$

 D. $1 - \left(\dfrac{1}{20}\right)^5$

37. Given the recursive function defined by

$$f(0) = 5,$$
$$f(n) = 2f(n-1) + 1 \text{ for } n \geq 1,$$

what is the value of $f(3)$?

 A. 11
 B. 23
 C. 47
 D. 95

38. How many different license plates can be made consisting of three digits followed by three letters?

 A. $3 \cdot 3$
 B. $({}_{10}C_3)({}_{26}C_3)$
 C. $10^3 \cdot 26^3$
 D. 36^6

39. A civic club has 150 members. A committee of 5 members is to be selected to attend a national conference. How many different committees could be formed?

 A. ${}_{150}C_5$
 B. ${}_{150}P_5$
 C. 150^5
 D. $150!$

40. Which of the following statements follows logically from the statement: "If it is raining, I will carry an umbrella."

 A. It is not raining, so I am not carrying an umbrella.
 B. It is raining, so I am carrying an umbrella.
 C. I am carrying an umbrella, so it must be raining.
 D. I am not carrying an umbrella, so it is not raining.

Part B

3 Constructed-Response Questions
(Suggested Time—40 minutes)

Directions: Questions 41–43 are constructed-response questions. Write your responses to these questions in the space provided in the lined pages following the questions. If a question has multiple parts, be sure to answer each part of the question.

Question 41

For a company the total amount of money received by the company for goods sold during a certain time period is called revenue (R). The cost (C) of production is the fixed costs plus the variable cost associated with producing the goods sold. (Fixed costs are costs like rent, salaries, and so forth that do not change with production levels.) When the revenue exceeds the cost of production, the company has a profit. When the cost of production exceeds revenue, the company has a loss. The point at which revenue and cost of production are equal is called the break-even point.

Suppose a small manufacturing company has daily fixed costs of $6000. Each unit the company manufactures costs $10 to produce and is sold for $40.

(a) Write an equation that gives the company's daily revenue, R, in terms of number of units sold daily, x. Write a second equation that gives the company's daily cost of production, C, in terms of number of units produced daily, x.

(b) Use the equations you wrote in part (a) to determine the break-even point for the company. Show your work.

(c) Graph the two equations you wrote in part (a) to show a graphical interpretation of the break-even point. First, graph daily revenue (on the y-axis) *versus* daily number of units. Next, graph daily cost (on the y-axis) *versus* daily number of units. Label each axis, show the units and scales used, and label the graph of each equation. Write a brief summary of what you can observe from the graphs in regard to the break-even point.

Question 42

Students at a community college participate in three different intramural sports: soccer, volleyball, and basketball. The director of intramural activities at the community college checks the number of participants one month into the school year and finds that 90 students participate in soccer, 70 in volleyball, and 50 in basketball. However, some students participate in more than one type of sport. The director finds that 20 students participate in both soccer and volleyball, 15 in both volleyball and basketball, 10 in both soccer and basketball, and 5 participate in all three sports.

(a) Draw a Venn diagram showing three circles that represent each type of sport. Include the number of student participants in each of the seven regions inside the circles. Explain your process and your reasoning.

(b) Using the Venn diagram you created in part (a), determine how many students participate in exactly two types of intramural sports. Explain your process and reasoning.

(c) Using the Venn diagram you created in part (a), find the total number of students who participate in the three types of intramural sports. Explain your process and your reasoning.

GO ON TO THE NEXT PAGE

Question 43

Richard leaves his house at 11:00 A.M., drives an average speed of 50 miles per hour, and arrives at his destination at 2:00 P.M. on the same day.

(a) How many miles was Richard's trip? Show your work.

(b) At what time would Richard have arrived if he had driven an average speed of 60 miles per hour? Show your work.

(c) Richard's car gets 30 miles per gallon when he drives at an average speed of 50 miles per hour and gets 25 miles per gallon when he drives at an average speed of 60 miles per hour. How many gallons of gas will Richard save by driving at the slower average speed on his trip? Show your work.

Begin your response to Question 41 here.

GO ON TO THE NEXT PAGE

Begin your response to Question 42 here.

Begin your response to Question 43 here.

Middle School Mathematics (0069) Practice Test 1 Answer Key

Part A: Correct Answers for the Multiple-Choice Questions

Question Number	Correct Answer	Content Category	Question Number	Correct Answer	Content Category
1.	C	I	21.	B	II
2.	B	I	22.	C	II
3.	D	I	23.	A	III
4.	D	I	24.	C	III
5.	C	I	25.	A	III
6.	B	I	26.	D	III
7.	A	I	27.	A	III
8.	B	I	28.	C	III
9.	A	I	29.	C	III
10.	C	I	30.	A	III
11.	D	I	31.	B	IV
12.	B	I	32.	C	IV
13.	B	II	33.	A	IV
14.	A	II	34.	D	IV
15.	C	II	35.	A	IV
16.	C	II	36.	B	IV
17.	B	II	37.	C	IV
18.	D	II	38.	C	IV
19.	D	II	39.	A	IV
20.	B	II	40.	D	IV

Answer Explanations for the Multiple-Choice Section

1. **C.** Analyze the problem. The number of degrees of change in temperature is $13 - (-2) = 13 + 2 = 15$. The best way to work this problem is to mentally work out the answer choices to see which yields 15 as a result. Only Choice C ($|13| + |-2| = 13 + 2 = 15$) gives a result of 15. All the other answer choices yield 11 as a result.

2. **B.** This question is an example of a multiple-response set question. One approach to answering this type of question is to do the following: First, identify choices that you know are incorrect from the Roman numeral options and then draw a line through every answer choice that contains a Roman numeral you have eliminated. Next, examine the remaining answer choices to determine which Roman numeral options that you are sure are correct. Eliminate answer choices, if any, that do not contain the Roman numerals you are sure are correct.

   Looking at the four expressions given in the Roman numeral options, you can immediately eliminate Roman II because $a^2 - ab + b^2$ is *not* factorable over the real numbers. Draw a line through choices A and C because each of these answer choices contains Roman numeral II. The remaining answer choices are B and D, which contain Roman numeral options I, III, and IV. Notice that both B and D contain Roman numeral options III and IV, so you know these are correct. Look at the factors of the one remaining option Roman numeral I.

   I. $a^2 - b^2 = (a + b)(a - b)$

Tip: If you have not memorized the special products given in the chapter "Basic Algebra," you should do so before the test.

   Roman numeral I is correct because $(a - b)$ is a factor of $a^2 - b^2$. You can eliminate Choice D because it does not contain Roman numeral I. This leaves answer Choice B as the correct response because it includes every Roman numeral option that is correct and no incorrect Roman numeral options.

3. **D.** Analyze the problem. The question asks: What is the *lowest* grade the student can make on the fourth test and still receive a B in the course? The average of the student's four test grades must be at least 80. This means the sum of the four test grades divided by 4 must be at least 80. Devise and carry out a plan.

   Method 1. You can find the answer by writing and solving an equation.

   Let x = the lowest grade the student can make on the fourth test and still have at least an 80 average.

   $$\frac{\text{sum of 4 test grades}}{4} = \frac{68 + 92 + 84 + x}{4} = 80$$

   Solve $\dfrac{68 + 92 + 84 + x}{4} = 80$ for x.

   $$\frac{68 + 92 + 84 + x}{4} = 80 \Rightarrow \frac{244 + x}{4} = 80 \Rightarrow 244 + x = 320 \Rightarrow x = 76$$

   Therefore, the lowest grade that will yield an average of at least 80 is 76, Choice **D**.

   Method 2. Another way to work this problem is to check the answer choices—a smart test-taking strategy for multiple-choice math tests. However, be careful with this problem. Because you have to find the *lowest* test score that will work, you must check all the answer choices even if you find an answer choice that gives an average in the 80s.

   Checking **A:** $\dfrac{\text{sum of 4 test grades}}{4} = \dfrac{68 + 92 + 84 + 99}{4} = 85.75$, too high

   Checking **B:** $\dfrac{\text{sum of 4 test grades}}{4} = \dfrac{68 + 92 + 84 + 82}{4} = 81.5$, too high

   Checking **C:** $\dfrac{\text{sum of 4 test grades}}{4} = \dfrac{68 + 92 + 84 + 80}{4} = 81.0$, too high

   Checking **D:** $\dfrac{\text{sum of 4 test grades}}{4} = \dfrac{68 + 92 + 84 + 76}{4} = 80.0$, correct because 76 is the *lowest* grade needed.

4. **D.** $\dfrac{3}{x} + \dfrac{4}{y} = \dfrac{3y}{xy} + \dfrac{4x}{xy} = \dfrac{3y + 4x}{xy} = \dfrac{4x + 3y}{xy}$, Choice D.

5. **C.** $\left(x^2 + 4\right)^{-\frac{1}{2}} = \dfrac{1}{\left(x^2 + 4\right)^{\frac{1}{2}}} = \dfrac{1}{\sqrt{x^2 + 4}}$, Choice C.

6. **B.** Analyze the problem. You know the number of gallons needed for a 204-mile trip is 8.5 gallons, and you want to know how many gallons are needed for a 228-mile trip. Devise a plan. Set up a proportion and solve for the number of gallons needed for the 228-mile trip. Carry out the plan.

$$\frac{x}{228 \text{ miles}} = \frac{8.5 \text{ gal}}{204 \text{ miles}} \Rightarrow x(204 \text{ miles}) = (8.5 \text{ gal})(228 \text{ miles}) \Rightarrow x = \frac{(8.5 \text{ gal})(228 \text{ miles})}{204 \text{ miles}} = 9.5 \text{ gal, Choice B.}$$

> **Tip:** Be sure to check the units to make sure that (mathematically) they work out to be the desired units for the answer.

7. **A.** $4^x + 12^x = 4^x + (3 \cdot 4)^x = 4^x + 3^x \cdot 4^x = 4^x(1 + 3^x)$, Choice A.

8. **B.** The illustration shows that you can group complex numbers in a sum in any way you want and still get the same answer. This property is called the associative property of addition, Choice B.

9. **A.** Analyze the problem. Since x and y are whole numbers and $z = x + y = x + 3x = 4x$, then z is a multiple of 4. Therefore, z represents a whole number that is divisible by 4. A number is divisible by 4 if and only if the last 2 digits form a number that is divisible by 4. Looking at the answer choices, you can see that only Choice A fails the test for divisibility by 4—because the last two digits of 314 are 14, which is not divisible by 4.

10. **C.** $2x^3y(x + 3)(3x - 1) = 2x^3y(3x^2 + 8x - 3) = 6x^5y + 16x^4y - 6x^3y$, Choice C.

11. **D.** Express $2x(x - 2) = 1$ in standard form: $2x(x - 2) = 1 \Rightarrow 2x^2 - 4x = 1 \Rightarrow 2x^2 - 4x - 1 = 0$.

    Thus, $a = 2$, $b = -4$, $c = -1$ (include the $-$ signs).

    Plug into the quadratic formula $x = \dfrac{-(-4) \pm \sqrt{(-4)^2 - 4(2)(-1)}}{2(2)} = \dfrac{4 \pm \sqrt{16 + 8}}{4} = \dfrac{4 \pm \sqrt{24}}{4} = \dfrac{4 \pm 2\sqrt{6}}{4} = \dfrac{2 \pm \sqrt{6}}{2}$, Choice D.

12. **B.** $\begin{cases} 2x - 3y = 16 \\ 4x + 5y = 10 \end{cases} \Rightarrow \begin{cases} -4x + 6y = -32 \\ 4x + 5y = 10 \end{cases} \Rightarrow 11y = -22 \Rightarrow y = -2$, Choice B.

13. **B.** The **maximum possible error** of a measurement is half the magnitude of the smallest measurement unit used to obtain the measurement. The most accurate way of expressing the measurement is as a tolerance interval. Thus, a measurement of 10 grams, to the nearest gram, should be reported as 10 grams $\pm$ 0.5 grams, Choice B.

14. **A.** The angle bisectors of a triangle are concurrent in a point that is equidistant from the three sides, which means Choice A is the correct response.

15. **C.** Mark on the diagram.

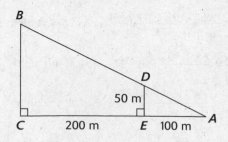

Analyze the problem. From the figure, you can see that triangle *ABC* is a right triangle. To find the area of a right triangle, you find $\frac{1}{2}$ the product of the lengths of the two legs. You can determine the length of leg $\overline{CA}$ by adding the lengths of the two segments, $\overline{CE}$ and $\overline{EA}$. Since right triangles *ABC* and *ADE* have two congruent right angles and an acute angle in common, namely angle *A*, they are similar triangles. Thus, the length of $\overline{BC}$ can be determined by using properties of similar triangles. Devise a plan. To find the area of triangle *ABC* will take three steps. First, find the length of leg $\overline{CA}$ by adding the lengths of the two segments, $\overline{CE}$ and $\overline{EA}$. Next, find the length of leg $\overline{BC}$, by using the proportionality of the corresponding sides of the similar triangles *ABC* and *ADE*. Then, find the area of triangle *ABC* by calculating $\frac{1}{2}bh = \frac{1}{2}$(length of $\overline{CA}$) (length of $\overline{BC}$). Carry out the plan.

Step 1. Find the length of leg $\overline{CA}$: $\overline{CA}$ = 200 m + 100 m = 300 m

Step 2. Find the length of $\overline{BC}$, call it *x*: $\dfrac{x}{300 \text{ m}} = \dfrac{50 \text{ m}}{100 \text{ m}} \Rightarrow 100x = 15{,}000 \text{ m} \Rightarrow x = 150 \text{ m}$

Step 3. Find the area of triangle *ABC*: area = $\frac{1}{2}bh = \frac{1}{2}$ (300 m)(150 m) = 22,500 m², Choice C.

16. C. Analyze the problem. Angles *x* and *y* are angles formed when parallel lines are cut by a transversal. Devise a plan. Use the properties of angles formed when parallel lines are cut by a transversal to find *x* and *y*. Carry out the plan. Angle *y* and the angle adjacent to angle *x* are congruent because they are corresponding angles. Thus, angles *x* and *y* are supplementary angles. Recall that the sum of supplementary angles is 180°. It is given that *x* = 8*y*, so *x* + *y* = 180 $\Rightarrow$ 8*y* + *y* = 180 $\Rightarrow$ 9*y* = 180 $\Rightarrow$ *y* = 20. Thus, *x* = 8*y* = 8(20) = 160, Choice C.

Tip: Make sure you answer the question asked. This problem asks for the value of *x*, so after you find *y*, you keep going and find *x*.

17. B. First sketch a diagram to illustrate the problem.

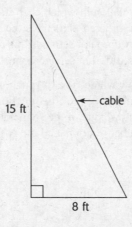

Analyze the problem. The pole, the cable, and the ground form a right triangle. From the diagram, you can see that the length of the cable is the hypotenuse of a right triangle that has legs of 15 feet and 8 feet. You can use the Theorem to find the hypotenuse denoted by *c*.

$c^2 = a^2 + b^2 = (15 \text{ ft})^2 + (8 \text{ ft})^2 = 225 \text{ ft}^2 + 64 \text{ ft}^2 = 289 \text{ ft}^2 \Rightarrow c = 17 \text{ ft}$, Choice B.

18. D. Analyze the problem. From the figure, you can see that right angle *ACB* is an inscribed angle. The measure of an inscribed angle is half the degree measure of its intercepted arc. Thus, the degree measure of arc *AB* is 180°, making the chord *AB,* which is the hypotenuse of right triangle *ABC,* a diameter of the circle. Devise a plan. To find the length of the hypotenuse, multiply the radius by 2. Carry out the plan. Length of the hypotenuse = 2(5.5 cm) = 11 cm, Choice D.

19. D. Analyze the problem. The volume V of a cube with edge s is given by $V = s^3$. The volume of the original cube will equal the sum of the volumes of the two smaller cubes. Devise a plan. To find the length of an edge of one of the smaller cubes will take three steps: First, find the volume of the original cube. Next, find the volume of one of the smaller cubes. Finally, find the length of an edge of one of the smaller cubes. Carry out the plan.

Step 1. Find the volume V_o of the original cube: $V_o = (4 \text{ cm})^3 = 64 \text{ cm}^3$.

Step 2. Find the volume V_s of one of the smaller cubes: $V_s + V_s = V_o = 64 \text{ cm}^3 \Rightarrow 2V_s = 64 \text{ cm}^3 \Rightarrow V_s = 32 \text{ cm}^3$

Step 3. Find the length, call it e, of an edge of one of the smaller cubes: $e^3 = 32 \text{ cm}^3 \Rightarrow e = \sqrt[3]{32 \text{ cm}^3} = \sqrt[3]{8 \text{cm}^3 \cdot 4} = 2\sqrt[3]{4}$ cm, Choice D.

20. B. Analyze the problem. From the diagram, you can see that the area of the figure is the sum of the area of the fourth of the circle and the area of the rectangle. The formula for the area of a circle is πr^2, and the formula for the area of a rectangle is lw. Devise a plan. To find the area of the figure, find the sum of the area of the fourth of the circle and the area of the rectangle. Carry out the plan. From the diagram, you can determine that the radius of the fourth of the circle is 4 m and that the length of the rectangle is 4 m + 3 m = 7 m. Hence, the area of the figure $= \frac{1}{4}\pi r^2 + lw = \frac{1}{4}\pi (4 \text{ m})^2 + (7\text{m})(3 \text{ m}) = 33.56637 \ldots \text{ m}^2$ or approximately 34 m^2, Choice B.

21. B. Analyze the problem. You want to know how many years it would take to spend $1.6 billion per second. Devise a plan. The best way to determine which answer is correct is to use dimensional analysis to find out how many years are 1.6 billion seconds. Write $1.6 billion as a fraction with denominator 1 and let unit analysis tell you which conversion fractions to multiply by, keeping in mind that you want years as your final answer. Carry out the plan.

$$\frac{\$1,600,000,000}{1} \times \frac{1\ \cancel{s}}{\$1} \times \frac{1\ \cancel{\text{min}}}{60\ \cancel{s}} \times \frac{1\ \cancel{h}}{60\ \cancel{\text{min}}} \times \frac{1\ \cancel{d}}{24\ \cancel{h}} \times \frac{1 \text{ yr}}{365\ \cancel{d}} = 50.73566 \ldots \text{ or approximately 50 years, Choice B.}$$

22. C. Analyze the problem. You can plug into the midpoint formula to find the midpoint between $(2, -2)$ and $(3,4)$:

$$\left(\frac{x_1 + x_2}{2}, \frac{y_1 + y_2}{2} \right) = \left(\frac{2+3}{2}, \frac{-2+4}{2} \right) = (2.5, 1), \text{ Choice C.}$$

23. A. Analyze the problem. A function is a relation in which each first component is paired with *one and only one* second component. In other words, no two ordered pairs have the same first components and different second components. Only the relation in Choice A does not satisfies this requirement because the ordered pairs (3,1) and (3,10) have the same first components, but different second components, namely 1 and 10.

24. C. Analyze the problem. You want to know which type of function best models the cost of renting a Jet Ski. Devise a plan. Make a rough graph of a portion of the cost function to get a visual picture of the function. Then decide on the best model based on your knowledge of the shape of the graphs of the functions listed in the answer choices. Carry out the plan. Since the number of hours and the cost are both always nonnegative, you can restrict your graph to the first quadrant.

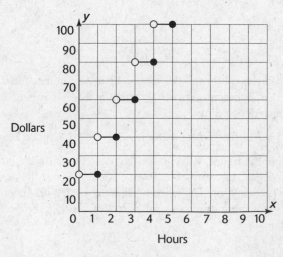

Since the graph looks like a series of "steps," the best model for the cost of renting a Jet Ski is a step-function, Choice C.

25. A. Analyze the problem. Since the function $y = \dfrac{x^2 + 40x - 500}{500}$, has no excluded values, its domain is the set consisting of all its possible x-values; that is, $D_f = \{x \mid 500 < x < 750\}$. Since $y = f(x)$ is increasing over its domain, the range of $y = \dfrac{x^2 + 40x - 500}{500}$ is the set consisting of all its possible y-values; that is,

$$R_f = \left\{ y \,\middle|\, \frac{500^2 + 40(500) - 500}{500} < y < \frac{750^2 + 40(750) - 500}{500} \right\} = R_f = \{y \mid 539 < y < 1184\}.$$

Thus, Choice A is the correct response.

> **Tip:** After you compute the y-value corresponding to $x = 500$, use the Recall Entry feature of your graphing calculator to compute the y-value corresponding to $x = 750$.

26. D. Analyze the problem. Since the problem states that the relation is a function, by definition, each first component (age value) is paired with one and only one second component (hours value). Thus, only the statement given in Choice D will always be true about the social scientist's function. None of the other statements are guaranteed to be true about the social scientist's function.

27. A. Analyze the problem. A graph of a function must pass the vertical line test: Any vertical line in the plane will intersect the graph of a function in no more than one point. Examining the graph, you can see that the graph fails the vertical line test when $x > 0$. Only when the domain is restricted to $\{x \mid x = 0\}$ is the resulting relation, which is $\{(0,0)\}$, a function. Therefore, Choice A is the correct response.

28. C. Analyze the problem. You want to determine the equation of a line that passes through $(0, 5)$ and is perpendicular to the line that has equation $x - 3y = 10$. Observe that $(0, 5)$ is the y-intercept of the line. Also, when two lines are perpendicular, their slopes are negative reciprocals of each other. Make a plan. Use the slope-intercept form to write the equation. You need two steps. First, find the slope for the desired equation by writing the equation $x - 3y = 10$ in slope-intercept form, identifying its slope, and taking the negative reciprocal. Next, write the equation and put it in standard form (since the answer choices are in standard form). Carry out the plan.

Step 1. Find the slope for the desired equation: $x - 3y = 10 \Rightarrow -3y = -x + 10 \Rightarrow y = \dfrac{1}{3}x - \dfrac{10}{3}$. The slope of $x - 3y = 10$ is $\dfrac{1}{3}$, so the desired equation has slope -3.

Step 2. Write the equation and put it in standard form: $y = -3x + 5 \Rightarrow 3x + y = 5$, Choice C.

29. C. Analyze the problem. Subtracting a positive constant h from x will result in a horizontal shift of h units to the right. The graph of $f(x) = (x - 2)^3$ is the same as the graph of $f(x) = x^3$ shifted right by 2 units, Choice C.

> **Tip:** If you are unsure whether the shift is to the right or left, graph both functions on your graphing calculator to check.

30. A. $(g \circ f)(x) = g(f(x)) = g\left(\dfrac{2x + 6}{x + 2}\right) = \dfrac{2x + 6}{x + 2} + 2 = \dfrac{2x + 6}{x + 2} + \dfrac{2(x + 2)}{x + 2} = \dfrac{2x + 6}{x + 2} + \dfrac{2x + 4}{x + 2} = \dfrac{4x + 10}{x + 2}$, Choice A.

31. B. Analyze the problem. In an ordered set of numbers, the median is the middle number if there is a middle number; otherwise, the median is the arithmetic average of the two middle numbers. First, put the running times in order from smallest to largest: 61 s, 63 s, 64 s, 64 s, 66 s, 68 s, 69 s, 73 s. Since there is no middle number, average the two running times, 64 s and 66 s that are in the middle of the list: $\dfrac{64\text{ s} + 66\text{ s}}{2} = \dfrac{130\text{ s}}{2} = 65\text{ s}$, Choice B.

32. C. Analyze the problem. A pie chart is made by dividing the 360 degrees of the circle that makes the pie chart into portions that correspond to the proportion for each category. The central angle that should be used to represent the category science fiction/fantasy $= \dfrac{104}{320} (360°) = 117°$, Choice C.

33. A. Analyze the problem. A box and whiskers plot graphically summarizes a data set by showing five numbers in the following order: the minimum value, the first quartile, the median, the third quartile, and the maximum value. Thus, the vertical line at 5 indicates 5 is the median, Choice A.

34. D. Analyze the problem. This question asks you to find a conditional probability; that is, you already know that the subject is a smoker. Thus, when computing the probability, the number of possible subjects under consideration is no longer 400 subjects, but is reduced to the total number of smokers. You want the probability that if one of the 400 subjects is randomly selected, the subject was positively diagnosed with lung cancer, *given* that the subject is a smoker. After you can assume that the selected person is a smoker, you are dealing only with the subjects in the first row of the table. Devise a plan. First, find the total number of smokers. Next, among those, determine the number diagnosed with lung cancer, and then compute the conditional probability. Carry out the plan.

Step 1. Find the total number of smokers: Total smokers = 50 + 10 = 60 smokers.

Step 2. Among the 60 smokers, 50 were diagnosed with long cancer. Thus, P(diagnosed with lung cancer | given subject is a smoker) = $\frac{50}{60} = \frac{5}{6}$, Choice D.

35. A. Analyze the problem. This problem requires an application of the Multiplication Rule, which states that $P(A \text{ and } B) = P(A)\, P(B \mid A)$. P(thunderstorm and hail) = P(thunderstorm) P(hail | thunderstorm) = 60% · 10% = 6%, Choice A.

36. B. Analyze the problem. After 5 nondefective remote controls have been drawn, there are only 15 remote controls left in the box, one of which is defective. Therefore, the probability that the next remote control is defective = $\frac{1}{15}$, Choice B.

37. C. Analyze the problem. For the recursive formula given in the problem, you will need to find $f(1)$ and $f(2)$ before you can find $f(3)$. Since the problem tells you that $f(0) = 5$ and that $f(n) = 2f(n-1) + 1$ for $n \geq 1$, then

$f(1) = 2f(0) + 1 = 2(5) + 1 = 10 + 1 = 11$

$f(2) = 2f(1) + 1 = 2(11) + 1 = 22 + 1 = 23$

$f(3) = 2f(2) + 1 = 2(23) + 1 = 46 + 1 = 47$, Choice C.

38. C. Analyze the problem. Since there are six slots to be filled, so to speak, on a license plate, you can work this problem by extending the Fundamental Counting Principle to six events. There are 10 possibilities for each of the three digits and 26 possible values for each of the three letters, which means the total number of possible license plates is $10 \cdot 10 \cdot 10 \cdot 26 \cdot 26 \cdot 26 = 10^3 \cdot 26^3$, Choice C.

39. A. Analyze the problem. Since the order in which committee members are chosen does not make a difference regarding the composition of the committee, the number of different committees of size 5 that can be selected from the 150 members is $_{150}C_5$, Choice A.

40. D. Analyze the problem. The statement "If it is raining, I will carry an umbrella" is a conditional statement. It has the logical form "If p, then q," where p is the statement "it is raining" and q is the statement "I will carry an umbrella." In logic, the equivalent of "If p, then q" is its contrapositive, which is stated like so: "If not p, then not q." The contrapositive for the statement given is "If I will not carry an umbrella, then it is not raining." Only Choice D is compatible with this statement.

Part B: Solutions to the Short Constructed-Response Section

For questions 41–43, score your response 0 to 3 using the following criteria:

- Correctly answered all parts of the question
- Gave a complete and full explanation for answers
- Demonstrated a strong understanding of the mathematical content relevant to the question
- Demonstrated a thorough understanding of all aspects of any stimulus material provided

41. Sample correct constructed response

(a) Daily Revenue $R = \$40 \cdot x = 40x$, where x = number of units sold daily.

Daily Cost $C = \$6,000 + \$10x = 6000 + 10x$, where x = number of units produced daily.

(b) Break-even point occurs when $R = C$.

$40x = 6000 + 10x$

$30x = 6000$

$x = 200$ units

Thus, 200 units must be sold each day to break even. Thus, when $x = 200$ units, revenue and profit are equal; that is, $y = \$40x = \$40(200) = \$6000 + \$10(200) = \$8000$.

(c)

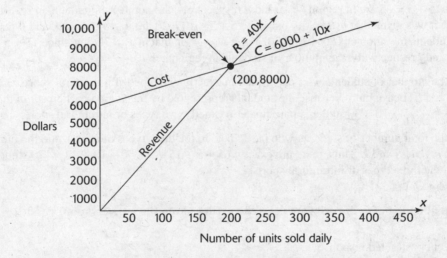

At the break-even point (200, 8000), the revenue and cost functions intersect. Thus, the company must sell 200 units each day to ensure no loss and no profit. When x < 200, the cost equation is above (exceeds) the revenue equation, resulting in a loss for the company. When x > 200, the revenue equation is above (exceeds) the cost equation so the company has a profit.

42. Sample correct constructed response

(a)

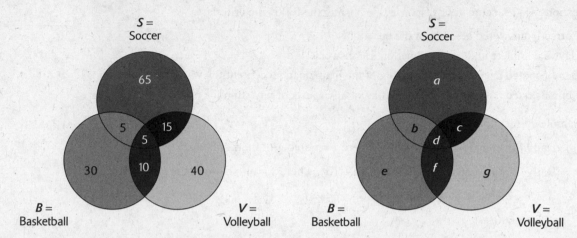

Explanation: Label the three circles S (soccer), V (volleyball), and B (basketball), and label the seven regions inside the circles a, b, c, d, e, f, and g.

Start with d, the intersection of the three sets. It was given that the $n(S \cap V \cap B) = 5$, so the number of students in region $d = \underline{5}$. Next, look at regions b, c, and f. It was given that $n(S \cap B) = 10$, but since 5 are in region d, then the number of students in region $b = 10 - 5 = \underline{5}$. In a similar way, the number of students in region $c = 20 - 5 = \underline{15}$ and the number of students in region $f = 15 - 5 = \underline{10}$. Then, look at regions a, e, and g. It was given that $n(S) = 90$, but since $5 + 15 + 5 = 25$ are in regions b, c, and d respectively, the number of students in region $a = 90 - 25 = \underline{65}$. Similarly, it was given that $n(B) = 50$, but since $5 + 5 + 10 = 20$ are in regions b, d, and f, respectively, the number of students in region $e = 50 - 20 = \underline{30}$; and it was given that $n(V) = 70$, but since $15 + 5 + 10 = 30$ are in regions c, d, and f respectively, the number of students in region $g = 70 - 30 = \underline{40}$.

(b) To find the number of students who participate in exactly two types of intramural sports, add the numbers in regions b, c, and f. (Leave out d because the students represented by this region participate in three types of sports.) Thus, $5 + 15 + 10 = \underline{30 \text{ students}}$ participate in exactly two types of intramural sports.

(c) To find the total number of students who participate in the three types of sports, add the numbers in all seven regions: a, b, c, d, e, f, and g. Thus, there are exactly $65 + 5 + 15 + 5 + 30 + 10 + 40 = \underline{170 \text{ students}}$ who participate in the three types of intramural sports.

Tip: For this problem underlining the answers helps the reader locate the answers more easily.

43. Sample correct constructed response

(a) distance = rate × time

time = 11:00 A.M. to 2 P.M. = 3 hours

rate = 50 mph

distance = $\dfrac{50 \text{ mi}}{\cancel{h}} \times 3\cancel{h} = 150 \text{ mi}$

Richard's trip was 150 miles.

(b) time = $\dfrac{\text{distance}}{\text{rate}} = \dfrac{150 \text{ mi}}{60 \text{ mi/h}}$ = 2.5 h = 2 hours 30 minutes

11:00 A.M. + 2 hours 30 minutes = 1:30 P.M.

Richard would have arrived at 1:30 P.M. if he had driven an average speed of 60 mph.

(c) No. of gallons at 60 mph = $\dfrac{150 \text{ mi}}{25 \text{ mi/gal}}$ = 6 gal

No. of gallons at 50 mph = $\dfrac{150 \text{ mi}}{30 \text{ mi/gal}}$ = 5 gal

Difference = 1 gal

Richard's will save 1 gallon of gas if he drives at the slower speed.

Scoring Your Practice Test

The testing company does not release the exact details of the way the Praxis Middle School Mathematics test is scored. Here is a method that will give you an approximation of your percentage score (out of a possible 100 percent) on this practice test, with the caveat that the scoring method used by the testing company could likely differ from what is shown here.

Your total percentage score is 67% of the percent of multiple-choice items correct plus 33% of your constructed responses percentage score for this practice test.

Here is an example.

Suppose that you get 38 multiple-choice items correct and full credit for each of the 3 constructed response questions. Your percentage score is computed as follows:

$$67\%\left(\frac{38}{40}\right) = 33\%\left(\frac{9}{9}\right) = 0.67(95\%) + 0.33(100\%) = 96.65\%.$$

Answer Sheet for Practice Test 2

1 Ⓐ Ⓑ Ⓒ Ⓓ		21 Ⓐ Ⓑ Ⓒ Ⓓ
2 Ⓐ Ⓑ Ⓒ Ⓓ		22 Ⓐ Ⓑ Ⓒ Ⓓ
3 Ⓐ Ⓑ Ⓒ Ⓓ		23 Ⓐ Ⓑ Ⓒ Ⓓ
4 Ⓐ Ⓑ Ⓒ Ⓓ		24 Ⓐ Ⓑ Ⓒ Ⓓ
5 Ⓐ Ⓑ Ⓒ Ⓓ		25 Ⓐ Ⓑ Ⓒ Ⓓ
6 Ⓐ Ⓑ Ⓒ Ⓓ		26 Ⓐ Ⓑ Ⓒ Ⓓ
7 Ⓐ Ⓑ Ⓒ Ⓓ		27 Ⓐ Ⓑ Ⓒ Ⓓ
8 Ⓐ Ⓑ Ⓒ Ⓓ		28 Ⓐ Ⓑ Ⓒ Ⓓ
9 Ⓐ Ⓑ Ⓒ Ⓓ		29 Ⓐ Ⓑ Ⓒ Ⓓ
10 Ⓐ Ⓑ Ⓒ Ⓓ		30 Ⓐ Ⓑ Ⓒ Ⓓ
11 Ⓐ Ⓑ Ⓒ Ⓓ		31 Ⓐ Ⓑ Ⓒ Ⓓ
12 Ⓐ Ⓑ Ⓒ Ⓓ		32 Ⓐ Ⓑ Ⓒ Ⓓ
13 Ⓐ Ⓑ Ⓒ Ⓓ		33 Ⓐ Ⓑ Ⓒ Ⓓ
14 Ⓐ Ⓑ Ⓒ Ⓓ		34 Ⓐ Ⓑ Ⓒ Ⓓ
15 Ⓐ Ⓑ Ⓒ Ⓓ		35 Ⓐ Ⓑ Ⓒ Ⓓ
16 Ⓐ Ⓑ Ⓒ Ⓓ		36 Ⓐ Ⓑ Ⓒ Ⓓ
17 Ⓐ Ⓑ Ⓒ Ⓓ		37 Ⓐ Ⓑ Ⓒ Ⓓ
18 Ⓐ Ⓑ Ⓒ Ⓓ		38 Ⓐ Ⓑ Ⓒ Ⓓ
19 Ⓐ Ⓑ Ⓒ Ⓓ		39 Ⓐ Ⓑ Ⓒ Ⓓ
20 Ⓐ Ⓑ Ⓒ Ⓓ		40 Ⓐ Ⓑ Ⓒ Ⓓ

CUT HERE

Part A

40 Multiple-Choice Questions

(Suggested Time—80 minutes)

Directions: Each of the questions or incomplete statements below is followed by four answer choices (A, B, C, or D). Select the one that is best in each case, and then fill in the corresponding lettered space on the answer sheet.

1. Which of the following equations defines y as a function of x?

   A. $9x - 16y^2 = 9$
   B. $36x^2 + 9y^2 = 36$
   C. $5y - 125x^2 = 10$
   D. $x = |y|$

Categories of 1200 Books Sold at World of Books in December

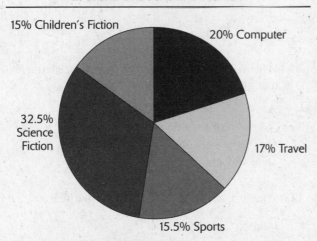

15% Children's Fiction

20% Computer

32.5% Science Fiction

17% Travel

15.5% Sports

2. The pie chart displays the categories, by percentages, of 1200 books sold at The World of Books bookstore. According to the information in the pie chart, how many fiction books were sold in December?

   A. 180
   B. 390
   C. 570
   D. 630

3. If a and b are real numbers, all of the following must be true EXCEPT

   A. $-|-x| = x$
   B. $|xy| = |x||y|$
   C. $\left|\dfrac{x}{y}\right| = \dfrac{|x|}{|y|}$, provided $y \neq 0$
   D. $|x + y| \leq |x| + |y|$

   1 cup = 16 tablespoons (T)
   1 tablespoon = 3 teaspoons (tsp)

4. A punch recipe calls for $2\frac{3}{4}$ cups of cranberry juice, $1\frac{1}{2}$ cups of orange juice, $\frac{3}{4}$ cup of water, 1 teaspoon cinnamon, and 3 tablespoons of sugar. What is the ratio of the total amount of juice to the total amount of cinnamon and sugar called for in the recipe?

   A. 5 to 100
   B. 204 to 10
   C. 68 to 1
   D. 227 to 1

5. Maria withdrew 25 percent of her money from her savings account. Later she withdrew another $150, leaving a balance of $975. How much money was in Maria's account originally if no other transactions were posted to her account?

   A. $1125.00
   B. $1500.00
   C. $1968.75
   D. $4500.00

GO ON TO THE NEXT PAGE

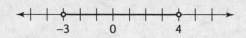

6. The graph on the number line shown represents the set of values of x satisfying which of the following inequalities?

   A. $\left|x - \frac{1}{2}\right| < \frac{7}{2}$

   B. $\left|x - \frac{1}{2}\right| > \frac{7}{2}$

   C. $\left|x - \frac{1}{2}\right| \leq \frac{7}{2}$

   D. $\left|x - \frac{1}{2}\right| \geq \frac{7}{2}$

n	1	2	3	4	...
m	0	1	4	9	...

7. If the pattern shown in the table continues indefinitely, which of the following expressions should be used to find m for a given value of n?

   A. $\sqrt{n}$

   B. n^2

   C. $n^2 - 1$

   D. $(n - 1)^2$

8. Which of the following statements is logically equivalent to the statement, "If p, then q"?

   A.   If q, then p.

   B.   If not p, then q.

   C.   If not p, then not q.

   D.   If not q, then not p.

9. Given $\frac{a}{b} = 10$ and $\frac{b}{c} = 5$, where $b \neq = 0$ and $c \neq 0$. What is the value of $\frac{a}{b+c}$?

   A. $\frac{25}{6}$

   B. $\frac{25}{3}$

   C. $\frac{5}{3}$

   D.   12

10. Which of the following sets is closed with respect to the given operation?

   A.   the set of perfect squares with respect to multiplication

   B.   the set of whole numbers with respect to subtraction

   C.   the set of odd numbers with respect to addition

   D.   the set of integers with respect to division

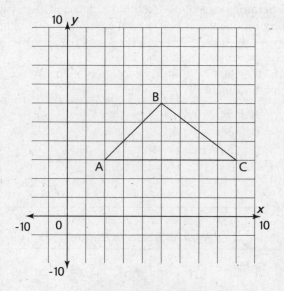

11. Which of the following properties associated with triangle ABC is an irrational quantity?

   A.   perimeter of triangle ABC

   B.   area of triangle ABC

   C.   length of side $\overline{BC}$

   D.   midpoint of side $\overline{AC}$

12. What is the x value of the ordered pair that is a solution to the system $\begin{cases} 2x - 3y = 16 \\ 4x + 5y = 10 \end{cases}$?

   A. -5

   B. -2

   C.   2

   D.   5

13. Measured to the nearest meter, the length of a rectangular yard is 60 m, and its width is 30 m. Which of the following is the most accurate way to express the area, *A*, of the yard?

    A. $1755.25 \text{ m}^2 \leq A \leq 1845.25 \text{ m}^2$

    B. $1784.75 \text{ m}^2 \leq A \leq 1814.75 \text{ m}^2$

    C. $1711 \text{ m}^2 \leq A\ 22 \leq 1891 \text{ m}^2$

    D. 1800 m^2

14. To estimate the population of fish in a lake, a parks and recreation team captures and tags 500 fish and then releases the tagged fish back into the lake. One month later, the team returns and captures 100 fish from the lake, 20 of which bear tags that identify them as being among the previously captured fish. If all the tagged fish are still active in the lake when the second group of fish is captured, what is the best estimate of the fish population in the lake based on the information obtained through this capture-recapture strategy?

    A.   100 fish

    B.   1500 fish

    C.   2500 fish

    D.   3000 fish

$$b2_{\text{seven}} = 134_{\text{five}}$$

15. In the equation shown, the subscript of each number identifies the base in which the number is expressed. What base-seven number does $b2_{\text{seven}}$ represent?

    A. 8_{seven}

    B. 26_{seven}

    C. 52_{seven}

    D. 62_{seven}

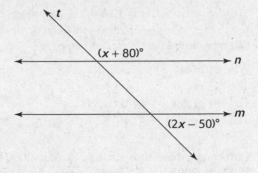

16. In the figure, line *t* is a transversal for lines *m* and *n*. For what value of *x* will lines *m* and *n* be parallel?

    A. $16\frac{2}{3}$

    B.   50

    C.   100

    D.   130

17. A length of cable is attached to the top of a 12-foot pole. The cable is anchored 5 feet from the base of the pole. What is the length of the cable?

    A.   7 feet

    B.   13 feet

    C.   17 feet

    D.   169 feet

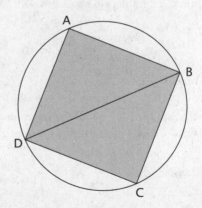

18. In the figure, the circle circumscribed about the square *ABCD* has a circumference of 8π cm. Find the area of the square *ABCD*.

    A.   It cannot be determined from the information given.

    B. $4\sqrt{2} \text{ cm}^2$

    C. $32\pi \text{ cm}^2$

    D. 32 cm^2

GO ON TO THE NEXT PAGE

Practice Test 2

19. The density of silver is 10.5 grams per cubic centimeter. What is the mass of a cube of silver that measures 2 centimeters on an edge?

A. 21 grams
B. 42 grams
C. 84 grams
D. 168 grams

20. Tara bought a precious stone pendant in 2000 for $500. By 2003 it had lost 10 percent of its value. In 2005 it was worth 10 percent more than in 2003. By 2008 it had lost 20 percent of its value from three years previously. What was the pendant worth in 2008?

A. $390
B. $396
C. $400
D. $404

21. A national health study estimates that 35 percent of the people over the age of 65 in the United States will get flu shots this year. According to the study, of the people who get flu shots, an estimated 2 percent will have some sort of adverse reaction. If N represents the number of people over the age of 65 in the United States, estimate how many people over age 65 will have an adverse reaction after getting flu shots this year?

A. $0.007N$
B. $0.02N$
C. $0.35N$
D. $0.37N$

22. For what value of $k > 0$ will the function $y = 16x^2 - kx + 25$ have exactly one real zero?

A. $40i$
B. -20
C. 20
D. 40

23. Which of the following functions have the same domain and the same range?

I. $\{(0, 0), (1, 1), (2, 4), (3, 9), (4, 16)\}$
II. $\{(x, y) \mid y = x^2\}$
III. $\{(0, 0), (1, 1), (2, 4), (3, 9), (4, 16), \ldots\}$
IV. $\{(x, y) \mid y = |x|\}$

A. I and III only
B. II and IV only
C. II, III, and IV only
D. I, II, III, and IV

24. A team of biologists introduces a herd of 1500 deer onto an uninhabited island. If the deer population doubles every eight years, which of the following functions models the growth of the deer population on the island if t is the time in years?

A. $(1500)^{0.125t}$
B. $(1500)2^{0.125t}$
C. $(1500)^{8t}$
D. $(1500)2^{8t}$

25. What is the equation of the line that is perpendicular to the line whose equation is $5x - 6y = 4$ and passes through the point $(3, 1)$?

A. $5x - 6y = 9$
B. $-6x + 5y = -13$
C. $6x + 5y = 23$
D. $6x + 5y = 21$

26. The exterior of a spherical tank with radius 12 feet is to be painted with one coat of paint. The paint sells for $24.50 per gallon and can be purchased in one-gallon cans only. If a can of paint will cover approximately 400 square feet, what will be the cost of the paint needed to paint the exterior of the tank?

A. $24.50
B. $98.00
C. $110.84
D. $122.50

27. An experiment consists of flipping a coin five times. How many different outcomes are in the sample space for this experiment?

A. $_5P_2$
B. 2^5
C. 5^2
D. $_5C_2$

$\otimes$	a	b
a	a	b
b	b	b

28. The table shown defines an operation $\otimes$ on the set $S = \{a, b\}$. All the following statements about S with respect to $\otimes$ are true EXCEPT

A. S is closed.
B. S is commutative.
C. S contains an identity element.
D. S contains inverses for all elements in S.

29. Given the cubic function $f(x) = x^3$, which of the following best describes the function $f(x) = (x + 3)^3$?

A. the same as the graph of $f(x) = x^3$ shifted up by 3 units
B. the same as the graph of $f(x) = x^3$ shifted down by 3 units
C. the same as the graph of $f(x) = x^3$ shifted right by 3 units
D. the same as the graph of $f(x) = x^3$ shifted left by 3 units

Weights (in pounds) of the 36 Members of a Females-Only Health Club

Stem	Leaf					
10	0	3	3	7	8	
11	1	1	1	4	7	8
12	2	6	8	8	9	
13	2	6	6	8		
14	1	2	4			
15	3	4	7	7	7	
16	3	7	8			
17	2	4	8			
18	3	6				

30. The graph shown is a stem-leaf plot of the weights of 36 women who comprise the membership of a females-only health club. What percent of the women in the club weigh less than 115 pounds?

A. 10%
B. 15%
C. 25%
D. 30%

31. At a grand-opening sale of an appliance store, 152 customers bought a washer or a dryer. Looking at the inventory, the store manager found that 94 washers and 80 dryers were sold. Of the 152 customers, how many bought only a washer?

A. 22
B. 58
C. 72
D. 130

GO ON TO THE NEXT PAGE

Practice Test 2

32. $\dfrac{a}{a^2-b^2} - \dfrac{b}{a^2+ab} =$

  A. $\dfrac{a-b}{b(a+b)}$

  B. $\dfrac{a-b}{a(a+b)}$

  C. $\dfrac{a^2-ab+b^2}{a(a+b)(a-b)}$

  D. $\dfrac{a^2-ab-b^2}{a(a+b)(a-b)}$

33. What are the units of the quantity $Y = \dfrac{Adv}{t}$, where A is measured in square centimeters (cm^2),

d is expressed in grams per cm^3 $\left(\dfrac{g}{cm^3}\right)$,

v is expressed in centimeters per second $\left(\dfrac{cm}{s}\right)$, and t is given in seconds (s)?

  A. g

  B. $\dfrac{g}{s^2}$

  C. $\dfrac{g\text{-}cm}{s}$

  D. $\dfrac{g\text{-}cm}{s^2}$

Resident Status of Second-Year Students (n = 500)		
	On-Campus	Off-Campus
Male	114	135
Female	156	95

34. The table shows the resident status, by sex, of 500 second-year students at a small community college. If one of the 500 students is randomly selected, what is the probability that the student resides off-campus, given that the student selected is a female student?

  A. $1 - \dfrac{156}{500}$

  B. $\dfrac{95}{500}$

  C. $\dfrac{251}{500} \cdot \dfrac{95}{500}$

  D. $\dfrac{95}{251}$

35. What is the volume of a right triangular prism that is 20 inches in height and whose bases are equilateral triangles that are 4 inches on a side?

  A. 7 in^3

  B. 46 in^3

  C. 80 in^3

  D. 138 in^3

36. Only three of 20 remote controls in a box are defective. The remote controls are tested one at a time. If the first five remote controls tested are not defective, what is the probability that the sixth remote control tested is defective?

  A. $1 - \left(\dfrac{17}{20}\right)^5$

  B. $\dfrac{1}{5}$

  C. $\dfrac{6}{15}$

  D. $\left(\dfrac{3}{20}\right)^5$

37. Given the recursive function defined by

  $f(0) = 1,$

  $f(n) = 3f(n-1) + 1$ for $n \geq 1,$

what is the value of $f(3)$?

  A. 4

  B. 13

  C. 40

  D. 121

38. If $f(x) = \dfrac{2x+6}{x+2}$ and $g(x) = x + 2$, then

$(f \circ g)(x) = f(g(x)) =$

  A. $\dfrac{4x+10}{x+2}$

  B. $\dfrac{2x+10}{x+4}$

  C. $\dfrac{4x+8}{x+2}$

  D. $\dfrac{2x+8}{x+4}$

39. A civic club has 300 members. A committee of six members is to be selected to attend a national conference. How many different committees could be formed?

- A. $_{300}C_6$
- B. $_{300}P_6$
- C. 300^6
- D. $300!$

40. What is the negation of the following statement: "All teenagers are curious"?

- A. Some teenagers are curious.
- B. Some teenagers are not curious.
- C. No teenagers are curious.
- D. All teenagers are not curious.

GO ON TO THE NEXT PAGE

Part B

3 Constructed-Response Questions

(Suggested Time—40 minutes)

Directions: Questions 41–43 are constructed-response questions. Write your responses to these questions in the space provided in the lined pages following the questions. If a question has multiple parts, be sure to answer each part of the question.

Question 41

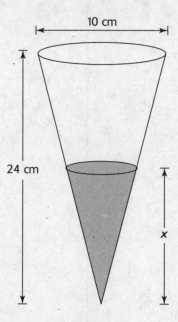

The funnel shown is a right circular cone with a diameter of 10 cm and a height of 24 cm.

(a) Using the information in the figure, write an expression that represents the radius of the circular surface of the fluid in the funnel in terms of h, the height of the fluid in the funnel. Explain your process and reasoning.

(b) Using the expression you wrote in part (a) of this question, write an expression that represents the volume of fluid in the funnel in terms of h. Show your work.

(c) Using the information in the figure and the expression you wrote in part (b) of this question, show that the ratio of the volume of the fluid in the funnel to the volume of the cone equals the ratio of h^3 to $(24)^3$, the cube of the height of the cone. Show your work.

Question 42

Given a positive counting number n such that when you write its digits, you have $d_p \cdots d_4 d_3 d_2 d_1 d_0$ indicating that d_0 is in the one's place, d_1 is in the 10's place, d_2 is in the 100s place, d_3 is in the 1000s place, and so on, in the base-ten representation of n.

(a) Prove that n is divisible by 2 if and only if its last digit is even. Explain your process and reasoning.

(b) Prove that n is divisible by 4 if and only if the number formed by deleting all but the last two digits of n is divisible by 4. Explain your process and reasoning.

(c) State a divisibility rule for 5 and explain in your own words the process you would use to prove it.

Question 43

The enrollment at a small community college for the fall semester is 10% higher than the enrollment in the fall semester a year ago. The number of female students increased by 5%, and the number of male students increased by 20%.

(a) What is the current ratio of female students to male students at the community college? Show your work.

(b) What fraction of the current enrollment at the community college is female? Show your work.

(c) What fraction of the current enrollment at the community college is male. Show your work.

Begin your response to Question 41 here.

Begin your response to Question 42 here.

GO ON TO THE NEXT PAGE

Practice Test 2

Begin your response to Question 43 here.

Middle School Mathematics (0069) Practice Test 2 Answer Key

Part A: Correct Answers for the Multiple-Choice Questions

Question Number	Correct Answer	Content Category	Question Number	Correct Answer	Content Category
1.	C	III	21.	A	I
2.	C	IV	22.	D	III
3.	A	I	23.	B	III
4.	B	II	24.	B	III
5.	B	I	25.	C	III
6.	A	I	26.	D	II
7.	D	III	27.	B	IV
8.	D	IV	28.	D	I
9.	B	I	29.	D	III
10.	A	I	30.	C	IV
11.	A	II	31.	C	IV
12.	D	I	32.	C	I
13.	A	II	33.	B	II
14.	C	I	34.	D	IV
15.	D	I	35.	D	II
16.	B	II	36.	B	IV
17.	B	II	37.	C	IV
18.	D	II	38.	B	III
19.	C	II	39.	A	IV
20.	B	I	40.	B	IV

Answer Explanations for the Multiple-Choice Section

1. **C.** Analyze the problem. You are asked to identify an equation of a function. Recall that a function is a set of ordered pairs in which each first component is paired with *one and only one* second component; that is, each x-value is paired with one and only one y-value. Looking at the answer choices, you can eliminate Choice D immediately because, except for 0, two different values of y correspond to each value of x. For example, both $(2, 2)$ and $(2, -2)$ satisfy the equation in Choice D. For A, B, and C, it is helpful to solve each equation for y as shown here.

   A. $9x - 16y^2 = 9 \Rightarrow -16y^2 = 9 - 9x \Rightarrow 16y^2 = 9x - 9 \Rightarrow 16y^2 = 9(x - 1) \Rightarrow y^2 = \frac{9}{16}(x - 1) \Rightarrow y = \pm\frac{3}{4}\sqrt{x - 1}$; therefore, eliminate A because for each x, you have two different values of y.

   B. $36x^2 + 9y^2 = 36 \Rightarrow 9y^2 = 36 - 36x^2 \Rightarrow 9y^2 = 36(1 - x^2) \Rightarrow y^2 = 4(1 - x^2) \Rightarrow y = \pm 2\sqrt{1 - x^2}$; therefore, eliminate B because for each x, you have two different values of y.

   Thus, Choice C is the correct response. You should go on to the next question; but, just so you know, for Choice C, $y = 25x^2 + 2$, which yields exactly one value of y for every x.

   Tip: When y is squared, the equation will *not* define a function.

2. **C.** Analyze the problem. The question asks: how many fiction books were sold in December? From the pie chart, you know the percentage of children's fiction books and the percentage of science fiction books. Devise a plan: To find how many fiction books were sold in December will take two steps: First, find the total percentage of fiction books sold. Next, find the total number of fiction books sold. Carry out the plan.

   Step 1. Find the total percentage of fiction books sold: $15\% + 32.5\% = 47.5\%$.

   Step 2. find the total number of fiction books sold: 47.5% of 1200 books $= (0.475)(1200 \text{ books}) = 570$ books, Choice C.

3. **A.** Analyze the problem. You must select which statement about absolute value is *NOT ALWAYS* true—even though it might be true for certain values of a and b. The best way to solve this problem is to substitute some values for a and b into the statements and check whether the statements hold. Only the statement in Choice A is not always true. For instance, when x is 8, you have $-|-x| = -|-(8)| = -|-8| = -8 \neq x = 8$. Choices B, C, and D are properties of absolute value that are always true.

   Tip: Be sure to memorize the properties for absolute value given in the chapter titled "Arithmetic and Basic Number Concepts" before you take the Praxis Middle School Mathematics Test.

4. **B.** Analyze the problem. The question asks: what is the ratio of the total amount of juice to the total amount of cinnamon and sugar called for in the recipe? The amount of each kind of juice is given in cups. The cinnamon is given in teaspoons, and the sugar, in tablespoons. To compare the total amount of juice to the total amount of cinnamon and sugar, both amounts will need to be in the same units. Devise a plan. To answer the question will take three steps: First, find the total amount of juice in cups; and then, using the conversion table, convert the answer to tablespoons. Next, using the conversion table, convert the amount of cinnamon into tablespoons; and then find the total amount of cinnamon and sugar in tablespoons. Finally, find the ratio of the total amount of juice to the total amount of cinnamon and sugar. Carry out the plan.

   Step 1. Find the total amount of juice in cups, and then in tablespoons: $2\frac{3}{4}c + 1\frac{1}{2}c = 4\frac{1}{4}c$; $4\frac{1}{4}c \times \frac{16\,\text{T}}{c} = 68$ T juice.

   Step 2. Convert the amount of cinnamon to tablespoons; and then find the total amount of cinnamon and sugar in tablespoons: 1 tsp cinnamon $= \frac{1}{3}T$ cinnamon; $\frac{1}{3}T + 3\,\text{T} = 3\frac{1}{3}T$ cinnamon and sugar.

   Step 3. $\frac{68\,\text{T}}{3\frac{1}{3}\,\text{T}} = 20.4$, which is the same as $\frac{204}{10}$ or 204 to 10, Choice B.

5. B. Analyze the problem. You are given information about Maria's transactions and how much is left in the account after the transactions. Devise a plan. Let x = the original amount in Maria's account, and then write an equation and solve for x. Carry out the plan.

$$x - 0.25x - \$150 = \$975 \Rightarrow 0.75x = \$1125 \Rightarrow x = \frac{\$1125}{0.75} = \$1500, \text{ Choice B.}$$

6. A. Analyze the problem. From your knowledge of solving inequalities, you know that the open-circles at -3 and 4 mean that -3 and 4 are not included in the solution set. Thus, the inequality symbol in the answer must be either $<$ or $>$, so you can eliminate choices C and D. Devise and carry out a plan.

Method 1. Test a number from the interval shown in the graph in each of the inequalities given in choices A and B. For convenience and ease of calculation select 0 as your test number.

A. When $x = 0$, $\left| x - \frac{1}{2} \right| = \left| 0 - \frac{1}{2} \right| = \left| -\frac{1}{2} \right| = \frac{1}{2} < \frac{7}{2}$, which is true. Thus, Choice A is the correct response.

B. Since you have determined that Choice A is the correct response, you should go on to the next problem. However, you can easily see that $x = 0$ does not satisfy the inequality in Choice B because $\frac{1}{2} > \frac{7}{2}$ is false.

> **Tip:** You also can use this method for testing a number in inequalities that contain the symbols $\leq$ or $\geq$. When you test a number from a given interval in these inequalities, do not select one of the endpoints of the interval as your test number because doing so might lead you to make a wrong decision about which inequality is the correct answer.

Method 2. Solve the inequalities given in choices A and B.

A. $\left| x - \frac{1}{2} \right| < \frac{7}{2} \Rightarrow -\frac{7}{2} < x - \frac{1}{2} < \frac{7}{2} \Rightarrow -\frac{7}{2} + \frac{1}{2} < x < \frac{7}{2} + \frac{1}{2} \Rightarrow -\frac{6}{2} < x < \frac{8}{2} \Rightarrow -3 < x < 4$, which is illustrated in the graph shown. Thus, Choice A is the correct response.

B. Since you have determined that Choice A is the correct response, you should go on to the next problem. However, for your information, the solution to Choice B is $x < -3$ or $x > 4$.

7. D. Analyze the problem. You are asked to find a rule or formula that can be used to find m when you know n. Devise a plan. Check the formulas given in the answer choices using the values in the table. Carry out the plan.

Checking Choice A: When $n = 1$, $\sqrt{n} = \sqrt{1} = 1$, not 0; eliminate Choice A.

Checking Choice B: When $n = 1$, $n^2 = 1^2 = 1$, not 0; eliminate Choice B.

Checking Choice C: When $n = 1$, $n^2 - 1 = 1^2 - 1 = 0$ ✓; when $n = 2$, $n^2 - 1 = 2^2 - 1 = 3$, not 1; eliminate Choice C. Therefore, you know that Choice D is the correct response. You should go on to the next problem.

For your information, here is the check for Choice D: When $n = 1$, $(n-1)^2 = (1-1)^2 = 0$ ✓; when $n = 2$, $(n-1)^2 = (2-1)^2 = 1$ ✓; when $n = 3$, $(n-1)^2 = (3-1)^2 = 4$ ✓; and when $n = 4$, $(n-1)^2 = (4-1)^2 = 9$ ✓.

> **Tip:** When simple math is involved, do the checks mentally to save time.

8. D. Analyze the problem. The statement, "If p, then q" is called a conditional statement. A conditional statement and its contrapositive are logically equivalent. The contrapositive of "If p, then q" is "If not q, then not p," Choice D.

9. B. Analyze the problem. You know the values of $\frac{a}{b}$ and $\frac{b}{c}$, and you are asked to find the value of $\frac{a}{b+c}$. Devise a plan. Express $\frac{a}{b+c}$ in terms of $\frac{a}{b}$ and $\frac{b}{c}$ by dividing each term in its numerator and denominator by b. Carry out the plan.

$$\frac{a}{b+c} = \Rightarrow \frac{\frac{a}{b}}{\frac{b}{b} + \frac{c}{b}} = \frac{\frac{a}{b}}{\frac{b}{b} + \frac{1}{\frac{b}{c}}} = \frac{10}{1 + \frac{1}{5}} = \frac{10}{\frac{6}{5}} = \frac{50}{6} = \frac{25}{3}, \text{ Choice B.}$$

Note: This solution is one way you might work this problem, but not the *only* way it can be worked.

10. A. Analyze the problem. A set is closed with respect to an operation if the result of performing the operation with any pair of elements in the set yields an element contained in the set. Therefore, to show a set is *not* closed, you need to find just *one* pair of elements that does not yield an element in the set when the operation is performed with that pair of elements. Devise a plan. Eliminate answer choices that are *not* closed by selecting arbitrary pairs of values and testing them with the given operation. Carry out the plan.

Tip: Use mental math to save time.

Eliminate Choice B because 5 and 9 are whole numbers, but $5 - 9 = -4$, which is not a whole number. Eliminate Choice C because 3 and 5 are odd numbers, but $3 + 5 = 8$, which is not an odd number. Eliminate Choice D because 1 and 2 are integers, but $1 \div 2 = 0.5$, which is not an integer. Thus, Choice A is the correct response. You should move on to the next problem. Notwithstanding, the following should convince you that the set of perfect squares is closed with respect to multiplication: Let a^2 and b^2 be any two perfect squares. Then $(a^2)(b^2) = (ab)^2$, which is also a perfect square.

11. A. Analyze the problem. From the figure, you can determine that the length of side $\overline{AC}$ is 7 units, and that the altitude of triangle *ABC*, from the vertex *B* to side $\overline{AC}$, is 3 units. Devise a plan. Draw the altitude from vertex *B* to side $\overline{AC}$, and label the point of intersection *D* as shown here.

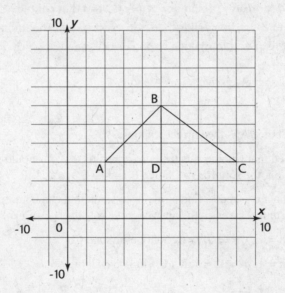

The line segment $\overline{BD}$ will create two right triangles: triangle *ADB* and triangle *CDB*. Use the information given and the properties of right triangles to check the answer choices. Start by eliminating answer choices that are obviously rational quantities. Carry out the plan. Eliminate Choice B because the area of triangle *ABC* is

$\frac{1}{2}\left(\overline{AC}\right)\left(\overline{BD}\right) = \frac{1}{2} = $ (7 units)(3 units), which is a rational quantity. Eliminate choice D because $\overline{AC}$ is 7 units,

so the distance from vertex *A* to the midpoint of $\overline{AC}$ will be a rational quantity. Eliminate Choice C because $\overline{BC}$ is the hypotenuse of a right triangle whose legs are 3 units and 4 units; thus, $\overline{BC}$ is 5 units, a rational quantity. Therefore, Choice A is the correct response. You should move on to the next problem, but just so you know, the perimeter of triangle *ABC* is irrational because it has a portion, namely $\overline{AB}$, that is the hypotenuse of a right triangle whose legs are each 3 units; thus, $\overline{AB} = \sqrt{3^2 + 3^2} = \sqrt{18}$ units, which is an irrational quantity.

12. D. $\begin{cases} 2x - 3y = 16 \\ 4x + 5y = 10 \end{cases} \Rightarrow \begin{cases} -4x + 6y = -32 \\ 4x + 5y = 10 \end{cases} \Rightarrow 11y = -22 \Rightarrow y = -2$. Be careful! The question asks for the *x* value

of the solution. Substitute the value you obtained for *y* into one of the equations and solve for *x*: $2x - 3y = 16 \Rightarrow 2x - 3(-2) = 16 \Rightarrow 2x + 6 = 16 \Rightarrow 2x = 10 \Rightarrow x = 5$, Choice D.

Tip: Always make sure you are answering the question asked.

13. A. Analyze the problem. The maximum possible error of a measurement is half the magnitude of the smallest measurement unit used to obtain the measurement. Therefore, the most accurate way of expressing the dimensions of the yard is as tolerance intervals. Thus, it is more accurate to express the length of the yard as 60 m ± 0.5 m, and its width as 30 m ± 0.5 m, and to determine the area as a tolerance interval based on these intervals (eliminate Choice D). Since area equals length times width, the tolerance interval for the area, A, of the yard is obtained as follows: $(60 \text{ m} - 0.5 \text{ m})(30 \text{ m} - 0.5 \text{ m}) \leq A \leq (60 \text{ m} + 0.5 \text{ m})(30 \text{ m} + 0.5 \text{ m}) = (59.5 \text{ m})(29.5 \text{ m}) \leq A \leq (60.5 \text{ m})(30.5 \text{ m}) = 1755.25 \text{ m}^2 \leq A \leq 1845.25 \text{ m}^2$, Choice A.

14. C. Analyze the problem. If all the tagged fish are still active in the lake when the second group of fish is captured, the proportion of tagged fish in the second group should equal to the proportion of tagged fish in the whole population, P, of fish in the lake. Devise a plan. Set up a proportion and solve for P.

$$\frac{20}{100} = \frac{500}{P} \Rightarrow P = \frac{100 \cdot 500}{20} = 2500 \text{ fish, Choice C.}$$

15. D. Analyze the problem. The question asks: "What base-seven number does $b2_{seven}$ represent? You need to determine the value of the digit b to answer the question. The number on the left of the equal sign is expressed in the base-seven system, while the number on the right is expressed in the base-five system. Devise a plan. To find the value of b (and thus $b2_{seven}$) will take two steps. First, expand the numbers in their respective bases to convert them to the base-ten system. Next, set the resulting base-ten expressions equal to each other, solve for b, and then put its value in the expression $b2_{seven}$. Carry out the plan.

Step 1. $b2_{seven} = b \cdot 7 + 2 = (7b + 2)_{ten} = 7b + 2$; $134_{five} = 1 \cdot 25 + 3 \cdot 5 + 4 = 44_{ten} = 44$

Step 2. $7b + 2 = 44 \Rightarrow 7b = 42 \Rightarrow b = 6 \Rightarrow b2_{seven} = 62_{seven}$, Choice D.

16. B. Analyze the problem. From the properties of parallel lines cut by a transversal, you know that one way that lines m and n will be parallel is for a pair of corresponding angles for the transversal t to be congruent. In the figure, the angle that measures $(x + 80)°$ corresponds to the angle above line m that is supplementary to the angle that measures $(2x - 50)°$. Label this angle θ.

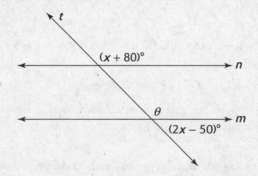

Devise a plan. To find the value of x for which lines m and n will be parallel will take two steps. First, find the measure of angle θ in terms of x. Next, write and solve an equation that ensures angle θ and the angle that measures $(x + 80)°$ will be congruent. Carry out the plan.

Step 1. Recall that the sum of supplementary angles is 180°. Thus, angle θ measures $180° - (2x - 50)°$.

Step 2. Lines m and n will be parallel when $(x + 80)° = 180° - (2x - 50)°$. Solving for x (and omitting the units for convenience), you have $(x + 80) = 180 - (2x - 50) \Rightarrow x + 80 = 180 - 2x + 50 \Rightarrow x + 2x = 180 + 50 - 80 \Rightarrow 3x = 150 \Rightarrow x = 50$, Choice B.

17. B. First sketch a diagram to illustrate the problem.

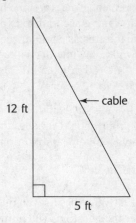

Analyze the problem. The pole, the cable, and the ground form a right triangle. From the diagram, you can see that the length of the cable is the hypotenuse of a right triangle that has legs of 12 feet and 5 feet. You can use the Pythagorean Theorem to find the hypotenuse, denoted by c.

$c^2 = a^2 + b^2 = (12 \text{ ft})^2 + (5 \text{ ft})^2 = 144 \text{ ft}^2 + 25 \text{ ft}^2 = 169 \text{ ft}^2 \Rightarrow c = 13$ ft, Choice B.

18. D. Analyze the problem. From the figure, you can see that right angle DAB is an inscribed angle. The measure of an inscribed angle is half the degree measure of its intercepted arc. Thus, the degree measure of arc DB is 180°. Therefore, chord $\overline{DB}$ is a diameter of the circle that has circumference 8π cm. Also, chord $\overline{DB}$ is the diagonal of the square $ABCD$ and the hypotenuse of right triangle DAB. The area of square $ABCD$ is $x \cdot x = x^2$. Devise a plan. To find the area of square $ABCD$ will take three steps: First, use the formula for the circumference of a circle to find the length of chord $\overline{DB}$. Next, use the Pythagorean Theorem to find the length of x, a side of the square. Finally, use the value obtained for x to find the area of the square. Carry out the plan.

Step 1. $C = \pi d \Rightarrow \pi d = 8\pi$ cm $\Rightarrow d = 8$ cm.

Step 2. Applying the Pythagorean Theorem in right triangle DAB, you have $x^2 + x^2 = (8 \text{ cm})^2 \Rightarrow 2x^2 = 64 \text{ cm}^2 \Rightarrow$ $x^2 = 32 \text{ cm}^2 \Rightarrow x = \sqrt{32}$ cm.

Step 3. area of square $ABCD = (\sqrt{32} \text{ cm})(\sqrt{32} \text{ cm}) = 32 \text{ cm}^2$, Choice D.

Note: Notice that in Step 2, you determine x^2, the area of the square, just before you obtain x. You actually can skip Step 3 in this problem by stopping when you find x^2.

Tip: In an isosceles right-triangle, the length of the hypotenuse is always twice the square of the length of a leg of the triangle.

19. C. Analyze the problem. You are to find the mass, in grams, of the cube. The units for density are grams per cubic centimeter $\left(\dfrac{g}{cm^3}\right)$, so unit analysis tells you that if you want to have grams as the units of your answer then you will need to "cancel" cm^3 from the denominator of the density quantity. Cubic centimeters are units of volume. Therefore, you need to find the volume of the cube. Devise a plan. To find the mass of the silver cube will take two steps. First, find the volume of the cube, and then multiply by the density of silver.

Step 1. Volume of cube $= (2 \text{ cm})^3 = 8 \text{ cm}^3$

Step 2. Mass of cube $= \left(8 \, cm^3\right)\left(\dfrac{10.5 \text{ g}}{cm^3}\right) = 84$ grams, Choice C.

20. B. Analyze the problem. You are asked to find the value of the pendant after a series of percent increases and decreases. Devise a plan. Systematically show the percent increases and decreases from year to year. Carry out the plan.

In 2000, the value is $500. In 2003, the value is $500 − 10%($500) = 90%($500) = 0.90($500) = $450. In 2005, the value is $450 + 10%($450) = $450 + 0.10($450) = $495. In 2008, the value is $495 − 20%($495) = 80%($495) = 0.80 ($495) = $396, Choice B.

21. A. Analyze the problem. The number of people over age 65 who get a flu shot is $35\%N = 0.35N$. Of this number, 2% will have an adverse reaction. Thus, the estimated number of people over age 65 that will have an adverse reaction after getting flu shots is $(0.02)(0.35)N = 0.007N$, Choice A.

22. D. Analyze the problem. The quadratic function $y = 16x^2 − kx + 25$ will have exactly one real zero when its discriminant $b^2 − 4ac = 0$. The coefficients for $y = 16x^2 − kx + 25$ are $a = 16$, $b = −k$, and $c = 25$. Thus, you have $(−k^2) − 4(16)(25) = 0 \Rightarrow k^2 − 1600 = 0 \Rightarrow$ the positive coefficient $k = 40$, Choice D.

23. B. Analyze the problem. You are to identify functions that have the same domain and the same range. The function given in Roman I is a finite function. None of the other functions are finite, so eliminate any answer choice containing Roman I. Eliminate A and D. Devise a plan. Compare the domains of the functions, and then compare the ranges. Carry out the plan. The domain of each of the functions given in Roman II and IV is the set of real numbers; however, the domain in Roman III is the set of whole numbers, so eliminate Choice C. Thus, Choice B is the correct response. You do not have to check the ranges; but, just so you know, the range of each of the functions in Roman II and IV is the nonnegative real numbers.

24. B. A good way to analyze this problem is to make a chart that shows the growth of the deer population as a function of time, t, at eight-year intervals.

Time in years	$t = 0$	$t = 8$	$t = 16$	$t = 24$	. . .
Deer population	1500	(1500)2	$(1500)2^2$	$(1500)2^3$	. . .

From your table, you can see that at eight-year intervals, you are multiplying by a power of 2. Therefore, the function that models the population growth must have an exponential factor that has base 2 in it, so you can eliminate choices A and C, which do not have an exponential factor with base 2. Now you must decide whether the exponent for 2 in the expression should be $0.125t$ (Choice B) or $8t$ (Choice D). Again, use your table to help you decide. When $t = 0$, $(1500)2^{0.125t} = (1500)2^{8t} = (1500)2^0 = (1500)1 = 1500$, which matches the table. When $t = 8$, $(1500)2^{0.125t} = (1500)2^{0.125(8)} = (1500)2^1 = 1500$, which matches the table; but $(1500)2^{8t} = (1500)2^{8(8)} = (1500)2^{64} = 4.6 \ldots \times 10^{22}$, which does not match the table. Therefore, Choice B is the correct response.

25. C. Analyze the problem. When two lines are perpendicular, their slopes are negative reciprocals of each other. You can write the equation of a line when you know the slope of the line and a point on the line. Devise a plan. To find the equation of the line that is perpendicular to the line whose equation is $5x − 6y = 4$ and passes through the point (3, 1) will take three steps. First, find the slope, m, of the line whose equation is $5x − 6y = 4$; next, find the negative reciprocal of m, which is $-\dfrac{1}{m}$; and then use the point-slope form to determine the equation of the line with slope $-\dfrac{1}{m}$ that passes through the point (3, 1).

Step 1. Rewrite $5x − 6y = 4$ as $y = \dfrac{5}{6}x − \dfrac{2}{3}$, which shows the slope of this line is $= \dfrac{5}{6}$.

Step 2. The negative reciprocal of $\dfrac{5}{6}$ is $-\dfrac{6}{5}$

Step 3. Determine the desired equation: $y − 1 = -\dfrac{6}{5}(x − 3) \Rightarrow 5y − 5 = −6x + 18 \Rightarrow 6x + 5y = 23$, Choice C.

26. D. Analyze the problem. You need to find the cost of the paint needed to cover the surface area of the sphere. Devise a plan. To determine the cost of the paint will take three steps. First, find the surface area of the sphere; next, find the number of gallons of paint needed; and then find the cost of the paint.

Step 1. $SA = 4\pi r^2 = 4\pi(12 \text{ ft})^2 = 1809.5575 \ldots \text{ ft}^2$ (Don't round this answer.)

Tip: Memorize this formula. You will not be given a formula sheet for the test.

Step 2. Number of gallons needed = 1809.5575 . . . ft² ÷ $\dfrac{400\ \text{ft}^2}{1\ \text{gal}}$ = 4.5238 . . . gallons, so 5 gallons will need to be purchased (since the paint is sold in gallon containers only).

Step 3. Cost of 5 gallons of paint = 5 gallons × $\dfrac{\$24.50}{1\ \text{gal}}$ = \$122.50, Choice D.

27. B. Analyze the problem. Since the coin is to be flipped five times, you can work this problem by extending the Fundamental Counting Principle to five events. There are 2 possibilities for each of the 5 coin flips, which means the total number of possible outcomes in the sample space is $2 \cdot 2 \cdot 2 \cdot 2 \cdot 2 = 2^5$, Choice B.

28. D. Analyze the problem. You want to determine which of the given properties does NOT hold for S with respect to $\otimes$. Devise a plan. Using the table, list the possible "products" and check for the properties given in the answer choices. Carry out the plan.

From the table, you have $a \otimes a = a$, $a \otimes b = b$, $b \otimes a = b$, and $b \otimes b = b$.

Checking Choice A: S is closed with respect to $\otimes$ because when $\otimes$ is performed on any two elements in S, the result is an element in S. Eliminate Choice A.

Checking Choice B. Since $a \otimes b = b$ and $b \otimes a = b$, S is commutative with respect to $\otimes$. Eliminate Choice B.

Checking Choice C. Since $a \otimes a = a$, $a \otimes b = b$, and $b \otimes a = b$, S contains an identity element, namely a, with respect to $\otimes$. Eliminate Choice C.

Thus, Choice D is the correct response. You should go on to the next problem. However, for your information S does not contain an inverse for every element in S. In particular, the element b does not have an inverse because there is no element in S such that $b \otimes$ (that element) = a (the identity element).

29. D. Analyze the problem. Adding a positive constant h to x will result in a horizontal shift of h units to the left. The graph of $f(x) = (x + 3)^3$ is the same as the graph of $f(x) = x^3$ shifted left by 3 units, Choice D.

Tip: If you are unsure whether the shift is to the right or left, graph both functions on your graphing calculator to check.

30. C. Analyze the problem. The stem-leaf plot shows three-digit weights for each member, with the first two digits under the "stem" column, and the third digit under the "leaf" column. Devise a plan. To find the percent of women in the club who weigh less than 115 pounds will take two steps. First, read the information in the stem-leaf plot to determine how many women weigh less than 115 pounds. Next, use the result to find the percent of women who weigh less than 115 pounds.

Step 1. Using the stem-leaf plot, count how many women weigh less than 115 pounds. There are 9 weights that are less than 115 pounds (100, 103, 103, 107, 108, 111, 111, 111, and 114).

Tip: Do this step mentally. Don't waste time writing down the weights.

Step 2. Find the percent: $\dfrac{9}{36}$ = 25%, Choice C.

31. C. Analyze the problem. If you let W = the set of customers who bought washers and D = the set of customers who bought dryers, you have $n(W) = 94$ and $n(D) = 80$. Consequently, $n(W) + n(D) = 94 + 80 = 174$, which is greater than 152, the total number of customers. Logically, you can conclude that there is overlap in the sets W and D. Devise a plan. Draw a Venn diagram showing two overlapping circle representing W and D. Label the three regions determined by the overlapping circles as follows: a, the region representing customers who bought only washers; b, the region representing customers who bought both a washer and dryer; and c, the region representing customers who bought only dryers. Use $n(a)$, $n(b)$, and $n(c)$ to write equations representing the information given in the problem with the goal of determining $n(a)$. Carry out the plan.

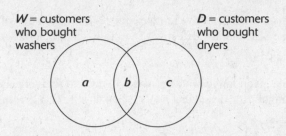

From the diagram and the information given in the problem, you have the following three equations:

(1) $n(a) + n(b) + n(c) = 152$, (2) $n(a) + n(b) = 94$, and (3) $n(c) + n(b) = 80$.

Adding (2) and (3) gives equation (4) $n(a) + n(b) + n(c) + n(b) = 94 + 80 = 174$.

Substituting (1) into (4) gives $152 + n(b) = 174 \Rightarrow n(b) = 174 - 152 = 22$, which is the number of customers who bought both a washer and dryer. Substituting $n(b) = 22$ into (2) gives $n(a) + 22 = 94 \Rightarrow n(a) = 94 - 22 = 72$. Thus, the number of customers who bought only a washer is 72, Choice C.

32. C. $\dfrac{a}{a^2 - b^2} - \dfrac{b}{a^2 + ab} = \dfrac{a}{(a+b)(a-b)} - \dfrac{b}{a(a+b)} = \dfrac{a \cdot a}{a(a+b)(a-b)} - \dfrac{b(a-b)}{a(a+b)(a-b)} =$

$\dfrac{a^2}{a(a+b)(a-b)} - \dfrac{ab - b^2}{a(a+b)(a-b)} = \dfrac{a^2 - ab + b^2}{a(a+b)(a-b)}$, Choice C.

Tip: Watch your signs! A minus sign before a fraction applies to the entire numerator, not just to the first term.

33. B. This is a unit analysis problem. Plug the units into the formula and simplify as you would for variable quantities.

$$Y = \frac{Adv}{t} = \frac{(cm^2)\left(\dfrac{g}{cm^3}\right)\left(\dfrac{cm}{s}\right)}{s} = \frac{\dfrac{g}{s}}{s} = \frac{g}{s^2} \text{, Choice B.}$$

34. D. Analyze the problem. This question asks you to find a conditional probability; that is, you want to find the probability when you already know that the student is female. Thus, when computing the probability, the number of possible students under consideration is no longer 500, but is reduced to the total number of female students. In other words, once you know that the selected person is a female student, you are dealing only with the students in the second row of the table. Devise a plan. First, find the total number of female students. Next, among those, determine the number who reside off-campus, and then compute the conditional probability. Carry out the plan.

Step 1. Total female students = $156 + 95 = 251$.

Step 2. Among the 251 female students, 95 reside off-campus. Thus, P(resides off-campus | given student is female) = $\dfrac{95}{251}$, Choice D.

35. D. Analyze the problem. The volume of a right prism is given by $V = Bh$. Devise a plan. To find the volume of the right triangular prism will take two steps. First, find the area, B, of one of the equilateral triangular bases, and then find the volume by multiplying B by 20 in, the height (h) of the prism.

Step 1. The area of an equilateral triangle with sides of 4 in is given by: Area = $\dfrac{\sqrt{3}}{4}s^2 = \dfrac{\sqrt{3}}{4}(4 \text{ in})^2 = 4\sqrt{3}$ in^2

Tip: If you forget the formula for the area of an equilateral triangle, you can derive it by using the Pythagorean Theorem to determine the height (altitude) of the triangle, and then using the formula, area = $\dfrac{1}{2}bh$ to find the area of the equilateral triangle.

Step 2. Volume = $(4\sqrt{3} \text{ in}^2)(20 \text{ in}) = 138.5640 \ldots$ or approximately 138 in^3, Choice D.

36. B. Analyze the problem. After 5 nondefective remote controls have been drawn, there are only 15 remote controls left in the box, three of which are defective. Therefore, the probability that the next remote control is defective = $\frac{3}{15}$ = $\frac{1}{5}$, Choice B.

37. C. For the recursive formula given in the problem, you will need to find $f(1)$ and $f(2)$ before you can find $f(3)$. Since the problem tells you that $f(0) = 1$ and that $f(n) = 3f(n-1) + 1$ for $n \geq 1$, then

$f(1) = 3f(0) + 1 = 3(1) + 1 = 3 + 1 = 4$

$f(2) = 3f(1) + 1 = 3(4) + 1 = 12 + 1 = 13$

$f(3) = 3f(2) + 1 = 3(13) + 1 = 39 + 1 = 40$, Choice C.

38. B. $(f \circ g)(x) = f(g(x)) = f(x + 2) = \dfrac{2(x+2)+6}{(x+2)+2} = \dfrac{2x+4+6}{x+2+2} = \dfrac{2x+10}{x+4}$, Choice B.

39. A. Analyze the problem. Since the order in which committee members are chosen does not make a difference as regards the composition of the committee, the number of different committees of size 6 that can be selected from the 300 members is $_{300}C_6$, Choice A.

40. B. In logic, the negation of a statement is a statement that has the opposite truth value; that is, when the given statement is true, its negation is false, and when the given statement is false, its negation is true. The given statement, "All teenagers are curious" contains the universal quantifier "All." You can eliminate choices C and D because the negation of a statement that contains a universal quantifier is a statement that contains an existential quantifier. To contradict that all teenagers are curious, you need only show that there exists at least one teenager who is not curious. In other words, since the given statement has the logical form "All t are c," the negation has the logical form "Some t are not c." Therefore, the negation of "All teenagers are curious" is "Some teenagers are not curious," Choice B.

Part B: Solutions to the Short Constructed-Response Section

For questions 41–43, score your response 0 to 3 using the following criteria:

- Correctly answered all parts of the question
- Gave a complete and full explanation for answers
- Demonstrated a strong understanding of the mathematical content relevant to the question
- Demonstrated a thorough understanding of all aspects of any stimulus material provided

41. Sample correct constructed response

(a) The circular base of the cone has diameter 10 cm; therefore, its radius is 5 cm. The funnel is a right circular cone, so to find r we can set up the following proportion:

$$\frac{r}{5 \text{ cm}} = \frac{h}{24 \text{ cm}} \text{ ; Thus, } r = \frac{5h}{24} .$$

(b) The formula for the volume of a cone is $V = \frac{1}{3}\pi r^2 h$.

The volume of fluid in the funnel $= \frac{1}{3}\pi\left(\frac{5h}{24}\right)^2 h = \frac{25}{1728}\pi h^3$.

(c) The ratio of the volume of the fluid in the funnel to the volume of the cone =

$$\frac{\frac{25\pi h^3}{1728}}{\frac{\pi(5)^2(24)}{3}} = \frac{\frac{25\pi h^3}{3\cdot 24^2}}{\frac{\pi(25)(24)}{3}} = \frac{25\pi h^3}{3\cdot 24^2}\cdot\frac{3}{\pi(25)(24)} = \frac{h^3}{24^3} .$$

42. Sample correct constructed response

(a) Proof: Write the number n in base-ten expanded form:

$$n = d_p \cdot 10^p + \ldots + d_4 \cdot 10^4 + d_3 \cdot 10^3 + d_2 \cdot 10^2 + d_1 \cdot 10^1 + d_0 \cdot 10^0$$

$$= d_p \cdot 10^p + \ldots + d_4 \cdot 10^4 + d_3 \cdot 10^3 + d_2 \cdot 10^2 + d_1 \cdot 10 + d_0$$

Except for the last term, rewrite each term as an equivalent expression with coefficient 10:

$$= 10d_p \cdot 10^{p-1} + \ldots + 10d_4 \cdot 10^3 + 10d_3 \cdot 10^2 + 10d_2 \cdot 10^1 + 10d_1 + d_0$$

Factor out 2 from all terms except the last term:

$$= 2(5d_p \cdot 10^{p-1} + \ldots + 5d_4 \cdot 10^3 + 5d_3 \cdot 10^2 + 5d_2 \cdot 10^1 + 5d_1) + d_0$$

Thus, since the steps shown are reversible, n is divisible by 2 if and only its last digit, d_0, is divisible by 2, which will occur only when d_0 is an even number.

(b) Proof: Write the number n in base-ten expanded form:

$$n = d_p \cdot 10^p + \ldots + d_4 \cdot 10^4 + d_3 \cdot 10^3 + d_2 \cdot 10^2 + d_1 \cdot 10^1 + d_0 \cdot 10^0$$

$$= d_p \cdot 10^p + \ldots + d_4 \cdot 10^4 + d_3 \cdot 10^3 + d_2 \cdot 10^2 + d_1 \cdot 10 + d_0$$

Except for the last two terms, rewrite each term as an equivalent expression with coefficient 100:

$$= 100d_p \cdot 10^{p-2} + \ldots + 100d_4 \cdot 10^2 + 100d_3 \cdot 10^1 + 100d_2 + d_1 \cdot 10 + d_0$$

Factor out 4 from all terms except for the two last terms:

$$= 4(25d_p \cdot 10^{p-2} + \ldots + 25d_4 \cdot 10^2 + 25d_3 \cdot 10^1 + 25d_2) + d_1 \cdot 10 + d_0$$

Thus, since the steps shown are reversible, n is divisible by 4 if and only if $d_1 \cdot 10 + d_0$ is divisible by 4. In other words, n is divisible by 4 if and only if the number formed by deleting all but the last two digits of n is divisible by 4.

(c) A number is divisible by 5 if and only if the last digit of the number is 0 or 5. To prove this statement, proceed in a manner similar to that used in part (a). Begin with a counting number n that has digits $d_p \cdots d_4 d_3 d_2 d_1 d_0$. Write n in expanded form. Then, except for the last term, rewrite each term as an equivalent expression with coefficient 10. Next, factor out 5 from all terms except the last term. Therefore, since the steps are reversible, n is divisible by 5 if and only its last digit is divisible by 5, which will occur only when the last digit is 0 or 5.

43. Sample correct constructed response

(a) Let f = the number of female students enrolled in the fall semester a year ago

Let m = the number of male students enrolled in the fall semester a year ago

Let F = the number of female students currently enrolled

Let M = the number of male students currently enrolled

Since the female student enrollment increased by 5%,

$$F = f + 0.05f = f(1.05) \Rightarrow f(1.05) = F \Rightarrow f = \frac{F}{1.05}$$

Since the male student enrollment increased by 20%,

$$M = m + 0.20m = m(1.20) \Rightarrow m(1.20) = M \Rightarrow m = \frac{M}{1.20}$$

Since the total enrollment increased by 10%,

$$F + M = (f + m) + 0.10(f + m) = 1.10(f + m) \Rightarrow 1.10(f + m) = F + M \Rightarrow (f + m) = \frac{F + M}{1.10}$$

Substituting $f = \frac{F}{1.05}$ and $m = \frac{M}{1.20}$ into $(f + m) = \frac{F + M}{1.10}$ gives

$$\frac{F}{1.05} + \frac{M}{1.20} = \frac{F + M}{1.10} \Rightarrow$$

$$\frac{F}{1.05} + \frac{M}{1.20} = \frac{F}{1.10} + \frac{M}{1.10} \Rightarrow$$

$$\frac{F}{1.05} - \frac{F}{1.10} = \frac{M}{1.10} - \frac{M}{1.20} \Rightarrow$$

$$F\left(\frac{1}{1.05} - \frac{1}{1.10}\right) = M\left(\frac{1}{1.10} - \frac{1}{1.20}\right) \Rightarrow$$

$$\frac{F}{M} = \frac{\left(\frac{1}{1.10} - \frac{1}{1.20}\right)}{\left(\frac{1}{1.05} - \frac{1}{1.10}\right)} = 1.75 = 1\frac{3}{4} = \frac{7}{4}.$$

Thus, the current ratio of female students to male students at the community college is 7 to 4.

(b) The fraction of the current enrollment at the community college that is female equals

$$\frac{F}{F + M} = \frac{1}{1 + \frac{M}{F}} = \frac{1}{1 + \frac{4}{7}} = \frac{7}{7 + 4} = \frac{7}{11}.$$

(c) The fraction of the current enrollment at the community college that is male equals

$$1 - (\text{the fraction that is female}) = 1 - \frac{7}{11} = \frac{4}{11}.$$

Scoring Your Practice Test

The testing company does not release the exact details of the way the Praxis Middle School Mathematics test is scored. Here is a method that will give you an approximation of your percentage score (out of a possible 100 percent) on this practice test, with the caveat that the scoring method used by the testing company could likely differ from what is shown here.

Your total percentage score is 67% of the percent of multiple-choice items correct plus 33% of your constructed responses percentage score for this practice test.

Here is an example.

Suppose you get 38 multiple-choice items correct and full credit for each of the 3 constructed-response questions. Your score is computed as follows:

$$67\%\left(\frac{38}{40}\right) = 33\%\left(\frac{9}{9}\right) = 0.67\left(95\%\right) + 0.33\%\left(100\%\right) = 96.65\% \ .$$

Answer Sheet for Practice Test 3

1 Ⓐ Ⓑ Ⓒ Ⓓ		21 Ⓐ Ⓑ Ⓒ Ⓓ
2 Ⓐ Ⓑ Ⓒ Ⓓ		22 Ⓐ Ⓑ Ⓒ Ⓓ
3 Ⓐ Ⓑ Ⓒ Ⓓ		23 Ⓐ Ⓑ Ⓒ Ⓓ
4 Ⓐ Ⓑ Ⓒ Ⓓ		24 Ⓐ Ⓑ Ⓒ Ⓓ
5 Ⓐ Ⓑ Ⓒ Ⓓ		25 Ⓐ Ⓑ Ⓒ Ⓓ
6 Ⓐ Ⓑ Ⓒ Ⓓ		26 Ⓐ Ⓑ Ⓒ Ⓓ
7 Ⓐ Ⓑ Ⓒ Ⓓ		27 Ⓐ Ⓑ Ⓒ Ⓓ
8 Ⓐ Ⓑ Ⓒ Ⓓ		28 Ⓐ Ⓑ Ⓒ Ⓓ
9 Ⓐ Ⓑ Ⓒ Ⓓ		29 Ⓐ Ⓑ Ⓒ Ⓓ
10 Ⓐ Ⓑ Ⓒ Ⓓ		30 Ⓐ Ⓑ Ⓒ Ⓓ
11 Ⓐ Ⓑ Ⓒ Ⓓ		31 Ⓐ Ⓑ Ⓒ Ⓓ
12 Ⓐ Ⓑ Ⓒ Ⓓ		32 Ⓐ Ⓑ Ⓒ Ⓓ
13 Ⓐ Ⓑ Ⓒ Ⓓ		33 Ⓐ Ⓑ Ⓒ Ⓓ
14 Ⓐ Ⓑ Ⓒ Ⓓ		34 Ⓐ Ⓑ Ⓒ Ⓓ
15 Ⓐ Ⓑ Ⓒ Ⓓ		35 Ⓐ Ⓑ Ⓒ Ⓓ
16 Ⓐ Ⓑ Ⓒ Ⓓ		36 Ⓐ Ⓑ Ⓒ Ⓓ
17 Ⓐ Ⓑ Ⓒ Ⓓ		37 Ⓐ Ⓑ Ⓒ Ⓓ
18 Ⓐ Ⓑ Ⓒ Ⓓ		38 Ⓐ Ⓑ Ⓒ Ⓓ
19 Ⓐ Ⓑ Ⓒ Ⓓ		39 Ⓐ Ⓑ Ⓒ Ⓓ
20 Ⓐ Ⓑ Ⓒ Ⓓ		40 Ⓐ Ⓑ Ⓒ Ⓓ

CUT HERE

Part A

40 Multiple-Choice Questions

(Suggested Time—80 minutes)

Directions: Each of the questions or incomplete statements below is followed by four answer choices (A, B, C, or D). Select the one that is best in each case, and then fill in the corresponding lettered space on the answer sheet.

1. If $f(x) = \dfrac{x+6}{x+2}$ and $g(x) = x + 1$, then $(g \circ f)(x) =$ $g(f(x)) =$

 A. $\dfrac{2x+8}{x+2}$

 B. $\dfrac{x+7}{x+3}$

 C. $\dfrac{4x+4}{x+1}$

 D. $\dfrac{2x+8}{2x+4}$

2. How many different passwords can be made consisting of four lowercase letters followed by two digits?

 A. $4 \cdot 2$
 B. $(_{26}C_4)(_{10}C_2)$
 C. $26^4 \cdot 10^2$
 D. 36^6

3. For what value of $k \geq 0$ will the graph of the function $y = \dfrac{k}{25x^2 + kx + 9}$ have exactly one vertical asymptote?

 A. 0
 B. 15
 C. 30
 D. 60

4. Using a protractor a student measures the acute angles in a right triangle and then adds the two measurements to obtain a sum of 81°. What is the percent error of the sum to the nearest percent?

 A. 0.10%
 B. 0.11%
 C. 10%
 D. 11%

5. For calls to China, a long-distance phone service charges $3.75 for the first minute (or fraction thereof) and $0.55 for each additional minute. Suppose that a customer using the service is charged $11.45 for a call to China. For how many minutes did the customer's phone call last?

 A. 12 minutes
 B. 13 minutes
 C. 14 minutes
 D. 15 minutes

6. $i^{254} =$

 A. -1
 B. $-i$
 C. 1
 D. i

GO ON TO THE NEXT PAGE

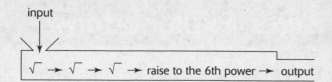

input

$\sqrt{} \rightarrow \sqrt{} \rightarrow \sqrt{} \rightarrow$ raise to the 6th power $\rightarrow$ output

7. If x^2 $(x \geq 0)$ is used as the input for the function machine shown, which of the following is equivalent to the output?

A. $x^{\frac{1}{24}}$

B. $x^{\frac{3}{4}}$

C. x

D. $x^{\frac{3}{2}}$

8. Grace runs the same distance each morning before going to work. For 10 days she records her running times for her target distance. Her recorded running times are 21 minutes, 35 minutes, 34 minutes, 30 minutes, 32 minutes, 36 minutes , 24 minutes, 35 minutes, 28 minutes, and 35 minutes. What is the difference between Grace's median running time and her mean running time for the 10 days?

A. 0 minutes

B. 2 minutes

C. 3 minutes

D. 4 minutes

9. $(a^{-1} + b^{-1})^{-1} =$

A. $a + b$

B. $\dfrac{1}{a} + \dfrac{1}{b}$

C. $\dfrac{ab}{a + b}$

D. $\dfrac{2}{a + b}$

10. In a mixture the ratio of cornmeal to wheat bran, by weight, is 2 to 3. Find the amount (in ounces) of a mixture that contains 30 ounces of cornmeal.

A. 30 oz

B. 40 oz

C. 50 oz

D. 75 oz

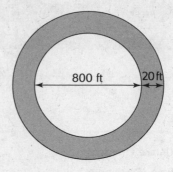

800 ft   20 ft

11. The figure shows two concentric circles. Find the area of the shaded region.

A. 8100π ft^2

B. $16{,}400\pi$ ft^2

C. $32{,}400\pi$ ft^2

D. $65{,}600\pi$ ft^2

12. On a number line, line segment x has endpoints $6\frac{1}{4}$ and $6\frac{1}{2}$, and line segment y has endpoints $\dfrac{5}{\sqrt{8}}$ and $\dfrac{3}{\sqrt{2}}$, What is the ratio of the length of y to the length of x?

A. $\dfrac{1}{\sqrt{2}}$

B. $\sqrt{2}$

C. $\dfrac{4}{\sqrt{2}}$

D. $4\sqrt{2}$

13. The ratio of the volume of sphere A to the volume of sphere B is 27 to 1. What is the ratio of the surface area of sphere A to the surface area of sphere B?

A. 3 to 1

B. 6 to 1

C. 9 to 1

D. 27 to 1

14. $(2x^2 - 3x - 2)^{-1}(2x^2 + 7x + 3)(x^2 - x - 2)(x^2 - 9)^{-1} =$

A. $\dfrac{x + 1}{x - 3}$

B. $\dfrac{x - 1}{x + 3}$

C. $\dfrac{(x + 7)(x + 1)}{(x + 3)(x - 3)}$

D. $-\dfrac{1}{3}$

15. $\dfrac{ab - b^2}{ab - a^2} - \dfrac{a^2 b - b^2}{ab} =$

   A. $-\dfrac{1}{a}$

   B. $-a$

   C. a

   D. $-\dfrac{a^2 + 2b}{a}$

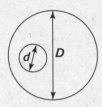

16. In the picture shown above, the diameter, *D,* of the larger circle is four times the diameter, *d,* of the smaller circle. What is the ratio of the area of the smaller circle to the area of the larger circle?

   A. $\dfrac{1}{16}$

   B. $\dfrac{1}{8}$

   C. $\dfrac{1}{4}$

   D. $\dfrac{1}{2}$

17. A 40-foot cable is attached to the outside wall of a four-story building. One end of the cable is anchored 24 feet from the base of the building. How high up on the outside wall of the building does the other end of the cable reach?

   A. 16 feet
   B. 32 feet
   C. 36 feet
   D. 47 feet

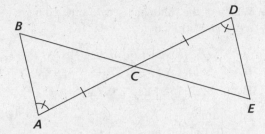

18. In the figure $\angle A \cong \angle D$ and $\overline{BE}$ bisects $\overline{AD}$. Which of the following methods should be used to show triangle *ABC* is congruent to triangle *DEC*?

   A. SSS
   B. SAS
   C. AAA
   D. ASA

19. If the surface area of a sphere is 144π cm^2, find the volume of the sphere.

   A. 36 cm^3
   B. 288 cm^3
   C. 216π cm^3
   D. 288π cm^3

20. Two identical machines can do a job in 10 days, how many days will take five such machines to do the same job?

   A. 4 days
   B. 5 days
   C. 8 days
   D. 25 days

21. Two vehicles leave the same location at 10:45 a.m., one traveling due north at 70 miles per hour and the other due south at 60 miles per hour. If the vehicles maintain their respective speeds, at what time will they be 325 miles apart?

   A. 12:15 P.M.
   B. 1:15 P.M.
   C. 2:15 P.M.
   D. 3 P.M.

GO ON TO THE NEXT PAGE

22. Which of the following sets of ordered pairs represents a function?

    I.   {(7, 5), (7, 9), (5, 12), (–3, 0)}

    II. {(5, 5), (5, 5²), (5, 5³), (5, 5⁴)}

    III. {(5, 5), (5², 5), (5³, 5), (5⁴, 5)}

    A. II only

    B. III only

    C. II and III only

    D. I, II, and III

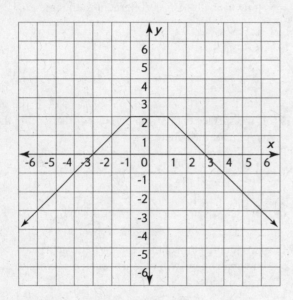

23. Which of the following sets is the range of the function shown?

    A. $\{y \mid y \text{ is a real number}\}$

    B. $\{y \mid y \text{ is a real number}, -3 \le y \le 3\}$

    C. $\{y \mid y \text{ is a real number}, -6 \le y \le 6\}$

    D. $\{y \mid y \text{ is a real number}, y \le 2\}$

24. Which of the following functions is the polynomial of lowest degree that has zeroes at $-4, -1, \frac{1}{2}$, and 2?

    A. $P(x) = x(x + 4)(x - \frac{1}{2})(x - 2)(x + 1)$

    B. $P(x) = (x - 4)(2x + 1)(x + 2)(x - 1)$

    C. $P(x) = (x + 4)(2x - 1)(x - 2)(x + 1)$

    D. $P(x) = 2x(x + 4)(x - \frac{1}{2})(x - 2)(x + 1)$

25. Which of the following expressions is equivalent to the expression $\log_{10}\left(\frac{x^3}{20}\right)$?

    A. $(\log_{10}x)^3 - 2$

    B. $3\log_{10}x - 2$

    C. $(\log_{10}x)^3 - \log_{10}20$

    D. $3\log_{10}x - \log_{10}2 - 1$

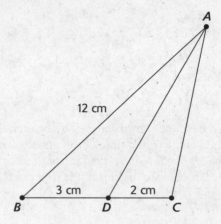

26. In triangle ABC, $\angle DAB \cong \angle DAC$. What is the length of $\overline{AC}$?

    A. It cannot be determined from the information given.

    B. 6 cm

    C. 7 cm

    D. 8 cm

27. Candi scored at the 85th percentile on a multiple-choice exam. The best interpretation of this information is that

    A. Candi answered 85 percent of the questions on the test correctly.

    B. Only 15 percent of the other students did worse on the test than did Candi.

    C. Candi answered 85 questions correctly.

    D. Candi did as well or better than 85 percent of the students who took the exam.

28. A water tank can be filled in 6 hours when the input valve is open and the outlet valve is closed. When the input valve is closed and the outlet valve is open, the same tank can be emptied in 10 hours. If a tank is filled with both valves open, how long will it take to fill the tank?

 A. 4 hours
 B. $7\frac{1}{2}$ hours
 C. 15 hours
 D. 16 hours

29. Given the cubic function $f(x) = x^3$, which of the following best describes the function $g(x) = (x - 5)^3 + 2$?

 A. the same as the graph of $f(x) = x^3$ shifted right by 5 units and up by 2 units
 B. the same as the graph of $f(x) = x^3$ shifted left by 5 units and up by 2 units
 C. the same as the graph of $f(x) = x^3$ shifted right by 5 units and down by 2 units
 D. the same as the graph of $f(x) = x^3$ shifted left by 5 units and down by 2 units

30. A realtor, who is selling houses located in an upscale housing development, has determined the following probabilities for two neighboring houses, one of which is a model home: the probability that the model home will be sold is 0.50, the probability that the house next door will be sold is 0.40, and the probability that at least one of the two houses will be sold is 0.80. Find the probability that the house next door will be sold given that the model home has already been sold.

 A. 10%
 B. 20%
 C. 30%
 D. 40%

31. Which of the following graphs does NOT contain an Euler path?

 A.

 B.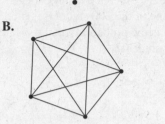

 C.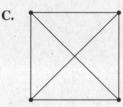

 D.

32. The compound interest formula is $P = P_0(1 + r)^t$, where r is the rate, compounded annually, and P is the value after t years of an initial investment of P_0. Suppose a couple establishes a trust fund account for their child's education with an investment of $10,000. Assuming no withdrawals and no additional deposits are made, approximately what interest rate compounded annually is needed to double the investment in 20 years?

 A. 3.5%
 B. 5.5%
 C. 10.0%
 D. 103.5%

33. What is the distance from the point $(-3, 7)$ to the line that has equation $4x + 3y = -5$?

 A. 0.6 unit
 B. 0.8 unit
 C. 2.0 units
 D. 2.8 units

GO ON TO THE NEXT PAGE

Practice Test 3

	Female	Male
Former Student	25	5
Current Student	93	77

	Exam 1	Exam 2	Exam 3	Exam 4
Student's Grade	85	77	92	90
Class Mean	75	78	86	80
Class Standard Deviation	5	2	4	10

34. The data in the table show the student status, by sex, of 200 library users at a small college for a given day. If one of the 200 students is randomly selected, what is the probability that the student is a male former student?

A. $\dfrac{1}{40}$

B. $\dfrac{1}{8}$

C. $\dfrac{5}{8}$

D. $\dfrac{5}{6}$

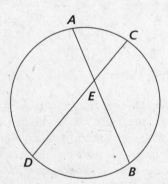

35. In the circle shown, chords $\overline{AB}$ and $\overline{CD}$ intersect at point E such that the length of $\overline{AE}$ is one-half the length of $\overline{EB}$. If the length of $\overline{CE} = 2$ cm and the length of $\overline{ED} = 6$ cm, find the length of chord $\overline{AB}$.

A. $\sqrt{6}$ cm

B. 4 cm

C. $2\sqrt{6}$ cm

D. $3\sqrt{6}$ cm

36. The data in the preceding table show a student's grades on four exams in an economics course along with the means and standard deviations of the grades for all the students in the class of 45 students? On which of the exams did the student perform best relative to the performance of the student's classmates?

A. Exam 1

B. Exam 2

C. Exam 3

D. Exam 4

37. A small town has four prefixes available—560, 562, 564, and 569— for the seven-digit telephone numbers in the town. How many different telephone numbers are possible if all four prefixes are used?

A. $4(_{10}C_4)$

B. $4 \cdot 10^4$

C. 10^8

D. 10^{16}

38. If $f(x) = -16x^{-4}$, then $f(-2)$ is

A. -1

B. 1

C. 128

D. 256

39. A box contains 25 wooden tiles of identical size, which are numbered 1 through 25. If one tile is drawn at random from the box, what is the probability that the number on the tile is a prime number?

A. $\dfrac{1}{25}$

B. $\dfrac{9}{25}$

C. $\dfrac{2}{5}$

D. $\dfrac{12}{25}$

40. Which of the following is a negation of "Some professors are entertaining"?

A. Some professors are not entertaining.

B. All professors are entertaining.

C. No professors are not entertaining.

D. No professors are entertaining.

GO ON TO THE NEXT PAGE

Part B

3 Constructed-Response Questions

(Suggested Time—40 minutes)

Directions: Questions 41–43 are constructed-response questions. Write your responses to these questions in the space provided in the lined pages following the questions. If a question has multiple parts, be sure to answer each part of the question.

Question 41

Several people attend a party. Each guest shakes hands with each of the other guests.

(a) Suppose that the number of guests in attendance at the party is eight, draw a model that represents the situation and then use the model to determine the number of handshakes that would take place. Explain your reasoning.

(b) Use your model from part (a) to help you write a general formula for the number of handshakes that would take place among n guests if each guest shakes hands with each of the other guests. Explain your reasoning.

(c) Using the formula you wrote in part (b) determine the number of people at a party where 45 handshakes were exchanged among the guests, assuming that each guest shook hands with each of the other guests.

Question 42

The figure shown is a **pendulum** of **length,** L. The **frequency,** f, of a pendulum is the number of times the pendulum makes one complete swing back and forth in one second. If the length, L, of the arm of the pendulum is given in centimeters, the frequency of the pendulum is given by the following formula:

$$f = \frac{1}{2\pi}\sqrt{\frac{g}{L}}$$, where g = acceleration due to gravity = 981 cm/s^2

(a) What is the approximate frequency, to the nearest tenth, of a pendulum with arm length 9 centimeters? Show your work.

(b) Determine an expression for the length, L, of the arm as a function of the frequency. Show your work.

(c) Using the expression you found in part (b), if the frequency of a pendulum is $\frac{1}{2}$ cycles per second, approximately how long, to the nearest tenth of a centimeter, is the arm of the pendulum? Show your work.

Question 43

Prices for tickets to a charity concert were $75, $45, and $20, depending on seat location. A total of 700 tickets were sold, with twice as many $20 tickets being sold than $45 tickets. The total amount of money collected was $24,500.

(a) Let x equal the number of $75 tickets sold and y equal the number of $45 tickets sold. Write an equation that shows the total number of tickets sold in terms of x and y. Explain your reasoning.

(b) Write an equation that shows the total amount of money collected in terms of x and y. Explain your reasoning.

(c) Use the equations you wrote in parts (a) and (b) to determine the number of tickets sold at $75, the number of tickets sold at $45, and the number of tickets sold at $20. Explain your process and show your work.

GO ON TO THE NEXT PAGE

Begin your response to Question 41 here.

Begin your response to Question 42 here.

GO ON TO THE NEXT PAGE

Begin your response to Question 43 here.

Middle School Mathematics (0069) Practice Test 3 Answer Key

Part A: Correct Answers for the Multiple-Choice Questions

Question Number	Correct Answer	Content Category	Question Number	Correct Answer	Content Category
1.	A	III	21.	B	I
2.	C	IV	22.	B	III
3.	C	III	23.	D	III
4.	C	II	24.	C	III
5.	D	I	25.	D	III
6.	A	I	26.	D	II
7.	D	I	27.	D	IV
8.	B	IV	28.	C	I
9.	C	I	29.	A	III
10.	D	I	30.	B	IV
11.	B	II	31.	C	IV
12.	B	I	32.	A	I
13.	C	II	33.	D	II
14.	A	I	34.	A	IV
15.	B	I	35.	D	II
16.	A	II	36.	A	IV
17.	B	II	37.	B	IV
18.	D	II	38.	A	III
19.	D	II	39.	B	IV
20.	A	I	40.	D	IV

Answer Explanations for the Multiple-Choice Section

1. A. $(g \circ f)(x) = g(f(x)) = g\left(\dfrac{x+6}{x+2}\right) = \dfrac{x+6}{x+2} + 1 = \dfrac{x+6}{x+2} + \dfrac{x+2}{x+2} = \dfrac{2x+8}{x+2}$, Choice A.

2. C. Analyze the problem. Since for a password there are six slots to be filled, you can work this problem by extending the Fundamental Counting Principle to six events. There are 26 possibilities for each of the four letters and 10 possible values for each of the two digits. Therefore, the total number of possible passwords is $26 \cdot 26 \cdot 26 \cdot 26 \cdot 10 \cdot 10 = 26^4 \cdot 10^2$, Choice C.

3. C. Analyze the problem. The graph of the function $y = \dfrac{k}{25x^2 + kx + 9}$ will have vertical asymptotes at values of x for which the denominator, $25x^2 + kx + 9$, equals zero. The trinomial, $25x^2 + kx + 9$, will have exactly one zero when it is a perfect square. Devise a plan. Find the value for $k \geq 0$ that makes $25x^2 + kx + 9$ a perfect square. Carry out the plan. For $25x^2 + kx + 9$ to be a perfect square, the coefficient, k, of x needs to be $2\sqrt{25}\sqrt{9}$, which is $2 \cdot 5 \cdot 3 = 30$, Choice C.

4. C. Analyze the problem. The sum of the acute angles of a right triangle is 90°. Devise a plan. To find the percent error of the student's sum will take two steps. First, find the absolute error by finding the difference between 90° and the student's sum. Next, find the percent error by dividing the difference by 90°. Carry out the plan.

Step 1. Find the difference: $90° - 81° = 9°$.

Step 2. Find the percent error: $\dfrac{9°}{90°} = 0.10 = 10\%$, Choice C.

5. D. Analyze the problem. Suppose x is the total number of minutes that the call lasted. Then x is the sum of the first minute and the total number of minutes talked after the first minute, which is $x - 1$. The charge for the first minute, \$3.75, plus the charge for the additional minutes, \$0.55$(x - 1)$, equals the total charge for the call, \$11.45. Devise a plan. Write an equation and solve for x. Carry out the plan.

\$3.75 + \$0.55$(x - 1)$ = \$11.45 $\Rightarrow$ \$3.75 + \$0.55x - \$0.55 = \$11.45 $\Rightarrow$ \$0.55x = \$8.25 $\Rightarrow$ $x = 15$ minutes, Choice D.

6. A. Analyze the problem. For the complex number i, $i = i$, $i^2 = -1$, $i^3 = -i$, $i^4 = 1$, $i^5 = i$, $i^6 = -1$, $i^7 = -i$, $i^8 = 1$, $i^9 = -1$, and so on. You can see that the powers of the complex number i are cyclic, such that $i^{4k+1} = i$, $i^{4k+2} = i^2 = -1$, $i^{4k+3} = i^3 = -i$, and $i^{4k+4} = i^4 = 1$. So to evaluate a power of i, you divide its exponent by 4 and use the remainder as the exponent for i. Thus, $i^{254} = i^2 = -1$, Choice A.

7. D. Analyze the problem. Since the answer choices are given as exponential expressions, the best way to work this problem is to perform on x^2 the sequence of operations indicated by the function machine, using the exponential form for the radicals:

$$\left[\left(\left(\left(x^2\right)^{\frac{1}{2}}\right)^{\frac{1}{2}}\right)^{\frac{1}{2}}\right]^6 = x^{\frac{12}{8}} = x^{\frac{3}{2}}, \text{ Choice D.}$$

8. B. Analyze the problem. You are asked to find the difference between Grace's median running time and her mean running time. Devise a plan. To find the difference between the median and the mean will take three steps. First, calculate the mean; next, calculate the median; and then find the difference between the two. Carry out the plan.

Method 1. The most efficient way to work this problem is to use the statistical features of your graphing calculator. For the TI-83, press **2ⁿᵈ STAT** to access the **LIST** menu. Select **MATH**, then press **3** to choose **3: mean (**. Enter the data inside braces and close the parentheses as shown here: **mean({21, 35, 34, 30, 32, 36, 24, 35, 28, 35})**. Press **ENTER**. The display will show **31**, which is the mean. Press **2ⁿᵈ ENTER** (for **ENTRY**) to recall the previous calculation. Use the arrow keys to go back until the cursor is on the **"m"** in **mean.** Press **DEL**. Press **2ⁿᵈ DEL** (for **INS**) so that you can insert a different function. Press **2ⁿᵈ STAT** to access the **LIST** menu. Select **MATH**, then press **4** to choose **4: median (**. Press **ENTER**. The display will show **33,** which is the median. Subtract to find the difference: 33 minutes – 31 minutes = 2 minutes, Choice B.

Tip: You should plan to use a graphing calculator when taking the test. However, make sure you practice using it so that you can access the features smoothly and efficiently.

Method 2. You can calculate the mean and median by using the appropriate formulas.

Step 1. Find the mean (omitting units for convenience): mean = $\dfrac{\text{the sum of the running times}}{\text{number of running times}}$ =

$\dfrac{21+24+28+30+32+34+35+35+35+36}{10} = \dfrac{310}{10} = 31$ min.

Step 2. Find the median: Put the times in order: 21, 24, 28, 30, 32, 34, 35, 35, 35, 36. Average the two middle

times: $\dfrac{32+34}{2} = 33$ min.

Step 3. Find the difference: 33 minutes – 31 minutes = 2 minutes, Choice B.

9. **C.** $\left(a^{-1}+b^{-1}\right)^{-1} = \dfrac{1}{\left(a^{-1}+b^{-1}\right)} = \dfrac{1}{\left(\frac{1}{a}+\frac{1}{b}\right)} = \dfrac{ab\cdot 1}{ab\left(\frac{1}{a}+\frac{1}{b}\right)} = \dfrac{ab}{b+a} = \dfrac{ab}{a+b}$, Choice C.

10. **D.** Analyze the problem. The amount (in ounces) in the mixture is the sum of the amount (in ounces) of cornmeal in the mixture and the amount (in ounces) of wheat bran in the mixture. You know how much cornmeal is in the mixture, but you will need to find the amount of wheat bran in the mixture. Devise a plan. To find the total number of ounces in the mixture will take two steps. First, set up a proportion and find the amount (in ounces) of wheat bran in the mixture. Next, find the total amount (in ounces) of the mixture. Carry out the plan.

Step 1. $\dfrac{30\text{ oz}}{x} = \dfrac{2}{3} \Rightarrow x = 45$ oz of wheat bran.

Step 2. Total amount of mixture = 30 oz + 45 oz = 75 oz, Choice D.

11. **B.** Analyze the problem. The shaded region is the difference between the area of the larger circle and the area of the smaller circle. The formula for the area of a circle is πr^2. Devise a plan. Calculate the two areas and subtract. Carry out the plan. From the figure, you have the diameter of the larger circle is 800 ft + 2(20 ft) = 840 ft, and the diameter of the smaller circle is 800 ft. Thus, the radius of the larger circle is $\dfrac{1}{2}$ (840 ft) = 420 ft, and the radius of the smaller circle is $\dfrac{1}{2}$ (800 ft) = 400 ft.

Area of shaded region = $\pi(420\text{ ft})^2 - \pi(400\text{ ft})^2 = 16{,}400\pi\text{ ft}^2$, Choice B.

12. **B.** Analyze the problem. You are given the endpoints of segments x and y, so you can find their lengths by subtracting endpoints. Devise a plan. To find the ratio of the length of y to the length of x will take two steps. First, find the lengths of each of the line segments. Next, find the ratio of the length of y to the length of x. Carry out the plan.

Step 1. Length of $x = 6\dfrac{1}{2} - 6\dfrac{1}{4} = \dfrac{1}{4}$; length of $y = \dfrac{3}{\sqrt{2}} - \dfrac{5}{\sqrt{8}} = \dfrac{3}{\sqrt{2}} - \dfrac{5}{\sqrt{4\cdot 2}} = \dfrac{3}{\sqrt{2}} - \dfrac{5}{2\sqrt{2}} = \dfrac{6}{2\sqrt{2}} - \dfrac{5}{2\sqrt{2}} =$

$\dfrac{1}{2\sqrt{2}} = \dfrac{1\cdot\sqrt{2}}{2\sqrt{2}\sqrt{2}} = \dfrac{\sqrt{2}}{4}$

Step 2. $\dfrac{y}{x} = \dfrac{\frac{\sqrt{2}}{4}}{\frac{1}{4}} = \sqrt{2}$, Choice B.

13. **C.** Analyze the problem. Upon first reading, you might think this problem will take some time to work out. However, recall that when the dimensions of a solid figure are multiplied by a scale factor, the surface area and volume are multiplied by the scale factor raised to the second power and third power, respectively. Devise a plan. To find the ratio of the surface areas of the spheres will take two steps. First, using the ratio of the volumes, determine the scale factor. Next, find the ratio of the surface areas by squaring the scale factor. Carry out the plan.

Step 1. The ratio of the volumes is $\dfrac{27}{1} \Rightarrow$ (scale factor)$^3 = 27 \Rightarrow$ scale factor = 3.

Step 2. The ratio of the surface areas is 3^2 to 1 = 9 to 1, Choice C.

Tip: Knowing how scale factors impact area and volume can be very helpful to you on the test.

Practice Test 3

14. A. $(2x^2 - 3x - 2)^{-1}(2x^2 + 7x + 3)(x^2 - x - 2)(x^2 - 9)^{-1} = \dfrac{(2x^2 + 7x + 3)(x^2 - x - 2)}{(2x^2 - 3x - 2)(x^2 - 9)} =$

$\dfrac{(2x+1)(x+3)(x+1)(x-2)}{(2x+1)(x-2)(x+3)(x-3)} = \dfrac{\cancel{(2x+1)}\cancel{(x+3)}(x+1)\cancel{(x-2)}}{\cancel{(2x+1)}\cancel{(x-2)}\cancel{(x+3)}(x-3)} = \dfrac{x+1}{x-3}$, Choice A.

15. B. $\dfrac{ab - b^2}{ab - a^2} - \dfrac{a^2 b - b^2}{ab} = \dfrac{b(a-b)}{a(b-a)} - \dfrac{b(a^2 - b)}{ab} = \dfrac{-b}{a} - \dfrac{(a^2 - b)}{a} = \dfrac{-b - a^2 + b}{a} = \dfrac{-a^2}{a} = -a$, Choice B.

> **Tip: Watch your signs! A minus sign before a fraction applies to all terms in the numerator, not just to the first term.**

16. A. Analyze the problem. The diameter, D, of the larger circle is four times the diameter, d, of the larger circle. One way to work the problem is to use the formula $A = \pi r^2$ to find the areas of the two circles in terms of D, and then find the ratio of the area of the smaller circle to the larger circle. However, you should remember that when the dimensions of a 2-dimensional figure are multiplied by a scale-factor, f, the area of the figure produced is f^2 times the area of the original figure. Therefore, the area of the larger circle in the diagram is $4^2 = 16$ times the area of the smaller circle. Hence, the ratio of the area of the smaller circle to the larger circle $= \dfrac{1}{16}$, Choice A.

> **Tip: Knowing how scale factors impact area and volume can save you time on the test.**

17. B. First sketch a diagram to illustrate the problem.

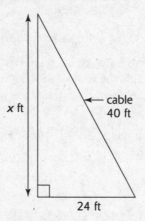

Analyze the problem. The building, the cable, and the ground form a right triangle. From the diagram, you can see that the length of the cable, 40 feet, is the hypotenuse of a right triangle that has legs of 24 feet and x feet. You can use the Pythagorean Theorem to find the missing leg, x.

Method 1. $c =$ hypotenuse $= 40$ ft, $a = 24$ ft, and $b = x$ ft

$a^2 + b^2 = c^2 \Rightarrow (24 \text{ ft})^2 + x^2 = (40 \text{ ft})^2 \Rightarrow 576 \text{ ft}^2 + x^2 = 1600 \text{ ft}^2 \Rightarrow x^2 = 1600 \text{ ft}^2 - 576 \text{ ft}^2 \Rightarrow x^2 = 1024 \text{ ft}^2 \Rightarrow x = 32$ feet, Choice B.

Method 2. The Pythagorean triple (3, 4, 5) and its multiples (6, 8, 10), (9, 12, 15), . . . , (24, 32, 40), . . . , which are also Pythagorean triples, satisfy the Pythagorean Theorem. Since you are given that the hypotenuse is 40 and one of the legs is 24, then you know that the third leg of the right triangle must be 32. Thus, $x = 32$ feet, Choice B.

18. D. Analyze the problem. Eliminate Choice C because this is not a method for proving congruence. Looking at the figure, you have $\angle ACB \cong \angle DCE$ because they are vertical angles. You know that $\overline{AC} \cong \overline{DC}$ because $\overline{BE}$ bisects $\overline{AD}$. You are given that $\angle A \cong \angle D$. Thus, you have two angles and the included side of triangle ABC congruent to two angles and the included side of triangle DEC. Therefore, ASA, Choice D, is the correct response.

19. D. Analyze the problem. The formula for the surface area of a sphere is $S = 4\pi r^2$. The formula for the volume of a sphere is $\frac{4}{3}\pi r^3$. Devise a plan. To find the volume of the sphere will take two steps. First, find the radius of the sphere. Next, use the radius to find the volume. Carry out the plan.

Step 1. Surface area $S = 4\pi r^2 = 144\pi$ cm^2 $\Rightarrow$ $r^2 = 36$ cm^2 $\Rightarrow$ $r = 6$ cm

Step 2. Volume $V = \frac{4}{3}\pi r^3 = \frac{4}{3}\pi (6 \text{ cm})^3 = \frac{4}{3}\pi(216 \text{ cm}^3) = 288\pi$ cm^3, Choice D.

Tip: Be sure to memorize the basic geometry formulas for area and volume before taking the test.

---

20. A. Analyze the problem. This problem is best analyzed as a "work problem." The key idea in a work problem is the rate at which work is done equals the amount of work accomplished divided by the amount of time worked: rate = $\dfrac{\text{amount of work done}}{\text{time worked}}$. For the situation in this problem, the work to be done is "a job." Devise a plan. To determine how many days it will take 5 machines to do the job will take two steps. First, determine the rate at which one machine works. Next, let d = number of days it will take 5 machines to do the job, and then write and solve an equation to find d. Carry out the plan.

Step 1. Let r = rate of 1 machine, then $2 \times r \times 10$ days $= 1$ job $\Rightarrow$ $20r = 1$ job $\Rightarrow$ $r = \dfrac{1}{20}$ job per day per machine.

Step 2. 5 machines $\times \dfrac{1}{20}$ job/day/machine $\times d = 1$ job $\Rightarrow$ $\dfrac{1}{4}d = 1$ (omitting units for convenience) $\Rightarrow$ $d = $ 4 days, Choice A.

21. B. Analyze the problem. Recall that distance = (rate)(time). The key idea in problems involving the distance formula is that a given distance is determined by the rate and the time traveled at that rate. For the situation in this problem, the two vehicles will travel the same amount of time. Devise a plan. To determine the time at which the two vehicles will be 325 miles apart will take two steps. First, Let t = the time traveled by the two vehicles. Write an equation and solve for t. Next, determine the time of day by adding the time traveled to the time of departure. Carry out the plan.

Step 1. Distance traveled by vehicle traveling north = (rate)(time) = $70 \frac{\text{mi}}{\text{h}}t$; distance traveled by vehicle traveling south = (rate)(time) = $60 \frac{\text{mi}}{\text{h}}t$. Therefore, the total distance traveled = 325 miles = $70 \frac{\text{mi}}{\text{h}}t + 60 \frac{\text{mi}}{\text{h}}t$. Solve for t (omitting the units for convenience): $325 = 70t + 60t \Rightarrow 325 = 130t \Rightarrow 130t = 325 \Rightarrow t = 2.5$ hours = 2 hours 30 minutes.

Step 2. 10:45 A.M. + 2 hours 30 minutes = 1:15 P.M., Choice B.

22. B. Analyze the problem. A function is a relation in which each first component is paired with *one and only one* second component. Only the relation in Roman numeral III satisfies this requirement, Choice B. In Roman I, the first component 7 is paired with two different second components, namely, 5 and 9. In Roman II, the first component 5 is paired with four different second components. In Roman numeral III, every first component has a unique second component.

23. D. Analyze the problem. You are to identify the range of the function shown. The range of a function is the set of possible second components. From the graph, you can see that the values of y are less than or equal to 2. Thus, Choice D is the correct response.

24. C. Analyze the problem. You are given the zeroes of the desired polynomial. If r is a zero of a polynomial, $P(x)$, then $x - r$ is a factor of $P(x)$. Looking at the answer choices and using the previous statement, you can see that choices A and D have the desired zeroes; however, Choice C also has the desired zeroes because the factor $(2x - 1)$ would yield a zero of $\frac{1}{2}$. Of the answer choices A, C, and D, Choice C is the polynomial of lowest degree. Therefore, Choice C is the correct response.

25. D. Method 1. Using the properties for logarithms, $\log_{10}\left(\dfrac{x^3}{20}\right) = \log_{10}x^3 - \log_{10}20 = 3\log_{10}x - \log_{10}(2 \cdot 10) =$

$3\log_{10}x - (\log_{10}2 + \log_{10}10) = 3\log_{10}x - \log_{10}2 - \log_{10}10 = 3\log_{10}x - \log_{10}2 - 1$, Choice D.

Method 2. Select a convenient value for x, say 5, and evaluate $\log_{10}\left(\dfrac{5^3}{20}\right)$, which is $0.79588\ldots$, and then evaluate

each of the expressions given in the answer choices for x equal to 5. Choice A yields $1.65851\ldots$; Choice B yields $.09691\ldots$; Choice C yields $-.95954\ldots$; and Choice D yields $0.79588\ldots$. Thus, Choice D is the correct response.

26. D. Analyze the problem. Since $\angle DAB \cong \angle DAC$, then $\overline{AD}$ bisects $\angle A$. Recall that the angle bisector of an angle

of a triangle divides the opposite side in the ratio of the sides that form the angle bisected. Thus, $\dfrac{BD}{DC} = \dfrac{AB}{AC}$ and

$\dfrac{BD}{DC} = \dfrac{AB}{AC}$. Devise a plan. Set up a proportion and solve for $\overline{AC}$. Carry out the plan.

$\dfrac{DC}{BD} = \dfrac{AC}{AB} \Rightarrow \dfrac{AC}{AB} = \dfrac{DC}{BD} = \dfrac{AC}{12\text{ cm}} = \dfrac{2\text{ cm}}{3\text{ cm}} \Rightarrow \overline{AC} = 8$ cm, Choice D.

27. D. Analyze the problem. The 85th percentile is a value at or below which 85 percent of the data fall. Therefore, the best interpretation of Candi's score is that she did as well or better than 85% of the students who took the exam, Choice D.

28. C. Analyze the problem. This problem is best analyzed as a "work problem." The key idea in a work problem is that the rate at which work is done equals the amount of work accomplished divided by the amount of time worked: rate = $\dfrac{\text{amount of work done}}{\text{time worked}}$. For the situation in this problem, the work to be done is to fill the tank. However, only the input valve works to fill the tank. The output valve works counter to the input valve because it works to empty the tank. Devise a plan. Let t = time it will take to fill the tank with both valves open. To find t will take two steps. First, determine the rate, r_{fill}, at which the tank can be filled when the input valve is open and the outlet valve is closed and the rate, r_{empty}, at which the tank can be emptied when the input valve is closed and the outlet valve is open. Next, write an equation and solve for t. Carry out the plan.

Step 1. The rate for filling the tank is $r_{\text{fill}} = \dfrac{1\text{ full tank}}{6\text{ h}} = \dfrac{1}{6}$ tank/h; The rate for emptying the tank is

$r_{\text{empty}} = \dfrac{1\text{ full tank}}{10\text{ h}} = \dfrac{1}{10}$ tank/h

Step 2. 1 full tank = $\left(\dfrac{1}{6}\text{ tank/h}\right)(t) - \left(\dfrac{1}{10}\text{ tank/h}\right)(t) \Rightarrow 1 = \dfrac{1}{6}t - \dfrac{1}{10}t$ (omitting the units) $\Rightarrow$

$1 = \dfrac{5}{30}t - \dfrac{3}{30}t \Rightarrow 1 = \dfrac{2}{30}t \Rightarrow 1 = \dfrac{1}{15}t \Rightarrow 15 = t \Rightarrow t = 15$ hours, Choice C.

29. A. Subtracting 5 from x will result in a horizontal shift of 5 units to the right. Adding 2 to $f(x)$ will result in a vertical shift of 2 units up. Thus, the graph of $g(x) = (x - 5)^3 + 2$ is the same as the graph of $f(x) = x^3$ shifted right by 5 units and up by 2 units, Choice A.

Tip: If you are unsure about the shifts, graph the two functions on your graphing calculator to check.

30. B. Analyze the problem. The problem asks: Find the probability that the house next door will be sold given that the model home has already been sold? This probability is a conditional probability. If A is the event that the model home will be sold and B is the event that the house next door will be sold, then you need to find $P(B|A) = \dfrac{P(A \text{ and } B)}{P(A)}$. Looking at the formula, you see that you are given $P(A) = 0.50$, but you are not given $P(A$ and $B)$, which is the probability that both houses are sold. The problem states "the probability that at least one of the two houses will be sold is 0.80." For this problem situation, the probability that at least one of the two houses will be sold is $P(A \text{ or } B)$. Recall that $P(A \text{ or } B) = P(A) + P(B) - P(A \text{ and } B)$. Thus, since you know $P(A) = 0.50$, $P(B) = 0.40$, and $P(A \text{ or } B) = 0.80$, you can determine $P(A \text{ and } B)$. Devise a plan. To find $P(B|A)$ will take two steps. First, determine $P(A \text{ and } B)$. Next, use the information obtained and information given in the problem to calculate $P(B|A)$. Carry out the plan.

Step 1. $P(A \text{ or } B) = P(A) + P(B) - P(A \text{ and } B) \Rightarrow 0.80 = 0.50 + 0.40 - P(A \text{ and } B) \Rightarrow 0.80 = 0.90 - P(A \text{ and } B) \Rightarrow P(A \text{ and } B) = 0.90 - 0.80 = 0.10$.

Step 2. $P(B|A) = \dfrac{P(A \text{ and } B)}{P(A)} = \dfrac{0.10}{0.50} = 0.20 = 20\%$, Choice B.

31. C. Analyze the problem. Recall the following: A path is a sequence of vertices such that from each vertex there is an edge to the next vertex, an Euler path is a path that uses each edge exactly once, and there is no Euler path for a graph that has more than two vertices of odd degree. (The degree of a vertex is the number of edges that are incident to that vertex.) Devise a plan. Count the number of vertices of odd degree in each graph to identify which graph has more than two vertices of odd degree. Carry out the plan. The graph in Choice A has exactly two vertices of odd degree. Eliminate A. The graph in Choice B has five vertices of even degree and no vertices of odd degree. Eliminate Choice B. The graph in Choice C has four vertices of odd degree, so it does not contain an Euler path. Choice C is the correct response. You should go on to the next problem; however, just so you know, the graph in Choice D has exactly two vertices of odd degree.

32. A. Analyze the problem. You need to find the rate, compounded annually, that will double an investment of $10,000 in 20 years. In other words, you need to find the rate, compounded annually, that will yield a value of $20,000 for P in 20 years. Devise a plan.

Method 1. The most efficient way to work this problem is to use the finance features of your graphing calculator. For the TI-83, press **2nd x^{-1}** to access the **FINANCE** menu. Press **ENTER** to select **1:TVM Solver...**. Use the information in the problem to fill in the values for the variables, including a zero for the unknown value of **I%** as shown in the table. *Note:* Because no payments are involved when you solve compound interest problems, **PMT** must be set to **0** and **P/Y** must be set to **1**.

N=20	number of payments
I%=0	unknown
PV=–10000	present value (entered as negative because it is an outflow of money)
PMT=0	not applicable
FV=20000	future value (entered as positive because it is an inflow of money)
P/Y=1	number of payments per year (must be set to 1 for this problem)
C/Y=1	number of compounding periods per year
PMT:END	BEGIN

Scroll to the **I%** line, and then press **ALPHA ENTER.** The **I%** line will show **I%=3.526492384**. Thus, 3.5% is the interest rate needed, Choice A.

Tip: Don't forget to enter PV as a negative number.

Method 2. Plug into the formula (omitting the units) and solve for r.

$P = P_0(1 + r)^t \Rightarrow 20,000 = 10,000(1 + r)^{20} \Rightarrow 2 = (1 + r)^{20} \Rightarrow \ln 2 = \ln(1 + r)^{20} \Rightarrow \ln 2 = 20 \ln(1 + r) \Rightarrow \dfrac{\ln 2}{20} = \ln(1 + r) \Rightarrow 1 + r = e^{\frac{\ln 2}{20}} \Rightarrow r = e^{\frac{\ln 2}{20}} - 1 = .03526\ldots$ or approximately 3.5%, Choice A.

Method 3. You can work this problem by checking the answer choices.

Checking A: $10,000(1 + 0.035)^{20} = 19,897.8886\ldots$ or approximately 20,000, indicating Choice A is the correct response.

In a test situation, you should go on to the next question since you have obtained the correct answer. You would not have to check the other answer choices; but for your information Choice B yields $29,177.5749\ldots$; Choice C yields $67274.9994\ldots$; and Choice D yields $1.4835\ldots \cdot E10$.

Tip: When feasible, working backward by checking answer choices is a clever strategy for the multiple-choice portion of the test.

33. **D.** Analyze the problem. The formula for the distance from point (x_1, y_1) to line $Ax + By + C = 0$ is given by
$d = \dfrac{|Ax_1 + By_1 + C|}{\sqrt{A^2 + B^2}}$. First, rewrite $4x + 3y = -5$ as $4x + 3y - 5 = 0$, and then apply the formula using the point $(-3, 7)$.

$$d = \frac{|Ax_1 + By_1 + C|}{\sqrt{A^2 + B^2}} = \frac{|4(-3) + 3(7) + 5|}{\sqrt{4^2 + 3^2}} = \frac{|-12 + 21 + 5|}{\sqrt{25}} = \frac{|14|}{5} = \frac{14}{5} \text{ or } 2.8 \text{ unit, Choice D.}$$

34. **A.** Analyze the problem. This question asks you to find the probability that a randomly selected student is a male former student. From the table, you can determine that of the 200 students, 5 are male former students. Thus, the
$= P(\text{male former student}) = \dfrac{5}{200} = \dfrac{1}{40}$, Choice A.

35. **D.** Analyze the problem. Recall that if two chords intersect within a circle, the product of the lengths of the segments of one chord equal the product of the lengths of the segments of the other. Let $x = $ length of $\overline{AE}$. Then $2x = $ length of $\overline{EB}$. Since chords $\overline{AB}$ and $\overline{CD}$ intersect at point E we have the following:

$x \cdot 2x = (2 \text{ cm})(6 \text{ cm}) \Rightarrow 2x^2 = 12 \text{ cm}^2 \Rightarrow x^2 = 6 \text{ cm}^2 \Rightarrow x = \sqrt{6} \text{ cm and } 2x = 2\sqrt{6} \text{ cm. Therefore, the length of}$
chord $= \sqrt{6} \text{ cm} + 2\sqrt{6} \text{ cm} = 3\sqrt{6} \text{ cm}$, Choice D.

Tip: Make sure you answer the question asked.

36. **A.** Analyze the problem. A good way to compare the student's performance on the four exams relative to the performance of the student's classmates is to compute the student's z-score for each of the four exams.

Exam 1: z-score $= \dfrac{\text{score} - \text{mean}}{\text{standard deviation}} = \dfrac{85 - 75}{5} = 2$. Therefore, the student scored 2 standard deviations above the mean on Exam 1.

Exam 2: z-score $= \dfrac{\text{score} - \text{mean}}{\text{standard deviation}} = \dfrac{77 - 78}{2} = -0.5$. Therefore, the student scored 0.5 standard deviation below the mean on Exam 2.

Exam 3: z-score $= \dfrac{\text{score} - \text{mean}}{\text{standard deviation}} = \dfrac{92 - 86}{4} = 1.5$. Therefore, the student scored 1.5 standard deviations above the mean on Exam 3.

Exam 4: z-score $= \dfrac{\text{score} - \text{mean}}{\text{standard deviation}} = \dfrac{90 - 80}{10} = 1$. Therefore, the student scored 1 standard deviation above the mean on Exam 4.

Since the student's z-score for Exam 1 is greater than any of the z-scores for the other exams, the student's best performance was on Exam 1 (Choice A) relative to that of the student's classmates.

37. B. You can extend the Fundamental Counting Principle to determine the number of possible telephone numbers for each prefix. After the prefix, there are four slots to fill. For each slot, 10 digits are available, which means the number of possible telephone numbers for each prefix is $10 \cdot 10 \cdot 10 \cdot 10 = 10^4$. By the Addition Principle, the total number of possible telephone numbers if all four prefixes are used is $10^4 + 10^4 + 10^4 + 10^4 = 4 \cdot 10^4$, Choice B.

38. A. $f(-2) = -16(-2)^{-4} \Rightarrow -16\dfrac{1}{(-2)^4} = \dfrac{-16}{16} = -1$, Choice A.

39. B. Analyze the problem. The box contains 25 tiles numbered 1 through 25. Devise a plan. If one tile is drawn at random, to find the probability the number on the tile is prime will take two steps. First, count how many numbers between 1 and 25 are prime, and then divide this answer by 25 and simplify, if possible. Carry out the plan.

Step 1. Count how many numbers between 1 and 25 are prime: The primes between 1 and 25 are 2, 3, 5, 7, 11, 13, 17, 19, and 23, which is a total of 9 primes (Remember, the number 1 is neither prime nor composite.)

Step 2. Divide by 25: $\dfrac{9}{25}$, Choice B.

40. D. In logic, the negation of a statement is a statement that has the opposite truth value; that is, when the given statement is true, its negation is false, and when the given statement is false, its negation is true. The given statement, "Some professors are entertaining" contains the existential quantifier "Some." You can eliminate choice A because the negation of a statement that contains an existential quantifier is a statement that contains a universal quantifier. The statement, "Some professors are entertaining" has the logical form "Some p are e." The negation has the form "No p are e." Therefore, the negation of "Some professors are entertaining" is "No professors are entertaining," Choice D.

Part B: Solutions to the Short Constructed-Response Section

For questions 41–43, score your response 0 to 3 using the following criteria:

- Correctly answered all parts of the question
- Gave a complete and full explanation for answers
- Demonstrated a strong understanding of the mathematical content relevant to the question
- Demonstrated a thorough understanding of all aspects of any stimulus material provided

41. Sample correct constructed response

(a) Model the situation in the problem with an eight-sided polygon, where each vertex represents a person at the party. Draw the diagonals between the vertices. Each diagonal and each line connecting a vertex to an adjacent vertex represents two people shaking hands at the party.

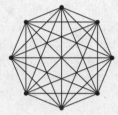

To count the handshakes, observe that at each vertex there are seven lines connecting that vertex to every other vertex. Since there are 8 vertices, there are $8 \cdot 7$ connections. However, the number of connection is twice the number of handshakes because it takes two people to make one handshake. Therefore, the number of handshakes is $\frac{8 \cdot 7}{2} = 28$ handshakes.

(b) In the polygonal model, the number of lines from each vertex is one less than the number of vertices in the polygon. For any n-sided polygon, this will always be the case because there would not be a line connecting a vertex to itself. In other words, each of n vertices is connected to $(n-1)$ other vertices. Hence, the total number of handshakes for n people is $\dfrac{n(n-1)}{2}$.

(c) $\dfrac{n(n-1)}{2} = 45$

$n^2 - n = 90$

$n^2 - n - 90 = 0$

$(n-10)(n+9) = 0$

$n = 10$ or -9 (reject because this is not consistent with the real-world situation)

$n = 10$ people

42. Sample correct constructed response

(a) $f = \dfrac{1}{2\pi}\sqrt{\dfrac{g}{L}} = \dfrac{1}{2\pi}\sqrt{\dfrac{981 \text{ cm/s}^2}{9 \text{ cm}}} = \dfrac{1}{2\pi}\sqrt{\dfrac{109}{\text{s}^2}} = 1.7$ cycles per second

(b) $f = \dfrac{1}{2\pi}\sqrt{\dfrac{g}{L}} \Rightarrow$

$2\pi f = \sqrt{\dfrac{g}{L}}$

$4\pi^2 f^2 = \dfrac{g}{L}$

$$L4\pi^2f^2 = g$$

$$L = \frac{g}{4\pi^2 f^2}$$

(c) $L = \frac{g}{4\pi^2 f^2} = \frac{981 \text{ cm/s}^2}{4\pi^2 \left(\frac{1}{2} \text{ /s}\right)^2} = \frac{981 \text{ cm/s}^2}{4\pi^2 \left(\frac{1}{4} \text{ /s}^2\right)} = 99.4 \text{ cm}$$

43. Sample correct constructed response

(a) Let x = the number of \$75 tickets sold and y = the number of \$45 tickets sold. Then $2y$ = the number of \$20 tickets sold. The sum of the number of tickets sold at each price = the total number of tickets sold. Thus, $x + y + 2y = x + 3y = 700$.

(b) The amount of money collected from the sales of each ticket = the total amount of money collected. Thus, $\$75x + \$45y + \$20(2y) = \$75x + \$45y + \$40y = \$75x + \$85y = \$24{,}500$.

(c) Solve $\begin{cases} x + 3y = 700 \\ 75x + 85y = 24500 \end{cases}$ by elimination.

$\begin{cases} -75x - 225y = 52500 \\ 75x + 85y = 24500 \end{cases}$ Multiply the first equation by –75.

$\begin{array}{r} -75x - 225y = -52500 \\ 75x + 85y = 24500 \\ \hline -140y = -28000 \end{array}$ Add the equations.

$-140y = -28000$ Solve for y and then determine $2y$.

$y = 200$, the number of \$45 tickets sold.

$2y = 400$, the number of \$20 tickets sold.

$x + 3y = 700 \Rightarrow x + 3(200) = 700$ Substitute 200 for y into the first equation.

$x + 600 = 700$ Solve for x.

$x = 100$, the number of \$75 tickets sold.

Scoring Your Practice Test

The testing company does not release the exact details of the way the Praxis Middle School Mathematics test is scored. Here is a method that will give you an approximation of your percentage score (out of a possible 100 percent) on this practice test, with the caveat that the scoring method used by the testing company could likely differ from what is shown here.

Your total percentage score is 67% of the percent of multiple-choice items correct plus 33% of your constructed responses percentage score for this practice test.

Here is an example.

Suppose you get 38 multiple-choice items correct and full credit for each of the three constructed-response questions. Your score is computed as follows:

$$67\%\left(\frac{38}{40}\right)+33\%\left(\frac{9}{9}\right)=0.67(95\%)+0.33(100\%)=96.65\%.$$

Simplifying Radicals

A radical is in **simplified form** when

- the radicand contains no variable factor raised to a power equal to or greater than the index of the radical;
- the radicand contains no constant factor that can be expressed as a power equal to or greater than the index of the radical;
- the radicand contains no fractions;
- no radicals are in a denominator; and
- the index of the radical is reduced to its lowest value.

For example,

$$\sqrt[3]{40a^6b^5} = \left(\sqrt[3]{8a^6b^3}\right)\left(\sqrt[3]{5b^2}\right) = 2a^2b\left(\sqrt[3]{5b^2}\right) \text{ in simplified form.}$$

$$\sqrt{18} = \left(\sqrt{9}\right)\left(\sqrt{2}\right) = 3\sqrt{2} \text{ in simplified form.}$$

$$\frac{\sqrt{54}}{\sqrt{6}} = \sqrt{\frac{54}{6}} = \sqrt{9} = 3 \text{ in simplified form.}$$

$$\frac{1}{\sqrt{2}} = \left(\frac{1}{\sqrt{2}}\right)\frac{\sqrt{2}}{\sqrt{2}} = \frac{\sqrt{2}}{2} \text{ in simplified form.}$$

$$\sqrt[4]{x^2} = \sqrt{x} \text{ in simplified form.}$$

Like radicals are radicals that have the same index and the same radicand. To add/subtract like radicals, add/subtract their coefficients and use the result as the coefficient of the common radical factor. For example,

$$4\sqrt{3} + 2\sqrt{3} = 6\sqrt{3} \,.$$

You might have to simplify the radical expressions before combining them. For example,

$$4\sqrt{3} + \sqrt{12} = 4\sqrt{3} + \left(\sqrt{4}\right)\left(\sqrt{3}\right) = 4\sqrt{3} + 2\sqrt{3} = 6\sqrt{3} \,.$$

You can only indicate the sum/difference of unlike radicals that are in simplified form. For example,

$$5\sqrt{2} + 4\sqrt{3} \text{ cannot be written as a single term.}$$

To multiply radicals that have the same index, multiply their coefficients to find the coefficient of the product, multiply the radicands to find the radicand of the product, and then simplify the results. For example,

$$\left(4\sqrt{3}\right)\left(2\sqrt{3}\right) = 8\sqrt{9} = 8(3) = 24.$$

When multiplying sums or differences, multiply the factors as you would binomials, being sure to simplify radicals after you multiply. Here are examples.

$$\left(2\sqrt{3} + 3\sqrt{5}\right)\left(\sqrt{3} - 3\sqrt{6}\right) = 2\sqrt{9} - 6\sqrt{18} + 3\sqrt{15} - 9\sqrt{30} =$$

$$2(3) - 6\sqrt{9}\sqrt{2} + 3\sqrt{15} - 9\sqrt{30} = 6 - 18\sqrt{2} + 3\sqrt{15} - 9\sqrt{30} \,.$$

$$\left(2 - \sqrt{3}\right)\left(2 + \sqrt{3}\right) = 4 + 2\sqrt{3} - 2\sqrt{3} - \sqrt{9} = 4 - 3 = 1.$$

Rationalizing is used to remove radicals from the denominator of a fraction. For radicals that contain a single term in the denominator, multiply the numerator and denominator of the fraction by the smallest radical that will produce a perfect square, a perfect cube, or so on in the denominator. For example,

$$\frac{6}{\sqrt{3}} = \left(\frac{6}{\sqrt{3}}\right)\left(\frac{\sqrt{3}}{\sqrt{3}}\right) = \frac{6\sqrt{3}}{3} = 2\sqrt{3} \text{ in simplified form.}$$

$$\frac{2}{\sqrt[3]{5}} = \left(\frac{2}{\sqrt[3]{5}}\right)\left(\frac{\sqrt[3]{5^2}}{\sqrt[3]{5^2}}\right) = \frac{2\sqrt[3]{5^2}}{\sqrt[3]{5^3}} = \frac{2\sqrt[3]{25}}{5} \text{ in simplified form.}$$

When the denominator contains a sum/difference of square roots, multiply the numerator and denominator by a difference/sum that will cause the middle terms to sum to zero when you multiply. For example,

$$\frac{-4}{1-\sqrt{3}} = \left(\frac{-4}{1-\sqrt{3}}\right)\left(\frac{1+\sqrt{3}}{1+\sqrt{3}}\right) = \left(\frac{-4\left(1+\sqrt{3}\right)}{1-3}\right) = -\left(\frac{-4\left(1+\sqrt{3}\right)}{-2}\right) = 2\left(1+\sqrt{3}\right) \text{ in simplified form.}$$

Synthetic Division

Synthetic division is a shortcut way to divide a polynomial in one variable, say x, by a binomial of the form $x - r$. To see how it works, divide $5x^3 - 2x + 3$ by $x - 2$:

$$
\begin{array}{r}
5x^2 + 10x + 18 \\
x - 2{\overline{\smash{)}5x^3 + 0x^2 - 2x + 3}} \\
\underline{5x^3 - 10x^2} \\
10x^2 - 2x \\
\underline{10x^2 - 20x} \\
18x + 3 \\
\underline{18x - 36} \\
\text{Remainder } 39
\end{array}
\qquad
\begin{array}{r}
5 + 10 + 18 \\
1 - 2{\overline{\smash{)}5 + 0 - 2 + 3}} \\
\underline{5 - 10} \\
10 - 2 \\
\underline{10 - 20} \\
18 + 3 \\
\underline{18 - 36} \\
\text{Remainder } 39
\end{array}
$$

On the left is the standard long division process; on the right is the same process using only the coefficients of the terms. Thus, you can perform the long division by working with the coefficients only, being sure to use 0 as a coefficient for missing powers of x. Here is the condensed procedure:

Divide $P(x) = 5x^3 - 2x + 3$ by $x - 2$.
Notice since $x - r = x - 2$, $r = 2$.

Step 1. Write the coefficients of the dividend in descending powers of x, using a coefficient of 0 when a power of x is missing as shown:

$5 + 0 - 2 + 3$

Step 2. Write $r = 2$, as shown:

$2|5 + 0 - 2 + 3$

Step 3. Leave a line space. Draw a line, and then bring down the first coefficient to below the line:

$$
\begin{array}{r}
2|5 + 0 - 2 + 3 \\
\underline{\;0} \\
5
\end{array}
$$

Step 4. Multiply the first coefficient by $r = 2$, write the product under the second coefficient of the first line, and then add:

$$
\begin{array}{r}
2|5 + 0 - 2 + 3 \\
\underline{10} \\
5 + 10
\end{array}
$$

Step 5. Multiply the sum by $r = 2$, write the product under the third coefficient of the first line, and then add:

$$
\begin{array}{r}
2|5 + 0 - 2 + 3 \\
\underline{10 + 20} \\
5 + 10 + 18
\end{array}
$$

Step 6. Repeat Step 5 until you have used all the coefficients in the dividend. Specify the final sum as the remainder, R, as shown:

$$
\begin{array}{r}
2\underline{|5 + 0 - 2 + 3} \\
\underline{10 + 20 + 36} \\
5 + 10 + 18 + R\,39
\end{array}
$$

Step 7. Using the coefficients in the third line, write the quotient and remainder as shown:

$5x^2 + 10x + 18\ R\ 39.$

[*Note:* The degree of the quotient is *one less* than the degree of $P(x)$.]

Therefore, $P(x) = 5x^3 - 2x + 3$ divided by $x - 2$ is $5x^2 + 10x + 18\ R\ 39$.

Appealing to the **remainder theorem** given in "Functions, Relations, and Their Graphs," you now know that

$P(2) = 5(2)^3 - 2(2) + 3 = 39.$

Thus, using synthetic division is a way to evaluate a one-variable polynomial at a given value.

Synthetic division is also a way to determine whether a given value is a zero of a one-variable polynomial. If the remainder is zero when you complete the division, the given value is a zero of the polynomial. Here is an example.

Is 3 a zero of the polynomial $P(x) = x^3 + 3x^2 - 9x - 27$?

$$
\begin{array}{r}
3\underline{|1 + 3 - 9 - 27} \\
\underline{3 + 18 + 27} \\
1 + 6 + 9\ \ R\ 0
\end{array}
$$

Since the remainder is zero, you know that $P(3) = 0$; thus, 3 is a zero of $P(x) = x^3 + 3x^2 - 9x - 27$.

Applying the **factor theorem** given in "Functions, Relations, and Their Graphs," you can say that since $P(3) = 0$, then $x - 3$ is a factor of $P(x) = x^3 + 3x^2 - 9x - 27$.

In summary, you have the following uses for synthetic division:

- To evaluate a polynomial $P(x)$ for a given value r: Divide $P(x)$ by $x - r$; $P(r)$ equals the remainder.
- To determine whether a given value r is a zero of a polynomial $P(x)$: Divide $P(x)$ by $x - r$; if the remainder is 0, r is a zero of $P(x)$; otherwise, r is not a zero of $P(x)$.
- To determine whether $x - r$ is a factor of a polynomial $P(x)$: Divide $P(x)$ by $x - r$; if the remainder is 0, $x - r$ is a factor of $P(x)$; otherwise, $x - r$ is not a factor of $P(x)$.

Measurement Units and Conversions

Length

English System	Metric System
1 foot (ft) = 12 inches (in)	1 centimeter (cm) = 10 millimeters (mm)
1 yard (yd) = 36 in	1 decimeter (dm) = 10 cm
1 mile (mi) = 1760 yd	1 meter (m) = 10 dm
= 5280 ft	= 100 cm
	= 1000 mm
	1 kilometer (km) = 1000 m

Area

English System	Metric System
$1\ ft^2 = 144\ in^2$	$1\ cm^2 = 100\ mm^2$
$1\ yd^2 = 9\ ft^2$	$1\ dm^2 = 100\ cm^2$
$= 1296\ in^2$	$1\ m^2 = 100\ dm^2$
$1\ acre = 4840\ yd^2$	$= 10{,}000\ cm^2$
$= 43{,}560\ ft^2$	$= 1{,}000{,}000\ mm^2$
$1\ mi^2 = 640\ acres$	$1\ km^2 = 1{,}000{,}000\ m^2$

Volume/Capacity

English System	Metric System
$1\ ft^3 = 1728\ in^3$	$1\ cm^3\ (cc) = 1000\ mm^3$
$1\ yd^3 = 27\ ft^3$	$1\ dm^3 = 1000\ cc$
$= 46{,}656\ in^3$	$1\ m^3 = 1000\ dm^3$
1 cup = 8 fluid ounces (oz)	$= 1{,}000{,}000\ cc$
1 pint (pt) = 2 cups	$= 1{,}000{,}000{,}000\ mm^3$
= 16 fl oz	$1\ km^3 = 1{,}000{,}000{,}000\ m^3$
1 qt = 2 pt	1 liter (L) = 1000 cc
= 32 fl oz	= 1000 milliliters (mL)
1 gallon (gal) = 4 qt	= 100 centiliters (cL)
= 8 pt	1 mL = 1cc
= 128 fl oz	1 kiloliter (kL) = 1000 L

Weight/Mass

English System	Metric System
1 pound (lb) = 16 ounces (oz)	1 gram (g) = 1000 milligrams (mg)
1 ton (T) = 2000 lb	= 100 centigrams (cg)
	= 10 decigrams (dg)
	1 kilogram (kg) = 1000 grams
	1 g = weight of 1 cc (1 mL) of water at 4 °C

Time

1 minute (min) = 60 seconds (s)

1 hour (h) = 60 min

= 3600 s

1 day (d) = 24 h

1 week (wk) = 7 days

1 month (mo) = 30 days (for ordinary accounting)

1 year (yr) = 12 months

= 52 weeks

= 365 days

1 leap year = 366 days

1 decade = 10 yr

1 century = 10 decades

= 100 yr

Approximate Equivalents

English to Metric	Metric to English
1 in = 2.54 cm (exactly)	1 cm $\cong$ 0.3937 in
1 ft $\cong$ 30.48 cm	1 m $\cong$ 39.37 in
1 yd $\cong$ 0.914 m	$\cong$ 1.094 yd
1 mi $\cong$ 1.609 km	1 km $\cong$ 0.621 mi
1 oz $\cong$ 28.349 g	1 g $\cong$ 0.035 oz
1 lb $\cong$ 0.454 kg	1 kg $\cong$ 2.205 lb
1 ton $\cong$ 907.18 kg	1000 kg $\cong$ 1.1 tons
1oz $\cong$ 29.574 mL (cc)	
1 cup $\cong$ 237 mL (cc)	
1qt $\cong$ 0.946 L	1 L $\cong$ 1.057 qt

Note: The symbol "$\cong$" is read "approximately equal to."

Other Approximate/Exact Equivalents

1 ft^3 $\cong$ 7.48 gal	0° C = 32° F freezing point of water
62.4 lb $\cong$ weight of 1 ft^3 of water	100° C $\cong$ 212° F boiling point of water

Conversion Factors for Metric System

*Kilo*unit = *1000* units
*Hecto*unit = *100* units
*Deca*unit = *10* units
*Deci*unit = *0.1* unit
*Centi*unit = *0.01* unit
*Milli*unit = *0.001* unit

Common Formulas

Temperature

F (degrees Fahrenheit) $= \dfrac{9}{5}C + 32$; C (degrees Celsius) $= \dfrac{5}{9}\left(F - 32\right)$

Percentage

$P = RB$ where P = percentage, R = rate, and B = base

Business Formulas

Simple Interest

$I = Prt$ where I = simple interest earned, P = principal invested or present value of S, r = annual simple interest rate, and t = time in years

$S = P(1 + rt)$ = maturity value of P

Compound Interest

$S = P\left(1 + \dfrac{r}{m}\right)^{mt}$ where S = maturity value, or the compound amount of P, P = original principal or the present value of S, r = stated annual percentage rate, m = number of compoundings per year, and t = time in years

$S - P$ = compound interest earned

Ordinary Simple Annuity

$S = R\left[\dfrac{(1+i)^n - 1}{i}\right]$ where S = amount of the annuity, R = periodic payment, r = stated annual percentage rate, m = number of payments (compoundings) per year, $i = \dfrac{r}{m}$ = interest rate per compounding period, and

n = total number of payments

Rn = total of payments

$S - Rn$ = interest earned

Amortization

$A = R\left[\dfrac{1 - (1+i)^{-n}}{i}\right]$ where A = amount financed, R = periodic payment, r = stated annual percentage rate, m = number of payments (compoundings) per year, $i = \dfrac{r}{m}$ = interest rate per compounding period, and

n = total number of payments

Rn = total of payments

$Rn - A$ = interest paid

Distance Formula

$d = rt$ where d = distance traveled, r = (uniform) rate of speed, and t = time

Basic Trigonometry Formulas

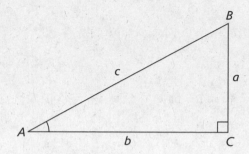

a = side opposite $\angle A$

b = side adjacent to $\angle A$

c = side opposite the right angle = hypotenuse

The basic trigonometry formulas relative to angle A in right triangle ABC are

sine of $\angle A = \sin A = \dfrac{\text{side opposite}}{\text{hypotenuse}} = \dfrac{a}{c}$ cosecant of $\angle A = \csc A = \dfrac{\text{hypotenuse}}{\text{side opposite}} = \dfrac{c}{a}$, $a \neq 0$

cosine of $\angle A = \cos A = \dfrac{\text{side adjacent}}{\text{hypotenuse}} = \dfrac{b}{c}$ secant of $\angle A = \sec A = \dfrac{\text{hypotenuse}}{\text{side adjacent}} = \dfrac{c}{b}$, $b \neq 0$

tangent of $\angle A = \tan A = \dfrac{\text{side opposite}}{\text{side adjacent}} = \dfrac{a}{b}$, $b \neq 0$ cotangent of $\angle A = \cot A = \dfrac{\text{side adjacent}}{\text{side opposite}} = \dfrac{b}{a}$, $a \neq 0$

Formulas from Science

Gas Laws

$\dfrac{p_1 v_1}{T_1} = \dfrac{p_2 v_2}{T_2}$ (General) $\dfrac{v_1}{T_1} = \dfrac{v_2}{T_2}$ (Charles's Law) $\dfrac{p_1}{p_2} = \dfrac{v_2}{v_1}$ (Boyle's Law)

where v_1 = volume at pressure p_1 and temperature T_1, and v_2 = volume at pressure p_2 and temperature T_2

Specific Gravity

Specific gravity of substance = $\dfrac{\text{weight of given volume of substance}}{\text{weight of equal volume of water}}$

Lever

$\dfrac{W_1}{W_2} = \dfrac{L_2}{L_1}$ where W_1 = force at distance L_1 from fulcrum, and W_2 = force at distance L_2 from fulcrum

Pulley

$\dfrac{R_1}{R_2} = \dfrac{d_2}{d_1}$ where R_1 = revolutions per minute of pulley of diameter d_1, and R_2 = revolutions per minute of pulley of diameter d_2